THE MIAMI DOLPHINS

THE
MIAMI DOLPHINS

by
Morris T. McLemore

Doubleday & Company, Inc.
Garden City, New York
1972

ISBN: 0-385-05263-4
Library of Congress Catalog Card Number 72–83147
Copyright © 1972 by Morris T. McLemore
All Rights Reserved
Printed in the United States of America
First Edition

To the gentle giants of the pits,
who hear bells other men never know.

Contents

Background . . .

On the night of Thursday, May 20, 1965, I was alone in the newsroom of the Miami *News*, the afternoon paper. A column had been hard to come by but finally was finished. With the last tap of the typewriter, my telephone rang and an old friend mentioned something that eventually would be fodder for bales of newspaper columns, weeks of air time and, at the crest of a long rise, this book.

"Have you heard that Danny Thomas, Anthony Abraham, and some other guys are making a strong move to put an American Football League franchise in here?" the friend asked. The answer was negative, of course, for I would have printed the story. "Well, they're pretty far along in their plans and have talked to some of the people at City Hall. . . . Maybe you could check it tomorrow."

I could check it that night. It was true. I got to a source who pleaded anonymity—as the first caller had done—and confirmed the report. So I chucked the earlier column and wrote another, the first story about the organization that eventually would become the Miami Dolphins. There have been a couple of times when it appeared the effort wasn't worth it but, in the long view, the Dolphins not only have been successful but they have survived. If that sounds a little screwy, you're not remembering the tales natives can dredge up about the town's first professional football team, the Miami Seahawks, who lived well, played poorly, and died by drowning.

It is better that you understand about the Seahawks so that your chances of understanding the Dolphins are advanced a few notches.

The Seahawks were formed in the afterglow of World War II,

when, in a major example of overreaction by those seeking normalcy and peacetime happiness, the All-America Conference was founded. We shall not dwell on its jerry-built structure. Luckily, space does not permit it. But the Seahawks are an example of the worst parts of the old A-A Conference, as the Cleveland Browns are examples of the best. Somewhere in between were the San Francisco Forty-Niners, the now extinct Buffalo Bisons, Brooklyn Dodgers, New York Yankees, Los Angeles Dons, and Chicago Rockets, the third team in a one-team town. The Browns and Forty-Niners were to live through the experience and become powerful members of the National Football League. But the others? Well, the Seahawks, for example, had a little hard luck.

Their backers were genial men from Atlanta, including Harvey Hester and Bill Bentley, with Harvey the chief executive and dining room check-picker. The late Mr. Hester was one of the delights of the Southland, but his devotion to his beloved part of the world and its football players blinded him to such things as size, speed, and talent available among players from north of the Smith and Wesson line. He hired the late Jack Meagher, a very successful coach before the war at Auburn and then for Iowa Pre-Flight, but few of the players furnished Meagher could make the breakfast table on opening day of practice of any current NFL team. Meagher's backfield averaged 182, his slow starting line a tense and underweight 200 pounds per man. There are players today with kneebones that weigh that much.

The Seahawks prepared for their ordeal in a North Carolina training camp, high above the sea-level Orange Bowl Stadium, where later they would gasp like lizards on a rail fence. The enterprising Hester also arranged that they should play their own exhibition games and the first three of the regular schedule on the road. In retrospect, this was not so silly as it sounds, for the Miami public didn't see the five defeats that resulted. However, they got the idea soon enough.

The one honor for the luckless Miami team occurred in the first game of that 1946 season, when they had the signal attention of being the first victims ever for Paul Brown's Cleveland Browns.

The magic of Brown's name drew 60,135 fans to the huge, Municipal Stadium in Cleveland—the all-time largest crowd ever to see a game in the AAC and largest to see the pros in Cleveland to that time. (The NFL's Rams had been located there. Brown chased them to Los Angeles). The Seahawks scrambled to a 44–0 loss and kept the pace with another two drops before showing up in the Orange Bowl against the San Francisco team.

Even the game date got fouled up. Miami's "blue laws" of that day did not permit Sunday afternoon games; the artful Hester was hemmed in by two other facts: The University of Miami long ago had nailed down Friday night for its own, and Miami High— then the toughest high school team south of Atlanta's Boys High— had a lock on Saturday nights. So Hester took Monday night.

A hurricane hit on the morning his first game was scheduled and the field couldn't even be seen under the water until Wednesday. Meanwhile, the Forty-Niners were in a downtown hotel, gulping steaks and looking bigger by the hour. When game time approached on Wednesday night, Harvey fervently asked a reporter pal for a prayer that they could reach a crowd of 15,000, the break-even point. Instead he could count a paid attendance of only 7534, although, knowing Harvey, we have to believe he had invited 3000 friends for free. Anyhow, San Francisco won the game, 34–7.

For the next five Monday nights, as if on cue, black clouds rolled in from the Everglades and over the Orange Bowl to dump a gulley-washer rain on poor Harvey Hester and his football team and its opponent—and almost nobody else.

To put it generously, the Seahawks were a disaster.

The shrewd Paul Brown, sensing impending doom for Hester, spent hours behind a potted palm in the McAllister Hotel lobby on one occasion, waiting to snare Hester, Bentley, or anyone else from the Seahawks' office. He finally collared Bentley and didn't turn loose until he got the $15,000 his Browns were guaranteed for a Miami game. Even when they finally won a second game, late in the season, and came home to play the Brooklyn Dodgers, the Seahawks drew only 2340 fans.

Hester threw in the towel and departed the premises with the only movable asset left—a station wagon. Later, he would make a fortune as a restaurateur outside Atlanta, but he was finished with football. The AAC commissioner, "Sleepy Jim" Crowley, took over and tried to find local investors in the Miami area who would take over the club. The locals weren't having any, so Crowley dealt with Bob Rodenberg, who headed a syndicate of Washington and Baltimore businessmen. When the AAC itself folded and surviving teams of the infant league were added to the National Football League, Rodenberg's group ultimately sold to the former Baltimore Colts' owner, Carroll Rosenbloom—and so the Seahawks, even now, come home to haunt Miamians.

Nineteen years after their demise here, on the day the column appeared suggesting the group headed by Danny Thomas would bid for a Miami franchise in the American Football League, the response included screams that the Seahawks had ruined the market. Danny Thomas probably never had heard of them, and the man who drilled the deal through all opposition for him, Joe Robbie, didn't care.

Robbie had a rendezvous with a gold mine, and he came out of the west to dig it in Miami. A compelling avarice drove him, perhaps, but an old schoolmate and bitter political opponent, Joe Foss, also was a forceful presence in the establishment of the club, for this former governor of South Dakota was commissioner of the American Football League when Robbie got the itch to make like a George Halas.

My description of Robbie in that first story—"Joe Robbie, a Minnesota attorney and investor"—hardly did him justice. He was and is a practicing attorney, but this investing has not been of the conventional kind; Joe has put 90 percent of his time and all of his money in and out of the Dolphins and a clutch of banks scattered from Minneapolis through Chicago to Miami but, mostly, he invested all his vast holdings of tenacity, imagination, and unmitigated gall.

There are some who say Joe Robbie is lucky, that he isn't even smart—while they stand back and stare at the organization he created almost on impulse.

If he isn't smart, he sure has been lucky. At this moment, he is the majority owner and lone general partner in a limited partnership with assets worth upwards of eleven million dollars—and his partners include seven or eight millionaires who can't tell him how to run the operation, while the First National Bank of Miami—Florida's largest and one of the nation's biggies—joins Chicago's LaSalle National in underwriting the whole business.

And it could be said, I suppose, that Robbie was lucky when he brought in pro football's most successful coach, Don Shula, and gave him a free hand to create football's most exciting team.

As a matter of fact, the only consistent thing about Joe Robbie has been his luck—if that's what you want to call it.

MORRIS McLEMORE

Coral Gables
January 1972

I

The Nearness of a Miracle

In the lowering dusk of a cold January afternoon in New Orleans, a couple of unhurried young citizens waded through the clutter of papers and boxes and cans and other trash immediately outside the now silent Tulane Stadium.

"We love you, Dolphins, yes we do. . . .

"We love you Dolphins, you know you're through. . . ."

The singer wasn't carrying the tune too well, for it seemed to have a gurgle in it now and then, but the theme of more than ten thousand bedraggled, road-weary followers of the Miami Dolphins was in the tall youngster's mind—love and despair, in almost equal parts, and perhaps a tearful regret for the cash lost on the wrong side of the six-point spread.

When Dallas dispatched the Miami football team, 24–3, in Super Bowl VI, Floridians were jarred out of a trance no less universal and hardly less exhilarating than The Boom—the mad ride on fragile clouds of slow paper that first fixed the world's attention on that funnel of sand "a thousand miles long, a hundred miles wide, and three feet high."

The Boom busted in the late 1920s, yet its scars and signs are indelibly intertwined with the glittering pleasure monuments of a half-century later. The deeds and then the ultimate defeat of the Miami professional team during and after the season of 1971 will live at least this long in the memories of those who took it as their own and, in a completely illogical but human reaction, quarrel among themselves over how it all happened.

That it happened at all is one of the great stories in the history of American sport . . . for no other professional team of an established league has ever accomplished so much in so short a span. Not even the New York Mets, Casey Stengel's lovelorn mob for so many seasons, who were led by Gil Hodges to victory in the World Series over the Baltimore Orioles after defeating the National Baseball League's best challengers in turn.

The Mets took most of a decade.

The Miami Dolphins, in six years from a standing start, clawed their way over and through twenty-four others to reach Super Bowl VI. That they did not humble a Dallas team that played a practically flawless game was a disappointment but, if any part of football in the United States at this point can be described thus, it was a rational happening after irrational happenings.

The way the Miami Dolphins seized upon the imagination and fancies of the American sports fan just before that New Orleans match is best illustrated, perhaps, in a Las Vegas oracle of odds.

"When you take the positives and the negatives of the Dallas and Miami teams and compare them, Dallas should be favored by ten points—certainly no fewer than eight," Jimmy (The Greek) Snyder reportedly figured aloud before the game. "But the people won't have it that way—not after Dick Anderson's run."

This run was only one feature of a splendid performance by the whole Miami squad in the American Conference championship game against Baltimore on January 2. The Dolphins cut down the champions of Super Bowl V by a shattering 21–0 in that final round of the conference play.

But it was the way that other Dolphins contributed to the superb sixty-two-yard runback of a Johnny Unitas pass that captured the imagination of football fans across the nation. When Anderson, Miami's strong-side safety, caught the ball after it was deflected out of the hands of Ed Hinton by cornerback Curtis Johnson, he turned and swept sixty-two yards to a touchdown— as six devastating blocks were delivered in his behalf by other Dolphins, defensive specialists unaccustomed to "laying the wood" to tacklers. One of those Colts chopped down by the dedicated colleagues of Anderson was Unitas himself. The greatest of all quarterbacks, now in the twilight of his career, went sprawling— and millions of football fans cheered across America.

It was unheard-of heresy. But, even to a hard-nosed realist in the dispassionate role of oddsmaker, it was negotiable testimony to the hold the Dolphins suddenly took on the emotions of the sports public.

Cinderella Team? A common descriptive used by writers who hardly could have employed it if they had noted the presence of Don Shula on the sideline of the Dolphins. If Cinderella had been escorted to the ball by Shula, he would have assured her victory over her witchy sisters in their competition for the prince. After a short workout and game plan review with Shula, Cinderella would have slung the prince over her shoulder and walked out the door with him, meanwhile declaring what a very fine party it was and how well the sisters had competed.

There in Tulane Stadium, his eyes a little misty but the chin still breasting the waves of questions thrown at him by newsmen, professional football's most successful coach faced up to inevitable comparisons of the thunderous defeat by Dallas and the far more surprising upset in Super Bowl III, when Shula saw his heavily favored Baltimore Colts upended by New York's Jets.

". . . I regret we didn't challenge Dallas. . . . The circumstances of this game bear little relation to the Baltimore-Jets game. . . . I'm so very proud of the accomplishments of this team, it deserves to finish with a better game than we turned in today. . . ." As always, his voice was controlled, never searching for a word.

In a far corner of the Dolphins' dressing room, beyond Norm Evans and near Dick Anderson's locker, a man one hardly would take for even an ex-athlete stared down the oblong chamber, not speaking to anyone. No one spoke to him as Joe Robbie stood there in his dark topcoat and bled inside, tears slowly dripping down his cheeks. His sharp tongue once made Robbie a national debating champion but, when a television reporter came up with the bright lights and a camera and asked his reaction to the day's events, Robbie said only: "I can't express how proud I am of this team. . . . It is unique. It will be here again. . . ."

Having said what was in him, he turned away and stood for a bit longer, silently looking about with his eyes brimming behind the glasses and then he departed—a man uneasy in the presence of those he wants to know best; a loyal friend to some, but the kind of man who attracts the spiteful quicker than lint finds a blue serge suit.

He has alienated thousands, yet his creation is the largest common denominator in a complex culture extending from the chickees of Seminole frog hunters to the poshest of pads for the most indolent lounge lizards of the jet set. In one week last winter, he brought South Floridians together as they've never been together before—each hungering for a piece of his pelt.

Trying to talk about the Dolphins without examining Joe Robbie early would be comparable to discussing electricity without mention of Benjamin Franklin. Both drew sparks because they had the key, if we can be forgiven the pun.

When T. E. Lawrence wrote, "There can be no honor in a sure success, but much might be wrested from a sure defeat," he might have been whispering in the ear of Joe Robbie. Long before he appeared in Miami with the notion of bringing together a group of people he didn't know, to buy a football team that didn't exist, with money that wasn't there, Robbie had proved he could fail gracefully and profitably.

This son of Lebanese and Irish parents returned from the Navy after World War II and won a seat in the South Dakota legislature, where he served as minority leader of both houses—it was a minority of nineteen Democrats nesting in a mob of 110 Republicans—before running for governor, in 1950. In that caper, he took a shellacking from Sigurd Anderson, who wasn't born Republican but found it the smart way when he shipped in from Norway. Not Robbie. He hung with the Democrats and later took another beating when he ran for Congress in Minnesota.

It is claimed by at least one magazine writer that Robbie was a twenty-five-thousand-dollar lawyer in Minneapolis when he parlayed an idea into a working football team in Miami, but Robbie claims otherwise. "We were living comfortably on high professional income but we had nothing more than a nest egg" is the way Robbie describes his family's financial position at the time the franchise was granted. Since his family included his wife, Elizabeth, and eleven children—a daughter since was drowned in a tragic accident in Mexico—the egg likely was malnourished.

A pal of former Vice President (now, again Senator) Hubert Humphrey since their association in Democratic politics in Minnesota, Robbie was responsible for Humphrey's arrangements for the inauguration of January 20, 1965, and went to Miami Beach for a rest when all that handshaking was finished. By what he later called "fortuitous chance," he arrived at the Eden Roc Hotel on February 2 and was asked to represent a man he had met during the 1964 campaign in a lawsuit involving the hotel's ownership interests. Actually, three persons were involved in the proceedings, and one of these, a Philadelphian, asked Robbie if he knew Joe Foss, commissioner of the American Football League. By chance, Robbie had known Foss as a classmate at the University of South Dakota and later as a jut-jawed opponent on the other side in state politics; Foss opposed and lost to Anderson in the Republican gubernatorial primary of 1960, but later won the governorship and, soon after leaving that position, became commissioner of the younger football league.

On Ash Wednesday, Robbie went to see Foss in Washington and asked, in behalf of the Philadelphian, what the commissioner thought of the possibility of a new franchise in Philadelphia. "You may as well forget Philadelphia because there is litigation over whether or not the National Football League has exclusive right to use the stadium," the onetime Marine aviator war hero told Robbie. "If you're in Miami and want an AFL franchise, apply for it. . . . Hell, it'll be the best franchise in the league, except for Oakland, where they're getting a new stadium, and the Jets in New York. . . ."

The Philadelphian was interested in the prospect until Robbie told him there would have to be seed money for expenses, that he would suggest a visit to each of the eight owners of AFL teams and perhaps repeated visits, since these owners would decide if they wished a Miami team. With this, the Philadelphian backed off and Robbie was faced with a hard decision—drop the whole thing or charge? Characteristically, he lowered his head and tested his skull on the roadblock. When the commotion ceased, neither ever would be itself again.

Stubbornly, Robbie held to his idea, through conversations with Lamar Hunt (Kansas City), Sonny Werblin (Jets), Ralph Wilson (Buffalo), Bill Sullivan (Boston), and other owners. Hunt was the AFL's founder and chairman of the expansion committee and, in the end, the key. Hunt started with the premise that Miami was no better than fourth, perhaps third, among prospective cities —with Atlanta and New Orleans, even Chicago and competition with the Bears, better places to put a franchise. Eventually, Hunt was partially convinced by Joe Haggar, a Dallas businessman who later became a Dolphins partner, that Miami is the center of a fertile commercial territory and alive with sports nuts. Hunt lowered his objections but did not discard them.

After a month or so of shopping and visiting with the owners, Robbie was convinced Miami would do well in the AFL, but he still had no financial backing. During a casual conversation with

Danny Thomas about St. Jude's Hospital, in Memphis, founded by Thomas and where both men serve on the board, Robbie mentioned the football opportunity. Thomas immediately was interested, reminding Robbie that he had tried to buy the Chicago White Sox when that American Baseball League member was sold to the Allyn brothers.

Thomas said Robbie could put his name on the application—and that small item meant life for the Dolphins. The AFL owners didn't know Danny Thomas in person, but they knew no Hollywood name of his stature could afford to blow the image with a shabby business connection so public as a football team.

A second critical point: the team would need a place to play, so the Vice President of the United States got involved in that, naturally.

Vice President Humphrey was entertaining mayors of major American cities in his Washington office one day and happened to mention to the late Miami Mayor Robert King High that Robbie was enthralled with the idea of obtaining an AFL franchise for Miami and would need the Orange Bowl Stadium. High, a political man with a terminal case of football fever, was instantly interested and, when Robbie called him some days later, asked the Minnesotan to join him at the Miami Beach Convention Center, where he was attending a meeting. They talked in the mayor's limousine, en route to High's law offices in the DuPont Building on Flagler Street, and Robbie won High's support. The mayor sent him straightaway to see City Manager Melvin Reese at Dinner Key but Reese was busy, so they met the next morning. This confrontation turned out more happily than have some later ones between these two; Reese said he could see no reason why Robbie couldn't have the stadium. Reese told him, however, that bonds sold to finance construction of certain seats at the bowl required rental of the stadium to be firm at 17½ percent, a figure AFL owners would never agree to for the new franchise. They wanted the new baby to remain solvent so they could be paid its expansion fees. Eventually, before the first game, this was lowered substantially, but the other users—University of Miami, the Orange Bowl

Committee, etc.—were bitterly unhappy that their rates per event were higher than those for the professionals. This remains a thorny barrier to cordial relations and, at this writing, there is a ridiculous standoff among Robbie, City Manager Reese, and the Orange Bowl Committee's Executive Vice President and veteran manager, Earnie Seiler. These three, with the University of Miami an interested but apparently impotent fourth, seem to irritate each other just for the hell of it—a sad commentary.

In the spring of 1965, such problems didn't exist, and Robbie's major concern was holding the parts of his possible deal together without the sure-fire coagulant, money. His nest egg went into the pot early, soon to be followed by money borrowed on his signature in Minneapolis. According to Robbie, Thomas's money appeared when the club actually was formed. Until then, it was a scrape and scrap proposition for the Westerner, long since captivated by his own rhetoric in praise of Miami to the AFL owners.

Sullivan Barnes, general counsel of the AFL in its earlier years and a Denver lawyer, was helpful in the earliest maneuvers but disappeared not long after the franchise was granted. Robbie estimates his own outlay of cash, covering travel and other expenses, to be about forty thousand dollars, plus a fee for Barnes, before the franchise was granted by the AFL.

"There was an agreed retainer of ten thousand dollars with Mr. Barnes and I would have lost that, plus the forty thousand, if we hadn't gotten the franchise. . . . It eventually came out of the jackpot, but there was a six-month period in my life that would have gone for naught if we had missed," is his way of saying it was a squeaker.

While Danny Thomas and Robbie were the only potential owners named on the application to the league, others joined the procession immediately after the grant of the Miami rights in August 1965.

A complete rundown of the owners—and, with the exception of Robbie and the Hagger brothers, of Dallas, they've changed completely—can be found in the Appendix. Robbie didn't come to a corporate plan until after the franchise was in hand; since that time, four vital shifts of emphasis in the board room have occurred:

the departure of Danny Thomas, the appearance of Bud Keland, the departure of Keland, and the participation as limited partners of the well-known Miami businessmen who still are associated with the club. These are Harper Sibley, Jr., H. Earl Smalley, Wilbur L. Morrison, James M. McLamore, Frank Callahan, William S. Frates, Judge Peter T. Fay, Robert L. Floyd, Ray H. Pearson, Morris S. Burk, and James L. Davis.

But the overriding fact through all these goings and comings through the office at 330 Biscayne Boulevard is the continued presence and gathering strength of Robbie, who seems to have thrown everything he had, and all he could beg or borrow, into the balance. That he won is old news now . . . that he was and is the sole general partner as an individual—the one with personal liability for all the partnership's debts—is not so widely recognized. Danny Thomas participated as a member of a company (Danny Thomas Sports, Inc.) that was itself a general partner in the Dolphins; this was at the suggestion of his advisers. Later, when the Thomas interest was sold to Bud Keland, a Wisconsin investor and developer, the reason given was that the Hollywood star was going into the production and personal backing of certain television spectaculars that would require all his energies. It is a coincidence that this occurred—in June 1967—after the entertainer reportedly got uptight about some of the things said of the Dolphins' enterprise by newsmen . . . but, no matter, he was supplanted by Keland. We'll note that gentleman's passing from the scene as the tale progresses.

Early in January 1969, a local group of prominent business men was interested in joining with Joe Robbie as partners. Most of these people were important customers of the bank . . .
At that time, the financial statement indicated the football team was losing money [with] projections of further losses. . . . However, increased television revenues were a certainty. . . . We were aware existing franchises were being sold at prices considerably in excess of the original cost of the Dolphins' franchise and we felt the financial and business resources of the prospective partners were such that we could make the loan

> . . . and buy out the existing partners (Bud Keland and
> several others) . . . the loan agreement gave the Dolphins a
> call on us for the amount to meet the annual league payments.
> While early forecasts did not come up to our expectations
> and hopes, the success of the team in the last two years . . .
> has been larger than anyone had any reason to project. . . .
> Accordingly, the financial success of the Dolphins is unques-
> tionably assured.
> —Bob Bruce (Vice Chairman, First National Bank of Miami)

Anthony Abraham, the Miamian originally figured into the bid, withdrew before the $7,500,000 deal was made with the AFL; John O'Neil, then a Miami newspaperman and now a part owner of the Harlem Globetrotters, was in from the start as a limited partner, but he and Robbie soon were at violent odds, and O'Neil cashed in and left after Keland lost a struggle for control and was bought out by the new, local partners.

It is perhaps miraculous that the Dolphins lived at all; it is more so when one recalls the tangles and snares Robbie danced among every time he took a step. "I had complete confidence that I wasn't going to get myself in a jackpot and lose whatever my family had at that time or thereafter required. . . . I was the only individual general partner and still am." The Dolphins' boss is neither sentimental nor lacking for words when talking business.

From time to time, and for a variety of purposes, Robbie and/or the Dolphins have done business with the Bank of Minneapolis; LaSalle National Bank of Chicago (still involved, LaSalle's Vice President Philip Butler funded the club payroll in a 1968 crisis); American National Bank of Chicago; the O'Hare International Bank of Chicago, and, more recently, the First National Bank of Miami. A substantial loan from the Brotherhood of Railway and Airline Clerks was forthcoming after Miami Mayor High introduced Robbie to C. L. Dennis, an officer of the union; this was floated when Danny Thomas was in the process of withdrawing from the team organization and later was repaid with funds from one of the banks listed above.

Like every franchise in the NFL, the Dolphins have been sought
by investors who wouldn't know a football from a hockey puck.
But some very knowledgeable citizens also tried to buy or trade for
it after the franchise was in business. Carroll Rosenbloom admits
he was one of the possibles; Robbie once said Rosenbloom—before their falling-out—wanted to swap the Colts for the Dolphins,
with Robbie sweetening the deal with substantial cash. This never
got very far.

Another one came closer, however.

After the season of 1966, the late Vince Lombardi was one of a
small group interested in purchasing the Dolphins. And the thing
might have worked if the approach had been made to Robbie—
who even then held the key—rather than Danny Thomas.

Joe McCrane, now treasurer of the State of New Jersey, and
son-in-law of Gene Mori, owner of Hialeah and Garden State race
courses, was a friend of Lombardi and had long been interested in a
football franchise. These two and another friend of Lombardi's, a
former Green Bay resident who had become a California businessman, Bud Levitas, were the principal figures. Red Blaik, former
great football coach at the U. S. Military Academy, where he was
Lombardi's chief, and later chairman of AVCO, reportedly was
interested, among others.

But the McCrane-Lombardi move perished in the wilds of the
Dolphins' internal organization. There was no way 100 percent—
or even 80 percent—of the club could be extracted from the maze
of interlocking relationships among the general and limited partners
of that day. McCrane recalls that their eventual withdrawal "was
strictly a business decision when we discovered the very complicated structure of the Dolphins."

A plump profit might have been realized even that early by
Robbie and associates, but they wouldn't bite. Robbie's position at
that time was such that "he controlled the situation in a negative
sense, in that he could block something, although he might not be
able to do something," is the way McCrane explains it. He says he
didn't blame Robbie; this just was the way it was arranged then.

At that time, Lombardi still was coach and general manager of the Packers—this was before his retirement from the field and subsequent move to Washington as part owner—but the attraction for him then was the same one that eventually brought him to the Redskins: "He would have been a substantial owner in our organization if we could have gotten the Dolphins. For Lombardi at that time, salary was not so important as a tax shelter," says McCrane.

We can only presume what might have happened had Lombardi—then at the peak of his effectiveness as a football leader—moved to Miami. His transfer at that moment would have struck the game with even more shattering impact than the later move by Don Shula from Baltimore. The reverberating happenings that characterize the Dolphins publicly are trumped by those behind the door at 330 Biscayne Boulevard.

Robbie vows he never has "gone out and gotten an expensive loan. We have been paying no more than 2 percent above prime [interest rate] and usually less than that through the whole period. . . . we've never given points, we've never given a premium. . . . I kept shuffling around. No use in selling what you own in order to finance keeping it. . . ."

The first four years were difficult and sometimes frantic but, in 1970, after the first winning season, the Dolphins' financial picture changed from red to black. After the 1971 season, it was even more so.

But that is for the moneychangers. Let us go to the field below.

2

"First, You Take Some Football Players . . ."

From the press box in the Orange Bowl, the view includes parts of Miami Beach and Manny Fernandez. Of these spectacular assets in the Gold Coast area of Florida, there's even more action where Manny plies his trade than across Biscayne Bay, where the girlies prance.

Watching Manny's furious charge from his defensive tackle position one afternoon last fall, Joe Thomas chuckled in appreciation. Joe is the kind of fellow who finds joy in the mighty thwack delivered to the noggin of the Baltimore guard before Manny wiped him out of the path toward the passer, Johnny Unitas.

"There he is. Manny's got all of it except tremendous size, and he doesn't need that," the Dolphins' hired hunter declared. "He's the only one I ever got for Miami from west of the Mississippi, and he's the best of the lot, my best ever. . . ."

Broken down, what Joe meant was that Manny Fernandez is the best "free agent" he ever signed for Miami. Such a citizen is a player not chosen by any of the pro teams at the annual, winter draft of college players. By instinct conservative with a buck, Thomas rightfully took particular pleasure from the success of a free agent, for the lad usually is signed without any bonus whatever; in the case of Fernandez, Joe didn't have to give him even a loud wristwatch. All Fernandez wanted in that winter of 1967–68 was a chance to knock heads with bigger boys than he had found opposite his spot in the University of Utah line.

The only reason he got the chance with the Dolphins, was a suspicion by Thomas that a coach had wandered from the normal channels of comment a scout might expect and that his wandering came from a personal grudge, rather than calm evaluation of Manny's abilities and potential.

During the autumn of 1967, Utah's coaches and players had a falling-out that soon received notice from coast to coast. Apparently none of the players liked any of the coaches and the feeling was likewise, ten times over, in the minds of Utah's coaches. Their season was a shambles. But nothing Thomas saw that fall entered his thinking. He recalled the moves and attitude of the Fernandez he had seen in the previous season. When he talked to one of the Utah coaches about the solid Californian, however, he was steered away from Fernandez.

"He's a sorehead and can't be coached," Thomas was told. "Sign Fernandez and you've got nothing but trouble until the day he leaves your squad."

Thomas listened, for a player's college coach is the prime source of information for a talent scout. But he couldn't shake the memory of Manny's quick reactions, his use of forearms the size of hams, and that certain quality sought more than all the others—instinct for the target, no matter where it is and no matter who stands in the way.

When the draft of that winter started, the name of Fernandez was still with Thomas, but he soon was ears deep in the drafting process. Not until the day after did Joe think of him again; a quick recheck of the draft lists, and he picked up the telephone. No team had snapped up Manny; now Joe found him willing to come to Miami for air fare. And he quickly signed.

A day or so later, Manny's former coach called Thomas, much upset.

"What's the idea, you signing Fernandez when I told you he's a no-good?" growled the former leader of men. "Don't ever ask me again what I think of a player!"

"Don't feel that way about it," Thomas responded, "Fernandez can be particularly valuable to us here in Miami at the gate . . . we've got a huge Latin-American population and we need a Spanish name to attract these fans. . . ."

The aggrieved coach subsided but hasn't been heard from since. Not so Fernandez. His compact form—250 pounds arranged in flat planes over a six-foot, two-inch frame—has been an island of constant violence in a defensive Front Four that only lately has matured and performed as a unit. No matter who else was doing what in the games since 1968, Manny Fernandez sought his target by the nearest trail and spared no prisoners in the process.

Manuel José Fernandez speaks no Spanish, but he speaks the language Dolphins fans understand, and—an interesting gauge of his personality—he is the easiest of all the senior operatives on the club to sign to contracts or deal with on any matter. He long since arrived at a financial state where the matter of air fare home is of little moment.

Until the day he departed the Dolphins in February 1972, Thomas refused to spend money for quick glances at dubious material . . . airline tickets for training-table athletes cost as much as for those who perform on the field. Since the Dolphins matured, even a Fernandez would not be invited across country, for the chances of any rookie being invited to workouts without prior notice from the club are almost nil today.

The scouting and recruiting processes of the Dolphins also have changed mightily. In his first years with the Dolphins, Thomas performed his amazing moves with flesh on a budget under fifty thousand dollars annually—including his own salary. It is testimony to the present prosperity of the franchise that now the same functions cost upwards of two hundred thousand dollars, with talent scouts popping about the country, in constant motion for the Dolphins. Today they seek the jewel who might ensure Super Bowl reappearances in the future. Initially, Joe Thomas sought working bodies whose owners spent sweat freely; later, he proved himself a superior jewel-setter, too.

When he departed the Dolphins, it was in hopes of moving forward to a general manager's position with another team. The skeletal outlines of Joe Thomas's pressurized career and personality are vital to this story of the Miami Dolphins, however.

With the Dolphins, his genius was proved early in seeing trouble and acting to eliminate or reduce it; his initial judgment of a player also was a paramount point in his hunter's game. As we shall see, Thomas had defeats of large denomination. The percentage of correct decisions on players is much in his favor, however.

In brief, a football team is accumulated through four devices: the signing of a free agent, as we have just noted in the case of Fernandez; the draft of college seniors, and—the one used immediately when George Allen recently transferred his coaching kit from Los Angeles to Washington—the trade of players already under contract. Then, in the case of teams being formed for new franchises (Cincinnati was the last), each of the other teams makes available a certain number of players in what is called a "stocking draft."

Of the three normal methods, the draft of college seniors is the usual route; the swapping of experienced players usually is a case of robbing Peter to pay Paul and, as for free agents, getting a goodie by such a piece of luck is all profit and all the sweeter to the man who finds one in this intensely competitive and, in the past few years, computerized hunting game.

For Thomas, the great adventure started in January 1960, during a vacation in Miami from his job as an assistant coach of the Toronto Argonauts. It was no accident that the National Football League was holding its winter convention of club owners here at the same time; Thomas sensed the great changes coming in the game. The American Football League, established and nourished by Lamar Hunt, was struggling in its birthing time. The older NFL looked upon the thrashing infant as more irritant than threat, although older hands recalled how Paul Brown got into and made a shambles of their own league . . . the now-extinct All-America Conference made a run at the NFL after World War II and came a cropper, but Brown busted into the NFL as a consequence. Other vestiges of it remained, too.

Tempered by coaching experience with Indiana high schools, DePauw University, the Baltimore Colts, and the Los Angeles Rams before he spent the season at Toronto, Thomas felt it was time to settle into a front office in American football. He happened into Miami while the NFL meeting stretched to interminable sessions of nominating, voting, and trying again for the club owners, as they sought a new commissioner.

At last, after twenty-three ballots, they compromised on the brilliant but young (thirty-four) general manager of the Rams, Pete Rozelle. It was a monumental piece of good luck, for the tall, alert young fellow quickly proved to be the most able administrator the game has known. We shall not dwell on Rozelle here, but his part in the career of Joe Thomas was typical of the part he has played in many others since his elevation to the commissioner's office.

When Max Winter, member of a Minneapolis group with a new NFL franchise for the Twin Cities, asked Rozelle whom he would recommend as a talent scout for the Vikings, the commissioner thought about it for a time and told him about Joe Thomas. The two had worked together briefly, when Thomas had scouted some for the Rams, and Rozelle liked his approach. So did Winter. In April 1960, Thomas became the first employee of the Vikings, and —though totally unschooled in the techniques of large-scale talent hunts—he hit the road immediately.

Fortunately, he was a bachelor, for that first swing in 1960 took Thomas three months without a return to Minneapolis. Instead, he visited ninety-two colleges and established a rapport with coaches that later paid off handsomely for the Miami club.

The ideal hunter must possess a shrewdness given to few men, a shrewdness that allows him to wait, to bide his time on one deal while striking as a shark might on another. Thomas has this shrewdness. Quick-witted and an essentially friendly man, he remains a loner in a restless world; the computer qualities of his mind are evident the moment Thomas is asked the fate of a player about whom he has heard nothing for years. He has complete recall of what he knew of the man a long time ago.

That the men Thomas hunts are football's blockers, tacklers, throwers, and catchers rather than wrong-doers in buckskin or a cowboy's chaps is only an accident of time. By nature and the hard training he underwent by force of circumstances at Minnesota, Joe is the kind of tracker who could lope across the Rockies in tireless pursuit or peer down a valley for weeks, awaiting a sign of his prey.

For Minnesota, his emphasis was on area scouts, with these checking on players recommended to Thomas by their coaches. As it later was to be when the Dolphins were being formed, Joe brought in free agents by the bunch to the Vikings; nine of these were still on hand in their second season and this, of itself, is testimony to the eye of this hunter. Later, ten free agents played or were activated by the Miami club in its first season. Early in the building of a team, the stress is on numbers, with excellence an extra dividend wherever it can be found.

"The 'skill positions' are what you've got to have first" is the Thomas approach. "The men who handle the ball, who throw and catch it—and those most responsible for stopping the other guys from throwing or catching it."

This means a quarterback, middle linebacker, running backs, and receivers, in that order or close to it, no matter what else applies.

At Minnesota, Thomas moved quickly to deal for a QB. He obtained George Shaw from the New York Giants for the Vikings' first-round draft of their second year, 1962. Then, as the Vikings' first choice in 1961, he drafted Tulane's Tommy Mason, a highly successful running back for Minnesota's early years; Rip Hawkins, of North Carolina, was the middle linebacker sought and signed and then—on the third round of that 1961 draft—Joe picked Fran Tarkenton, of Georgia, "because he was there and you can't let one like Fran pass by." Tarkenton was the great prize of that draft, of course, for he soon superseded Shaw and, in a very real sense, he was the key to the Minnesota franchise until his departure. (The latter followed an ill-concealed spat three seasons later with Coach Norm Van Brocklin, who left the Vikings shortly before Tarkenton was shipped to New York. Early in 1972, Tarkenton was traded back to the Vikings by the Giants.)

Another feature of that first draft for Minnesota tells more about Thomas, however: his selections of Chuck Lamson and Ed Sharockman in the fourth and fifth rounds sounded nutty, for both were quarterbacks in college. The key is that Thomas didn't draft them as quarterbacks but as defensive backs . . . in those days, the colleges were employing the "belly series" offense and other attacks that required all-around athletic ability at the quarterback position, rather than just passing expertise. Lamson and Sharockman were superior athletes with only ordinary capabilities as throwers. They found work immediately with the Vikings.

Building the player structure of the Dolphins later was far less complicated for Thomas than the building of the Vikes but, when he was hired by Joe Robbie for the Miami personnel job in September 1965, a new element that had nothing to do with a player's ability had everything to do with Thomas's destiny in pro ball.

The element, put at its simplest, was money.

Lamar Hunt's stubborn refusal to give up in the face of the National Football League's feverish efforts to stamp out his new American Football League was a gut factor, too, of course. But the wealthy Texan wasn't the only AFL club owner who roll the dice, so to speak, and risked hundreds of thousands of dollars in the money war that mounted to a state of white heat in the middle 1960s.

Even the most casual sideline observer got the sense of this struggle when—the day after Texas strangled Joe Namath's plucky but futile pair of sneaks that cost Alabama the 1965 Orange Bowl game—the most flamboyant figure ever in pro football, and perhaps its most gifted quarterback, signed with the American Football League rather than the older group. Namath's signature on the contract offered him by Sonny Werblin, of the New York Jets, was worth a lot more than the four hundred thousand dollars called for by its print. This contract not only proved the AFL was competitive; it proved for the most reluctant NFL mossback and the public that the younger league had a new grasp of show biz the NFL could not match. The St. Louis Cardinals—through a complicated process of draft swaps—ended up with rights to Namath among NFL teams. Evidence at hand indicated this was a blind, that the Cardinals were acting as a "beard" for the New York Giants, who wanted Namath but weren't wild-eyed for him, or didn't want to have a public struggle with the Jets for Joe's favor.

It's possible the Giants correctly, and—in the light of history—fortunately backed down. Werblin accurately read the personality and style of Joe Namath no less clearly than he read his talents on the football field; Weeb Ewbank and the other Jets' coaches also liked his talents there. It was the perfect matchup of hungers: Werblin wanted Namath's instinctive flair for the dramatic and calm-eyed confidence to charm and sometimes irritate the stuffy Provencals of the New York press and tube. This would turn them away from their comfortable acceptance of the Giants as the only football team in town worth watching, no matter how mediocre. The Jets' coaches needed a strong-armed quarterback with a highwayman's nerve, and Namath—he admitted it, bluntly, on the day he signed the contract—wanted to play football in New York.

And that clamorous village, though hardly recognizing the fact, wanted Joe Namath.

The moment Namath signed with Werblin, whose fortune had long since been made as a talent peddler in show business, the NFL went on the defensive. It wasn't any formal change of plan by Pete Rozelle, George Halas, and other NFL leaders that altered the emphasis; for the first time, the AFL had gone to the mat in a public struggle for a major star and in the center ring . . . and won. Football never would be the same.

The Namath signing needled the NFL people into doing and saying some things they'd never dreamed they might do or say. New York reporters galloped in Namath's wake as he gyrated around their town, and the Giants took a back seat. The AFL now had the initiative . . . a force no less powerful than Lamar Hunt's cash and/or determination. It would be months before the blockbuster announcement by Pete Rozelle that peace had broken out between the warring leagues, but the principal ingredient for that peace now was at work. This ingredient was a recognizable state of near-equality in player negotiations.

It was in this atmosphere that the idea for the Dolphins germinated and in it that Joe Thomas assembled the squad, that Joe Robbie hired the veteran George Wilson as the Dolphins' first coach, and that the South Florida football public was asked to support a successor to the Seahawks of rancid memory.

The war between the leagues reached its peak in the autumn of 1965 and the subsequent drafts by the NFL and AFL. Ordinary talents were plied with gold, and the watching public was bug-eyed at all the tales of fortune and enterprise, many of them purest baloney. However, enough were true to keep talent scouts sleepless and their club owners with one foot on the steps of airplanes bound for Brazil.

In sharp contrast to his posture when Max Winter hired him to put together the Minnesota franchise, Thomas was a proved hunter when Robbie offered him the Miami personnel job. With dozens of able operatives at his beck in the provinces and his own remarkable noggin stuffed with players' names and details about every one of them, Thomas was ready with weapons for the mortal war then in full fury.

Joe Foss, commissioner of the AFL, talked to Thomas about Miami's upcoming franchise in the younger league when the two attended the 1965 Coaches' All-America game, then in Buffalo.

Thomas shrugged him off, but then—another vital milestone for the AFL—the National Broadcasting Company signed with the AFL to telecast its games across the nation on a basis comparable to CBS telecasts of NFL games. The latter factor was even more important than the millions of dollars involved, although these, too, were a life-ring for the younger league. NBC's immediate plunge into promotions of its new programs, blended with the fresh awareness of the AFL at bargaining tables and the swift acceptance of tube-watching on Sunday afternoons by whole families, not just the males, accelerated the NFL's uneasy feeling.

It also convinced Thomas that a move might be right for him.

Foss talked to him again; Thomas called Robbie, whom he had never met, though both lived in Minneapolis. They made a deal and, two weeks later, in September 1965, Thomas—who was to remain a bachelor for another three or so years—moved his kit to a downtown Miami hotel. He and Robbie lunched with Max Winter during their talks about the move, and Winter had proved friendly to the last, but Thomas left the safety of the NFL's fastest-growing team family anyhow. Joe had had his own problems with the temperamental Dutchman, Norm Van Brocklin; these had left scars.

Of the several things he brought with him to Miami, none was more valuable at that tense moment than the certain knowledge of NFL methods and practices in the signing of draftees and free agents. Rozelle's "hand-holding" squads were on or near every college campus in America. The NFL commissioner's imaginative plan for cajoling the unready and nailing down college stars already leaning toward play in the NFL sent relays of personable young coaches and staff people from all league teams, plus some hired outsiders of proved loyalty and knowledge, swarming after the stars the moment the college coaches would allow their presence. Many were spirited off to glamorous hotels, etc., before some college coaches even knew the "baby sitters" were in their state.

The older league had more teams (fourteen to eight), a stronger league organization, and far more prestige. All these were thrown into the balance, as AFL clubs searched for the stars with accompanying "baby sitters" or "hand holders," if necessary, but preferably alone and agreeable to the sounds of green money being rubbed together. It was a great moment in history to be young, vigorous, and possessed of at least a small reputation as a college football player. Seldom has modern America seen such an outrageous display of punch and counterpunch between an established member of Big Business and an aspirant willing to take some lumps while getting topside, too.

That the Dolphins weren't nearly so well heeled as their competition was not apparent at the outset; it's certainly doubtful that Joe Thomas comprehended the depth of this explosive fact when he took on the chore of capturing players in the wildly changing scene. But, once committed, Thomas stayed the route.

As he did so, he realized a paramount truth: Any college player who seemed warm could be drafted by one league or the other, but the fatal error was to waste a high draft turn on a player who couldn't be signed. For all the flesh hunters in the NFL and AFL, a college star's natural affinity for one league or the other equaled in importance his speed or other physical charms.

In the draft of 1966—held in November 1965 by the AFL and shortly thereafter by the older league—Tommy Nobis was the perfect example of this. The great middle linebacker from Texas was determined to play in the NFL—"I want to test myself against the best," he later said—and Thomas knew it was foolish to try to persuade him otherwise. In many instances, less-confident college aces could be prevailed upon to sign with the AFL, for it was almost certain they could play first-string ball more quickly in the younger league.

It is worth noting, however, that even with extraordinary thought and complete concentration on the problems and opportunities before him in that draft, the gifted Thomas fell short of providing the Dolphins what he strived for hardest—a quarterback and a middle linebacker able to flower quickly and serve as the iron centerpiece for later drafts that would flesh out the predictably weak initial team structure and make it a contender in five seasons. That Joe succeeded a year later in obtaining such a quarterback and traded for the middle linebacker (Nick Buoniconti) in 1969 is historical fact.

The 1965 college season turned up two quarterbacks who seemed likely pro prospects.

Rick Norton, a tall, soft-spoken Louisville native, had rattled the Southeastern Conference consistently in his three varsity seasons at Kentucky. In those three years, he completed 302 of 573 attempts (52.7 percent) for 27 TDs. He was the hottest thing around, except for one factor: Norton injured his knee in a game against Houston late in that 1965 campaign. The subsequent operation was successful, but Norton turned out to be a slow healer. This last was not known when the two big leagues went after him.

The other prospect, Randy Johnson, of Texas A&I, enjoyed equally favorable reports from pro scouts, but Norton's SEC experience weighed in his stead, and Thomas drafted him in the first round. The best athlete in that draft—a college running back—was the powerful Jim Grabowski, of Illinois. Since the Dolphins had a "bonus" pick at the top of the AFL's first draft round, Thomas drafted Grabowski in that opportunity; he and Norton were considered, at the time, a glittering catch if both could be signed. When it got down to contracts, Norton signed for three hundred thousand dollars over a five-year period with the Dolphins, but Grabowski opted for Green Bay instead. Reports claimed outrageous figures for Grabowski from the Packers; it hardly is likely that the late Vince Lombardi, then at the peak of his powers and prestige, offered Grabowski the seven hundred thousand dollars bandied about at the time. Thomas admits reaching five hundred thousand dollars in a fit of generosity and, in the market of that day, Grabowksi was worth it. He later had a couple of excellent seasons with Green Bay, but a bum knee and other hurts stopped Jim before he reached the enormous potential seen for him.

Having satisfied his first requirement with Norton—"I told our owners that we had to have a quarterback above all others," Thomas has said, "even if it took our five top drafts in five years"—the hunter went looking for a middle linebacker, the defensive key around whom action revolves no less than around the quarterback on offense. The local press had approached the upcoming draft with bellows for Tommy Nobis, the burr-headed Texan with the élan of a cornered leopard . . . Miami reporters remembered the Orange Bowl game in which this great linebacker had stopped Joe Namath cold when it counted most. That was good enough recommendation.

This urging wasn't needed. Thomas knew about Nobis. But he also knew from a careful investigation that the big blond wouldn't sign with an AFL team—he wanted the NFL and knew he could have it. In the event, Houston of the AFL drafted Nobis in the first round and offered him everything but his pick of oil wells in East Texas; Tommy said "No" and signed with Atlanta, a young team in the other league. Having passed up the chance to negotiate with Nobis in the opening round, Thomas had two other linebackers in mind: Carl McAdams of Oklahoma and Frank Emanuel of Tennessee. McAdams was gone to the Jets when the Dolphins' second-round chance came and Emanuel, a big, handsome All-American from Tennessee, was selected.

Emanuel's reputation was no less impressive than was Norton's; established stars of the SEC generally are considered equal to any prospects in the nation by pro scouts, and Miami was considered fortunate, indeed, to have bagged this pair at the positions considered primary targets. But Emanuel—perhaps overmatched by demands made upon him—could not cash in the physical attributes that made him superior among college players. The bidding for this linebacker outstripped that for Norton, the quarterback; even after Thomas signed him for four hundred thousand dollars—again a five-year package—a report had the NFL trying to get him with another fifty thousand dollars on top. But Emanuel stuck with Miami. Apparently Frank was one of those prideful college stars who wanted quick acceptance on a pro team, a first-string job immediately. He got it with the Dolphins, but this may have contributed to his eventual frustration.

Emanuel was to spend the summer months of 1966 involved in a military obligation, the Coaches' All-America game, and the Col-

lege All-Star game at Chicago. When he finally appeared in the
Dolphins' camp, George Wilson and his assistant coach of linebackers, Bob Pellegrini, naturally tried to blend him into the
situation as quickly as Emanuel could absorb the demands upon
him. From that time forward, Frank always appeared to be trailing
the parade a bit. Any rookie playing middle linebacker will have
enough problems for a battalion of geniuses to deal with; in
Emanuel's case, he also had the worrisome job of calling signals for
the defensive platoon. These demands were compounded when his
arrival at the Dolphins' camp was delayed for weeks by the all-star
games of that summer. Those who have been close to the Dolphins
since their inception recall Emanuel's career with the team sym-
pathetically. While the Virginian had enough size and quickness,
his lateral agility wasn't of the best. But his troubles weren't rooted
in the physical problems of his position; it is ironic but Frank
Emanuel very well might still be playing professional football if he
had signed with a team that could afford to let him learn for a
couple of seasons before giving him prime responsibilities.

When Thomas reflects upon the Emanuel story it has to be
a humbling experience . . . but then Joe can recall the day he
signed Lonnie Warwick for Minnesota's Vikings and gave Lonnie a
free agent's contract and not a dime in bonus. Warwick became
one of football's best middle linebackers; Emanuel kicked around a
couple of other pro teams after the Dolphins shed him at the
start of the 1970 season. A year later, Frank was back on the
Tennessee campus as a student assistant coach.

The unrelenting pressure of pro football on its practitioners
hardly can be better illustrated than with Emanuel and Rick
Norton; we will consider Norton's tale of woe later.

Of the twenty draftees of that first Dolphin team, fourteen
were signed and appeared in training camp. When the 1971
Dolphins took the field, two survivors of that maiden batch were
still there or thereabouts. Bob Petrella, the eighth pick in 1966,
usually a reserve in the secondary troupe, proved especially valuable on the kicking teams; in this hard and painful world, the
slender Petrella survived through sheer, cussed courage, tackling

larger men than himself with a violence that brings the customers to their feet and a ringing to his own ears that must last until the following Thursday.

Howard Twilley, the other surviving first-draft Dolphin, is a man of elfin humor and, unfortunately, the size to go with it. At five feet, ten inches, and 185—or that's what he claims—and the kind of speed only a father could praise, Twilley still was there in the draft pot when the Dolphins' twelfth chance appeared; Thomas shrugged and took him. To this day, there are people who can't understand how Howard set ten National Collegiate Athletic Association records in his senior year at Tulsa. The 134 passes he caught that season must have been accidental, according to this school of reason. The 127 points he scored also were obscured by the stubby build and—for a wideout—all the swiftness of a fat lady falling downstairs. But, then and now, Thomas saw in Twilley not only hands that matched any in football but a stubborn spirit equal to any.

In his rookie year, Twilley survived a jaw cracked in two places and—in 1969—a fractured elbow that doctors said would prevent the pale-eyed receiver from straightening his right arm for years and probably forever. A week before he was supposed to make even the first effort toward rehabilitating the elbow, Twilley was soaking it, flexing it, wincing, and gritting his teeth but trying to overcome the odds. He won. But then, with the appearance of Paul Warfield and, to a lesser extent, Willie Richardson, Twilley's speed—or lack of same—was brought into focus once more. The mulish Texan didn't back down; blazing speed he never had, but courage he had in plenty, and it won for him. In the 1970 season, Year of the Turnabout for the Dolphins, Bob Griese threw to Twilley, Warfield, or Jim Kiick in key situations and, it seemed, to nobody else.

The early character and characteristics of the Dolphins were neither established nor embellished by Petrella and Twilley, however. The innards and the attitude of George Wilson's first team was to come from the stocking draftees and, in a unique byplay, from the son of the coach.

3

The Old Hands

While Robbie's struggles to put together a front office force and coaching staff simultaneously seemed slow producers, they paid off rapidly in January 1966.

Charlie Callahan was brought in from Notre Dame, where he had become a personality of national reputation while serving as public relations staffer for the football operations of Frank Leahy, his predecessors and heirs. Two weeks later, on January 29, George Wilson was named the first head coach of the Miami club.

But the draft of players already under contract to other teams—the stocking draft—was accomplished by Thomas before Wilson appeared. The scout got about as mixed a bag as one can imagine from that highly charged gathering of AFL owners and coaches at Houston. Even so, from the high ground of success today, Thomas looks back and admits he did better there than he did for the Vikings in that earlier time when other NFL teams sliced into their squads to equip Minnesota with football players.

Much of this difference came from guidelines established by the league in each case. The American Football League's scheme was more likely to produce a competitive new member than was the NFL's. It was simple necessity. The Dolphins were the ninth member of the AFL; the NFL's new Atlanta franchise was its fifteenth, with New Orleans on the drawing boards. If the AFL couldn't produce parity in numbers, it had to combat the older group's geographical advantages—the NFL was firmly fixed in every region of large population—with excitement for TV watchers. The AFL could attract attention only with competitive new teams. The reader must not think the guidelines were established out of charitable impulses. These seldom surface in modern pro football.

A comparison of the stocking plans of the two leagues, governing the establishment of the Minnesota and Miami franchises:

The National Football League, for the 1960 roster of the Vikings, told each of the other teams it could "freeze" thirty players (these could not be lifted by the Vikings); then Thomas picked three of the remaining eight, for the NFL player limit was thirty-eight in those days. Obviously, the last eight players of a thirty-eight-man roster were not the cream of the crop.

In stocking Miami, the AFL, having witnessed what happened at Minnesota and Dallas, for example, laid down a more generous set of rules. AFL teams already in business could "freeze" only twenty-three players; Thomas then could pick two men from each club. After this, each club—having surveyed the situation anew in the light of Miami pickoffs and its own needs—could freeze one player each, before the Dolphins could pick off two more per club. Altogether, the Dolphins got a basic squad of thirty-two players from the other eight AFL teams.

For weeks ahead of time, Thomas prepared for the Houston meeting. Since the college draft was completed in November and afterward he was furiously fighting off efforts of NFL teams to abolish him in contract competition for drafted collegians, there already was plenty of activity to keep him busy. But the stocking draft couldn't wait. It was scheduled for mid-January.

Some ideas about who could and who could not do a job around the league were formed during the 1965 season—between watching and evaluating college players—but Thomas did his main scouting for talent among the other AFL teams with a movie projector. Fourteen hours a day for a solid week, he sat in the office of the American Football League in New York, ceaselessly stopping and starting films of AFL games of the 1965 season; these were made available by Mark Duncan, chief of officials in the office of Commissioner Joe Foss. When Thomas finally got on the plane back for Miami and closed his weary peepers, he at last felt he had reasonable knowledge of the skills available among AFL players. But he didn't get the "freeze" list until ten days had passed in January. Decisions had to be made hurriedly.

There were no Joe Namaths or Ernie Ladds on these lists, of course. But youth—so conspiciously missing from the players in the NFL's stocking draft for Minnesota—was available to Thomas now. It became a matter of blending experienced veterans, many of whom were approaching the sunset of their careers, with fresh blood already tempered somewhat by a season or two or three in AFL competition. In the years since that foray among the other squads at Houston, the Dolphins profited constantly from the young players Thomas picked off that first freeze list— after each of the other teams withheld twenty-three players. Norm Evans, the powerful and intelligent offensive right tackle of the current Miami squad, was one of those youngsters. Norm is just arriving at his full powers, and years of play still lie before him. When Miami took him off Houston's roster in the stocking draft, Evans was a six-foot, five-inch, 235-pounder, one year off the TCU campus and, at twenty-three, still with baby fat on his bones. There's none there now.

Maxie Williams also was in that first batch and, as an offensive tackle and guard, was on the "injured reserve list" in 1971. A big (six-four, 240 pounds), cheerful man, Maxie already was twenty-five when Thomas netted him off the Houston roster. Maxie laughs and admits he was "the world's oldest rookie" in 1965, for he had served an enlistment term in the Army before he entered Southeast Louisiana. Despite injuries that would fell a bull, the soft-spoken Virginian plied his trade season after season. While they were valuable for other, obvious reasons, Maxie and Norm Evans were ties to the pioneer past for the youngsters who joined the Dolphins later, in more palmy days. A bum back forced Maxie to the injured reserve list in 1971. He was waived later and is currently a free agent.

Some of the others in that first squad showed zip for an entirely different set of reasons, most of them tied to the pride trampled on by their original clubs: Invariably, they played well against the team that made them available to the Dolphins, the one that wouldn't freeze them in its roster. While these people—usually the tired, the slow, or the marginal—could get "up" psychologically for a great effort against their former teammates, they couldn't maintain any such pace through a season.

"Look at the records of expansion teams," says Joe Thomas. "They win three apiece. . . . It happened at Minneapolis, Cincinnati, Atlanta, and New Orleans, in addition to Miami, because the fellows playing for these teams were tall as a Georgia pine the day they played against their old clubs. Then they fell back after the great effort of it all. . . . Wilson knew he had four guys 'ready' for every game he played that first season. They would play with broken legs against the clubs that let them get away, just to prove how wrong those clubs were.

"It didn't work at Dallas. I don't know what happened there, but I guess it's the exception that proves the rule. Dallas didn't even win the three. . . ."

The target in Miami's drafting of the stocking group was balance; difficult enough to attain when the hunter is leisurely picking among high-grade college stars, it is infinitely more so in the circumstances we've described. From close up, one is amazed

that Thomas and the other men in the perilous trade don't go daft
in almost any season . . . 1965–66 will go down as the maddest
of all times for the talent hunters involved in building new squads,
for the whole panorama of problems was overlaid by the pervasive
odors of money burning.

Danny Thomas, Joe Robbie, and associates could enjoy tax
writeoffs from their heavily mortgaged investment only by amortiz-
ing the $7,500,000 commitment to the American Football League
for the franchise over a period of five years. This commitment
could be established as a capital investment in goods or—in the
Dolphins' case—players.

> *It's a fast track. . . . I've had every hustler and promoter
> from all over America come in here and try to take a nick out
> of my hide. Miami people are deeply suspicious of anyone who
> comes in from the outside; we suffered from that.*
> —Robbie

For this reason, each of the thirty-one players obtained by the
Miami club from other AFL teams was evaluated on the ledgers
at a price of $234,375 on the hoof. For such a kingly sum, one
would expect to find at least a Bronko Nagurski, if not a Jim
Brown, now and then. But this hardly was the case. Instead, the
first Dolphins were as ordinary a band as one can imagine, their
ages and experience stretching from Norm Evans to Mike Hudock,
a former University of Miami center picked off the Jets. At thirty-
one, Mike was the original grandpappy of the Dolphins. Others
nearing thirty (and perhaps a natural reluctance to leave the
comfort of the twenties entered their recitation of vital statistics)
included Bo Roberson, of Cornell and Buffalo; Dick Wood, from
Auburn and Oakland; Laverne Torczon, of Nebraska and the
Jets; and Mel Branch, a surviving member of LSU's once-famous
"Chinese Bandits," who came to Miami from Kansas City's Chiefs.

This was the high end of the age scale Thomas accepted from
the stocking draft. Later, and rapidly, he paid the carfare of a
human chain of prospects who—washed up with other teams—

figured Wilson needed them and came in as free agents; usually they didn't hang around long, but a few proved valuable.

One of these was to be the grand old man of the squad, Rick Casares, a onetime Florida ace whose name still makes Gator alumni break out in goosebumps, but who made it even bigger in the NFL with Chicago's Bears. Now thirty-five and a few beers later, Rick volunteered his person, and Wilson said he'd like to have the old bull on the grounds; Thomas brought Casares over from his Tampa bar-restaurant, and Rick was a large contributor in several games of that first season.

In the stocking draft itself, the catch definitely was a cut above the cull class; hardly typical but proof of this point was Dave Kocourek.

At twenty-nine, Kocourek could look back upon five years as an all-league selection in his six seasons with San Diego; with the Chargers, the Wisconsin graduate was the player representative and, indeed, served as the AFL player rep—a guarantee that he was a natural leader. A 235-pound tight end, Kocourek was named the Dolphins' offensive captain and caught more passes than anyone else in the club in 1966. Dealt two seasons later to Oakland, Dave returned to make his home in Miami and today is a key executive in one of Florida's large community development companies.

Kocourek's presence on the freeze list submitted by San Diego was proof that the twenty-three-man hold rule worked in the Dolphins' favor; there was further proof in another Charger found on the list. This was Dick Westmoreland, a four-year pro corner-back who had missed most of the previous season because of a badly cracked arm. Fast and extremely agile, Westmoreland's career at Miami was to be filled with ebbs and flows—much of his public acceptance, or lack of it, intimately tied to the quality, or lack of it, in the Dolphins' rush line . . . for it is here that pass defense begins. But Westmoreland kept his own counsel about this feature of his life with the Dolphins. Let it be said Joe Thomas did not regret snapping him up from the Chargers, who bucked like crazy when Westmoreland was lost to them in the stocking draft.

Apparently it was presumed he would be passed over by Miami, since his previous season (1965) was not outstanding. Thomas confessed later that he went for Westmoreland because of things he had seen him do as a college boy at North Caroline A&T . . . surely a long-shot basis after four years, but this is the hunter's way.

Space forbids recollections of all those first veteran Dolphins (see the Appendix), but a scan of those who occupied the "skill positions" mentioned earlier is proper, since later drafts and trades can be understood more clearly with these in mind.

If anything, the quarterback situation was more marginal than most, since only madmen would make available passers and field generals of long-range value. Unfortunately for the Dolphins, the only madmen at that Houston meeting were owners, general managers, and coaches of AFL teams upset with their NFL opposite numbers in the fight for survival. The Dolphins did get a couple of quarterbacks, but—as the first season developed—they were to assume smaller and smaller roles.

The senior quarterback from the moment he was picked off Oakland was Dick Wood, the six-foot, five-inch giant from Auburn; after a couple of autumns in the NFL with Baltimore, Wood had drifted over to the San Diego Chargers for a season before joining the Jets, with whom, in two seasons, he threw 329 passes for 4500 yards and 35 touchdowns—impressive statistics, indeed.

Wood could sling a football from Miami to Fort Lauderdale if he could stand up long enough to bring his arm around. But the cheerful giant needed props, for his poor legs long since had knees of jelly. Wood had undergone *seven* knee operations, for everything from cartilage to explorations for gold before he reached Miami; yet he had enough physical resources left to attract the thoughtful eye of scouts in both leagues. One doesn't often see a quarterback with the height and arm—plus the football mind—of a Dick Wood. But he was lost, once the pocket of protecting blockers was broken, for he scrambled with all the agility of a drunken seal on a wet rock.

Since the Miami line of those days seldom forbade at least a passing shot at the quarterback to any rusher with a positive approach, Wood was to be batted mercilessly on those occasions when he could play. Although he was to throw more passes (230) than any Dolphin in the first season, his completion percentage of 36.1 hardly did his arm justice, and Dick would retire after that 1966 season.

It isn't cruel to say that Dick Wood was a total loss at any offense save that calling for a drop-back, pocket-style quarterback. With the Dolphins of that day, the emphasis was otherwise; perhaps out of necessity because of uncertain power in his offensive line, George Wilson was to lean more and more heavily upon rollouts. And the other veteran quarterback obtained in the stocking draft was to have health problems similar to Wood's, except more so.

Eddie Wilson—no kin to the coach—probably was a shade shorter than the six feet his stat sheet claimed, but he was tall enough. A crackerjack at Arizona, Eddie was drafted in the third round by Kansas City in 1961 and signed, although the NFL's Detroit Lions (where George Wilson was the reigning coach, by the way) picked him in the older league's second round. Eddie figured he could play quicker with the Chiefs; he did that but also took some wounds and, after three seasons, was dealt to Boston. The Patriots made him available to the Dolphins, and Thomas—knowing of a knee problem—took him anyhow. The idea here was to go with Wood, if possible. But if Eddie Wilson blossomed, he would be No. 1, for Eddie was a superb athlete in several sports and doubtless could be fitted into any kind of attack Coach Wilson laid out for Miami. But none of this came to pass, for Wilson's knee was to be a bother all season and, after very sparing action in 1966, he left the game. So much for veteran quarterbacks.

The problems that were to accrue around big Frank Emanuel, the college senior drafted to be the middle linebacker, already have been noted. From the stocking draft the Dolphins obtained a total of three linebackers, all aggressive by nature and obviously of a mind to battle anybody. But their talents weren't always so evident.

The central figure among these—and in almost any group he passed through in his football years—was Edward "Wahoo" McDaniel, an Oklahoma Choctaw of cherubic countenance. Wahoo also had been around, for a fellow in his twenty-ninth year. After good work for Bud Wilkinson at Oklahoma, he had wandered from the Dallas Cowboys to San Diego, Houston, Denver, and the New York Jets. Between these, Wahoo's campfire had been seen in almost every nook and cranny of the land, for he wrestled every wintertime. At 230 pounds or so and under six feet—the figures said—he was a compact citizen.

It is possible that McDaniel was more valuable as a center of attention for the fans than as a traffic director on defense. A quick-witted man, Wahoo usually could be found within earshot of the coaches, who delighted in his sallies no less than the paying customers. Instead of "McDaniel," the name on his jersey was "Wahoo," and spectators enjoyed hooting it in the most unlikely situations. Altogether, he had a unique place in the affections of those around him, including some opposing teams.

The other veterans, Tom Erlandson and Jack Rudolph, basically were outside linebackers. Capable of exceptional games occasionally, none of these older players had the kind of sure-fire talent and natural leadership that makes the good middle linebacker vital and necessary to a winning football team. The other AFL clubs hardly could be expected to furnish such a jewel in the expansion draft—no team has more than one—and the Dolphins didn't get one in that first draft of college seniors. In addition to Emanuel, Bob Bruggers came in from Minnesota and Jack Thornton from Auburn. Each was to have some good days, but none of this trio was the answer, either.

It could be said that few American League teams of that time had linebackers of the level enjoyed by NFL teams. Such a statement defies proof, but the observer had the feeling that linebackers born to the trade were of such a malevolent turn of mind that they naturally leaned toward work in towns where they could be hit hardest. The good ones actually seem to enjoy life most when their bells are rung loudest. Be that as it may, the Boston

Patriots had one of the AFL's few linebackers of national reputation in 1966. This citizen's name was a jawbreaker first renowned at Notre Dame: Nick Buoniconti. Not large (five-eleven, 220), he was quick, aggressive, and with built-in sensors that told him things about the opposition's offense; a trained lawyer, Nick also could dredge up defensive sets that might confound the other side, no matter the heat of the fight. He was to come to Miami for the 1969 season after recovering from a knee problem that led Boston to a mood for trading him. It was one of the most fortunate moves the Dolphins have made, ranking in importance with the sensational acquisition of Paul Warfield a year later; but in 1966, this was all in the future.

In a nutshell, the linebackers—including the crucial middle one—were of spotty quality for George Wilson's first Miami team.

Another of the "skill" positions—running back—was only lightly populated from the drafts of college seniors and other AFL players, but free-agent prospects, old and young, lined up as if for an Army chow line to tryouts in training camp.

The eleventh-round draftee, Illinois' Sam Price, was the lone collegian tapped as a runner. Sam had established his claim as a blocker while brushing aside tacklers who tried to reach Jim Grabowski, and it was felt that he would blossom as a ball carrier with the Dolphins. With better-than-average speed for a 215-pounder, Price had the equipment. Perhaps a stronger line ahead of him and steadier quarterbacking could have made his story a happier one; Sam never was able to reach high-average consistency for the Dolphins.

This left it up to old hands, the stocking draftees. And Thomas picked off several.

For power, Billy Joe certainly appeared the ideal answer. AFL Rookie of the Year in 1963 at Denver, the former Villanova star began having trouble with bunions, of all things, the following year. His high production of 649 yards and seven TDs for Denver shrank to 377 for Buffalo, in 1965, but Billy brought his sore tootsies to the Dolphins with the declaration that they felt fine, really. When Coach Wilson saw him, he had to be impressed:

240 pounds well distributed over a frame six feet, two inches tall. Joe was one of those athletes everybody in all football expects will become a great player, for he has the size, power, and speed to make things happen whenever he wishes. Today, Larry Csonka —almost a duplicate of Joe in physical dimensions—is such a one. The man who can determine before—or even after—why a Billy Joe falls short while a Larry Csonka reaches his potential will have all the answers there are in football.

Billy Joe was not the answer for the Dolphins, although he looked like a dandy when first he loomed up the turnpike. Another big back, Jack Spikes, a veteran of sound experience at Dallas and Kansas City, balked when drafted from Houston and was traded to Buffalo.

Fortunately, all these factors and failures weren't known to Coach Wilson as the first training camp approached in the early summer of 1966. On paper, the Dolphins had running backs. Later, they were to discover that their only successful people at the two deep-back positions were free agents—with Joe Auer foremost among them.

Surely Auer was one of the curious talents of his time, a fellow who did everything a little differently, leaving his own mark on teams and backfields with which he was associated during a career that began in Coral Gables, at the local high school, when the blond kid with the lazy blue eyes was an all-state whiz. At Georgia Tech, Bobby Dodd got a larger percentage of Auer's considerable ability for a longer stretch than any of the other coaches along his way. Even so, observers with a grasp of the national scene muttered that Joe Auer should be the greatest, but that he wasn't quite able to handle day-to-day discipline that superiority demands of an athlete. This, perhaps, is the nub of the frustrations that Joe met in camp after camp . . . at Kansas City, Buffalo, and Los Angeles. In the Rams' camp of 1966, Joe sensed he wasn't doing so swell and made a move on his own. He called George Wilson and came to the Dolphins as a free agent in the preseason period. He was to become the team's most valuable player in that first season.

Auer had deceptive speed: with long strides chewing up ground he seemed to be gliding across, he was at his best when defenders were loosely arranged. At such times, the 205-pounder's pacing and changing of gears was a delight to watch. Then, when he had to take a plastering or flee for the sidelines, he stood his ground and got what he could out of the situation. Joe Auer was a good football player.

The historian leafing back through files and old accounts is struck by the way Auer's off-field life got more attention than what happened to him or around him while he played football. The fact Joe enjoyed animals seemed to fascinate some reporters—among other things, when in college, his uncle's veterinary clinic gave him access to a pet lion for a while—and the notion got around that Auer was listening to a different drummer. This was reinforced by small arguments that seemed to follow him through every football organization; if he wasn't wrestling the front office on one matter, it soon would be two. As a consequence, Auer remained in the thoughts of his contemporaries, and they may have been inclined to load him up with suspicions he didn't deserve.

An example of this occurred the second summer the Dolphins went to training camp; Auer was driving a "dune buggy" when it failed to make a turn near the dormitory. Joe was bruised somewhat—but Larry Csonka also was in the buggy and might have had his neck broken . . . this was the general reaction to the incident. Such small tempests, never matters of national concern, seemed to follow Joe throughout his playing days.

He was to score a touchdown on the opening kickoff of the Dolphins' first official game—against the powerful Oakland Raiders, at that—and was a dramatic figure in that eventful first season. That he later was to move on to Atlanta's Falcons in a small storm of argument with the Dolphins' front office was a footnote typical to his story.

There were other running backs who contributed modestly to that first effort, but they quickly appeared and departed. The legendary "Cookie" Gilchrist was brought in after the season opened, but he was nothing close to the buster he had been at Buffalo two years before.

The reader will agree, perhaps, that the Dolphins were uncertain at the first three of the "skill positions"—quarterback, middle linebacker, running back—in the season of their beginning. This was not true, however in the fourth of the positions, that of receivers. There was balance and talent here in both the young and old players brought to camp.

We already have discussed Howard Twilley, the wideout. While injuries were to hamper Howard in that rookie year, his presence gave Coach Wilson and associates reason to think they could have a passing attack when they could get a quarterback to throw strikes. And the stocking draft was more generous with receivers than one might expect.

Foremost among the goodies Thomas found there was Frank Jackson, an engaging citizen who came from Southern Methodist via Kansas City. Fast and possessing excellent intuition, this twenty-six-year-old had caught sixty-two passes in one season (1964) of the five he spent with Kansas City; he also scored nine touchdowns in that year. Although injury cut him down to one TD and twenty-nine receptions in 1965, Jackson had maintained his average of fifteen yards per reception. This wasn't close to the average (twenty-six) Paul Warfield later was to produce for the Dolphins, but how many Paul Warfields have been produced by all of football?

In retrospect, Jackson did not attain the performance level for Miami that he did for Kansas City. Injuries were to bother him, and other, younger players nudged him aside as the seasons wore on, but Jackson had that undefinable "it" that sets aside the football player of real quality, until his retirement a couple of seasons later.

Bo Roberson, mentioned earlier, was older than Jackson but a proved receiver who had done very well with Buffalo's AFL champions; when Roberson was shrugged off by the Bills and Miami snapped him up, a furor among Buffalo fans ensued. But the moody wideout was not to prosper in Miami. Perhaps Lou

Saban, Harvey Johnson, or another of the Buffalo people who made the decision to make Bo available had seen something that wasn't obvious to an outside observer. A silver medal winner in the long-jump event of the Olympic games of 1960, Roberson had brilliant speed that served him well on kickoff returns, no less than as a receiver. With the Dolphins, however, even this skill was lost in the shuffle of events, for some reason.

Among the college draftees, John Roderick was a stickout. The SMU flanker had blazing speed—he turned the 40-yard dash in 4.4 seconds and the 100-yard dash in 9.3—and came to camp with the predictable reputation of being "the next Lance Alworth." The then San Diego flash was the standard by which other receivers were judged, in those days, and Roderick seemed well qualified to be placed in his class. But this was not to be. He was an injury-prone fellow, and his performances for the Dolphins were modest in the extreme.

But the net of the bag of receivers was positive in that foundation year for the Dolphins, and they have maintained a higher-than-average level of receivers ever since. This is true, too, of the tight ends, the bigger, heavier men who are eligible to catch passes but whose primary service to any team is in blocking for the running game; any tight end who has exceptional hand skills is way ahead of the percentages. Kocourek was such a tight end, and LSU's Doug Moreau—who came to the Dolphins as a split end (a wide-out receiver)—developed into one. Moreau was a team member until Marv Fleming appeared in 1970, and would still be present if he had more size. At six-one and 210 or so, Doug was one of those unfortunate athletes who had ability in several fields but could not overwhelm the odds, à la Howard Twilley.

And so it was with the first Dolphins in the "skill positions." They were good enough to be competitive, but not good enough to threaten any of the big boys more often than once a month.

We shall speak of other members of that first squad as the season of 1966 develops on the following pages, after a quick look at the most ridiculous training camp any pro team has endured since the invention of pigskin.

4
George Wilson Begins

The natural choice for the Dolphins' first head coach was George Wilson. There was no serious effort by Joe Robbie to sign anybody else, once his personal favorite, Ara Parseghian of Notre Dame, turned him down.

It is a permanent memorial to the natural optimism of football people—despite their often gloomy estimates of their chances to win a big game—that they run toward a new franchise like ants to a cube of sugar. When Robbie was identified as manager of the new outfit in Miami, he heard from coaches in every part of the spectrum.

He talked a couple of times with Paul Brown, the private man who then was cooling his heels in La Jolla, California, although still being paid eighty thousand dollars or so by the Cleveland Browns for not coaching them. Brown's pride was just as tough as his intellect and neither suffered from the layoff, as was proved when he finally put together the new Cincinnati franchise and—as he did at Cleveland after World War II—formed the Bengals into one of football's most powerful units.

Brown was forthright with Robbie: The coach wanted no part of any professional team in which he did not have a financial interest, and he also required complete control of the club's football operation, including player control at all levels. Robbie, his thoughts somewhat unformed about his own day-to-day relationship with the Dolphins, once the team was in business, moved carefully in his talks with Paul Brown. Tales of the showdown between Brown and Art Modell, after he bought control of the Browns, may have influenced Robbie's thinking. Other factors were pertinent, too. Chief among these was recognition that anyone hiring Paul Brown in 1965 or thereabouts had to content himself with fretting over ticket sales and other important but subsidiary aspects of the football operation—Brown would have to be the boss. Robbie's experience in football was zilch; Brown's was without compare. In the years since the eventual decision about the head coach, Robbie has demonstrated a remarkable talent for survival; he did not test this talent with Brown. What conversations there were on the subject amounted to the most preliminary of explorations and soon were forgotten by both parties.

Wilson's credentials were of the highest and apparently he was not difficult to deal with, once personal contact was established. George had spent considerable time in Florida between seasons with the Chicago Bears as a player and coach and, later, as head coach at Detroit and then as an assistant to Otto Graham at Washington. He made no secret of his happiness at making this decisive move to Miami, where he said he would remain for the rest of his life. When he and the Dolphins eventually parted, after the 1969 season, Wilson was true to his word. He and his wife, Claire, moved to the north end of Dade County, where

George is engaged in the building business and is quite successful at it.

When he signed a three-year contract to coach the Dolphins, in January 1966, he had a building job of another kind, however. Joe Thomas had accumulated the rough materials and some of the trim. It was up to Wilson to make the Dolphins' structure presentable. One great advantage he brought to this task was a large reputation for loyalty to players and his assistant coaches, the latter point having been proved the hard way: The story goes that his whole staff of assistants was fired by the Lions' owner, William Clay Ford, after the disappointing season of 1964, but that Wilson was told he was rehired. George quit rather than accept the canning of his friends, the men he had as assistants.

This notable and public demonstration of loyalty wasn't lost on football's people; it is worth remembering, however, that it got Wilson nowhere. He joined Otto Graham's staff at Washington for the 1965 season, although he had proved his leadership as a head coach with some of the toughest clubs ever seen. Wilson's first Detroit team, in 1957, won the National Football League championship in a period when the game might have reached its zenith in quality, for this was prior to the AFL's creation, when available talent naturally was watered down to some extent, and prior to the larger, forty-man squads we know today.

Certainly the Detroit Lions of the Wilson era put their mark on football—their battles with Green Bay and the Chicago Bears remain legendary and might be compared favorably to struggles between dinosaurs in the prehistoric bog. Wilson was an expert on defenses, a fact easily traceable through his Miami teams. If he had not been so gifted, the early Dolphins doubtless would have been blown to Bimini by Kansas City, Oakland, and San Diego teams that stressed attack. His years with Bobby Layne at Detroit had their effects, too, and George was perfectly willing to let his quarterbacks throw the football despite his personal emphasis on stopping the other people. One could fault neither his philosophy nor his approach to the game.

In the NFL's hard Western Division of those days, Wilson's Detroit teams were 57–45–6, including three second-place finishes in the division, a statistic that always got under Wilson's thick hide; he detested finishing second at anything, yet first established himself with Miami fans when those three Lions' teams played in the Orange Bowl's pro Playoff Bowl game, in January of successive seasons. Since he won all three of those "playoff" things, Wilson's name was a positive force with Miami fans. There was no bickering or outcry when he was named the man to form the team from a squad Thomas had dredged up from every level of skill and geography.

Within four days, Wilson had summoned his longtime associate at Detroit, the late Les Bingaman—as a player the epitome of the middle guard, a powerful symbol of line strength in the 1950s—to be his defensive line coach; Ernie Hefferle, a veteran of many fields, came in from the Steelers to teach the offensive line; Bob Pelligrini, a player at Washington, was brought in to coach linebackers. Soon thereafter, the initial staff was completed: John Idzik, offensive backfield; Tom Keane, defensive backfield; and Bobby Walston, receivers. Wilson, most comfortable in surroundings where relationships are warm and easy, was to feel at home with these staffers, although Pelligrini and Walston were to depart after the 1967 season and were not replaced by the head coach.

Other organizational moves made in the formative months included a contest to name the team, with Robbie and Julian Cole appearing on talk shows and everywhere else they could find welcome to whomp up interest in the project. Eventually, Mrs. Robert Swanson, of West Miami, won the contest and its two lifetime passes with "Miami Dolphins," and James Broome, of Opa Locka, was the runner-up. It was a fortuitous selection, for the happy mammal has proved instantly recognizable across the nation—especially when television's late "Flipper" was seen live and in color, gamboling in a tank at the east end of the Orange Bowl Stadium during games in the first couple of seasons.

Robbie was to recall Flipper's workouts with mixed emotions in the years after this, for negotiations with the owners of the engaging beast broke down, and icebound Yankees no longer could watch him leap in the end zone. Robbie's penchant for controversy was well served by the incident, for he was written up in a national magazine that accused him—among numerous other, less complimentary charges—of being "the man who fired Flipper," a dismal blast indeed. To charges that he had cast away the most easily recognizable and enjoyable signature in American sports in a fit of pinch-purse, Robbie reacted with violent denials . . . but Flipper was not flipping in the end zone, and the kiddies weren't able to see their favorite sardine have fun. Poor Robbie never has lived it down.

Although it was to be influential mostly among insiders, including a high percentage of Miami area newsmen, the personality clash between the managing partner and Julian Cole properly is a part of this story. For a long time afterward and perhaps to the present, it colored Robbie's reception in certain South Florida circles; since both have prospered since, detailed analysis would be academic, but it was significant at the time.

Cole apparently was an almost unanimous nominee by Miami editors when Robbie asked for leads to a knowledgeable public relations man who could serve in the formative months of the franchise. This was an important move, actually, for the peripatetic Robbie was flying off in all directions, hiring staffers and scrambling among bankers, partners, and other AFL people, nailing down innumerable loose ends morning and night. Cole's experience as a top hand at local racetracks and dozens of important expositions and promotions filled the requirements perfectly, and, for a time, the relationship was a congenial one; it became otherwise in the heat and misery of St. Petersburg Beach—or at least this is where others became aware of the division between the two. Sensing Robbie's uneasy position in the summer of 1966, dissident elements of several persuasions joined in the nitpicking, and Cole's usefulness to the football club was destroyed amid accusations and acrimony all hands could ill afford.

This was only one of the unfortunate results of the St. Petersburg expedition, surely the milepost from which all progress by the

Dolphins—on the field and off—must be measured for all time to come.

The ingredients for the disaster were simple: A group of St. Petersburg men, with perfectly good intentions and wild-eyed enthusiasm for Florida's pro team, came to Robbie and offered to underwrite the summer preseason camp if the Dolphins would work at St. Petersburg Beach.

A dozen or more sites in the general area of Miami already had been surveyed, and the most logical among these was St. Andrew's School, an Episcopal institution just south of Boca Raton, some forty-five miles up the Sunshine State Parkway from the Dolphins' home base. St. Andrew's had many appealing aspects, but none so appealing as the free ride offered at St. Petersburg Beach. Even with the barebones operation of those early Dolphin days, a normal preseason camp would chew up in excess of thirty-five thousand dollars.

The decision was made on that basis, with the business-booster club talking about a fifty-thousand-dollar kitty and all sorts of fringe goodies, too. To say the whole dream turned to dust is to put it very mildly, indeed. You could say it turned to the finest of beach sand, mixed with chunks of grass roots, coral rock, and slivers of seashells, with an occasional few square yards of sandspurs to break the monotony.

This was the practice field after the first hour of work on July 5, 1966.

A base of sand overlaid by a carpet of grass, it had a deceptively firm look when Wilson and associates first appeared there in the morning. By the time eighty-four players dug their cleats into the greenery in the morning drill, fears for the footing were being expressed by receivers and runners; by the time a scrimmage on that first afternoon set giant linemen against each other, the awful truth became apparent: This was a miserable field, with the grass —cut into swatches about one foot by two feet in size—being churned up before the first day of work was finished.

By the end of the first week, receivers obviously fearful of turning on real speed found their necks cramped as they attempted to run with one eye on the ball and another on the footing. Potholes developed in the sand, which swirled into dust-devils in the stifling heat. Altogether, it was a place of misery and frustration. Wilson, the dogged trouper, tried to keep smiling, but it was a pitiful situation, compounded by off-field conditions that were no better than those among the seashells.

There was no dressing room, as such. Each player kept his uniform gear in his own room at a motel down the road from the practice field. The reader can imagine the odors and flowering fungi that quickly permeated each chamber. The food leaned heavily toward chow mein and dry sandwiches, with emphasis on shingles of rubbery cheese.

The rookies who swarmed into the camp had to be even more astonished than were some of the veterans of earlier camps when the AFL was in its infancy. Facilities at major universities of the LSU, Ohio State, Michigan, Southern California, etc., cut are the finest money can buy. Players accustomed to luxuries and pampered treatment had approached the pro camp with expectations of moving up in class . . . and the mental letdown by these young bucks had to be the most serious part of the grim situation. Coach Wilson and the other elders at headquarters had lived through the Great Depression and knew privations that went with it. But the young players had no such yardstick, and visitors soon found them dull-eyed and uncommunicative.

With the camp rapidly assuming the general aspects of the battlefield at St.-Lô, another situation arose that complicated the already uneasy financial situation: A nationwide strike of major airlines marooned Joe Robbie in Minneapolis, where he had gone on business, and made the easy or economical movement of players into and out of the St. Petersburg area almost impossible.

Joe Thomas, elbow deep in communications to and from free agents and other personnel chiefs, felt this strangulation most keenly, perhaps, but Coach Wilson was in no less a bind.

"I couldn't spend a hundred dollars without thinking it out very, very carefully," Wilson said later. "It wasn't that Robbie was trying to hold up on expenses, it was just that there wasn't any money for him to send us for the daily operation."

Chuck Burr, Buffalo's publicity director until he came to Miami as business manager of the Dolphins, was in the middle of this squeeze, too, and his experiences later brought him to violent disagreements with Robbie. Burr departed after that first season.

The real crunch was most apparent in the workaday elements common to all football operations—in the training facilities, for example. Trainer Bob Lundy and his helpers tried to do what they could for dozens of players at a time while packed into three adjoining rooms of the motel. These could be identified by the long lines of meaty citizens queued up outside their doors, waiting to have their ankles wrapped and other customary things or— because of the peculiar nature of the practice field—nasty abrasions that somehow seemed different from the ones they knew in college ball at Texas or Tennessee or Notre Dame or wherever.

"The situation got so bad that I talked to the doctor about some new problems that popped up. Before we left St. Pete, I was reading books about the special infections one could expect from being cut by coral rock or seashells. It was a strange and rather terrifying experience," says Lundy.

In the way strong men do, Coach Wilson, Thomas, Lundy, and the other club employees tried to get by without constantly bleating to Robbie for relief. Robbie, in turn, was trying to meet at least the bare necessities of the situation from Minneapolis and Chicago—where he raced among bankers, arranging money matters—and do so without throwing Danny Thomas and his Hollywood crowd into some kind of a panic. As suggested, the airline strikers kept Robbie from flying back and forth between the camp and his banker targets, but the fates may have been kinder than they seemed at the time. If Robbie had been on the grounds at St. Petersburg more often, passions very easily might have got out of hand. They were strained to the breaking point over long-distance telephone lines but, somehow, neither the Dolphins' brass nor the St. Petersburg zealots who had failed so miserably in their grand scheme lost their cool in public. When the chaos was at its height, Robbie finally came south again and, in a couple of brief but pointed statements, told his embarrassed hosts that he was moving his football players elsewhere.

The switch was scheduled for the weekend of the first exhibition game, August 6, when they would play in San Diego. The players were told they would not return to the St. Pete base but would go across the state—a matter of 125 miles or so—to Boca Raton and St. Andrew's School. Jim Davis, coach and athletic director there, had a few frantic days of work, but all was arranged quite well when the Dolphins appeared in their new camp. They were to use the St. Andrew's facility for the rest of that preseason and for the next three summers, until Don Shula's appearance as head coach and the establishment of the present team base at Biscayne College.

Thus the nightmare of St. Petersburg Beach ended. Its legacy was neither pleasant nor profitable to the Dolphins, for bitter things said and written there and attitudes formed there proved highly volatile at a time when the organization could not afford them.

Hangovers and hangups from that dismal experience still shadow the club, but time and distance have blunted their effects.

Yet, with all this agony, an enduring good came from the St. Petersburg expedition: nothing that has happened to the Dolphins since even mildly approaches it in disappointments. It can be said truly and forever by all Dolphins and their fans:

"Well . . . at least this ain't as bad as St. Petersburg."

5

The Wilson Years

THE FIRST SEASON—1966

Some days before they bailed out of the misery of St. Petersburg Beach, the Dolphins moved their practices to the Boca Siega High School grounds and—for the first time—enjoyed sound footing. It was a distance from their motel digs, five miles on a slow bus.

Before embarking for San Diego and their first preseason game, they checked out of the motel and packed their gear for a truck haul across the peninsula to Boca Raton; they were finished with St. Petersburg, and all breathed easier. Now they could get down to the real adventure, football against other people. For that first game, the other people were in San Diego and included Lance Alworth, then the game's finest receiver, and John Hadl, a fellow who could throw with the good ones.

Business Manager Chuck Burr was half out of his wits for weeks trying to pry loose an airplane for the long flight across the country. The extended airline strike still had the nation in a knot. Burr finally contracted for a DC-7C from a charter outfit. The team left from Tampa's airport at eight-thirty on Friday morning and arrived in San Diego seven hours later, breathing heavily. A problem with the pressurization system restrained the plane to twelve-thousand feet, an unpleasant footnote to the previous unpleasant weeks of training camp.

Dave Kocourek and Tom Erlandson were appointed captains for the season by Wilson, and the pleasant weather in San Diego increased the mood of anticipation. The realists knew better, but some of those first Dolphins thought they would withstand the Chargers. Sid Gillman's team was attack-oriented and the defending champion of the AFC West. Tough.

Gillman and George Wilson had been rivals since college days, when Gillman was playing at Ohio State in the years of "Gates of Mercy" Schmidt, a coach who enjoyed pounding opponents to pieces long after they could resist. Wilson played at Northwestern. The rivalry increased when Wilson's Detroit teams enjoyed an edge over Gillman's Los Angeles Rams. It was to boil over in Balboa Stadium on the night of August 6, 1966.

It was only a matter of moments after the opening kickoff until Hadl indicated the flow of events. He hit five of his first six passes in the first period, and his Chargers had a score in just ninety-two seconds.

Wilson, knowing he must pull every stunt known to the game to give his people even a thin chance, had Dick Wood sling a bomb toward John Roderick on Miami's first play from scrimmage, but Kenny Graham, a safety for San Diego, covered Roderick so well that the rookie shoved Graham, and Roderick's penalty pushed the Dolphins back from their own thirty-three to the eighteen. Two plays later, Wood passed again and Graham intercepted, bringing it back for a thirty-eight-yard touchdown. Before the Dolphins could manage a new series San Diego scored again on a fullback pass from Keith Lincoln to Alworth, who breezed into the end zone.

Further details would be meaningless, except that three interceptions in the first half ruined the Dolphins, who yielded ground stubbornly when the Chargers tried to run. Early in the third period, Bob Petrella recovered a fumble inside the Chargers' ten and, after three plays and a holding penalty, the Dolphins were at the four. George Wilson, Jr., in relief of Wood and Eddie Wilson at quarterback, faked a pass and scored the Miami Dolphins' first touchdown, ever.

Thus the twenty-three-year-old rookie son of the head coach struck a psychological blow that loomed large at the time, for he accomplished more in that game than did the others competing for the quarterback job. George, Jr. probably was one of the most knowledgeable rookies ever to show up in a pro camp. He had been his father's shadow every fall as a boy and, while he had no great physical gifts, he proved he didn't spook easily under pressure. Slightly over six feet, the book probably gave him the best of it when it claimed that George, Jr. weighed 185. Yet he had been drafted by Buffalo and dealt to Miami despite a college career as a second-stringer. More important than all this, however, was the combustible situation revolving around George, Jr.'s effort to win the job over Rick Norton, the high-priced Kentuckian. While controversy swirled about them—and there was heat in the front office over young Wilson's presence—he and Norton became fast friends and roomed together at camp and on the road.

In San Diego, however, there were other things for George, Sr. to grapple with, for his team was wobbly, indeed, in that first game.

It wound up 38–10, with Wilson furious that Gillman had kept Hadl and his veteran associates in action into the fourth period, after which Steve Tensi—with twenty seconds to go—intentionally passed out of bounds to stop the clock. He was trying to score. Wilson told Gillman his innermost thoughts before witnesses outside the dressing rooms later, and they were sulphurous.

The next week, after a painful flight home, Wilson opened with George, Jr. at quarterback against Kansas City. At the time, he told Bill Bondurant of the Fort Lauderdale *News,* "I don't care what people think, deep in my heart I honestly believe George deserves this chance. He has consistently improved and looked best in practice. He did the best job last week against San Diego." It was a large responsibility for young George, who had started no games at Xavier University, where running dominated the offense.

In their death throes, the old Miami Seahawks played their last game in the Orange Bowl on Friday, December 13, 1946. Now the pros were back, with 34,277 witnesses as Kansas City smothered Miami, 33–0, in an impressive display of muscle. The Dolphins had the satisfaction of at least worrying their tormentors a trifle, for they reached the Chiefs' five-yard line after a seventy-four-yard drive early in the game. A high snap from center fouled up a field goal try by Gene Mingo. After this, it was all Kansas City, with Norton the most effective of Miami's quarterbacks during a heavy rain in the second half that almost drowned out Phil Napoleon's band near an end zone but bothered Flipper, who was in his tub under the scoreboard, not at all.

Losses to the Jets and Denver completed the preseason.

When Oakland appeared in the Orange Bowl to begin the real season on the night of September 2, only 26,776 fans showed up. In the first seconds of that one they saw Joe Auer contribute a run that added zest to the Dolphins' dreams all year. Joe took the opening kickoff and ran right up the gut, leaned to his left, and scored a ninety-five-yarder that stunned the crowd. Oakland's seventeen-point favorite's role didn't look so swell, and the final loss of 23–11 was respectable in Dolphin eyes. It could have been a whopping upset, perhaps, had Mingo not blown field-goal attempts of nineteen and sixteen yards in the second half. Four of Wood's passes were grabbed off by Oakland in the opening two quarters—one more than Dick completed. It was a very uneven performance, to say the least, but the Dolphins' eagerness and

aptitude with unusual defensive sets—"hell, we didn't have the
talent or the depth to play them straight," growls Wilson—kept
them in the battle.

Oakland made only nineteen yards in twelve rushing plays
against Miami—a statistic the modern Dolphins would accept with
celebrations. McDaniel was the middle linebacker in the five-front,
two-linebacker defense, instead of the normal three-linebacker arrangement. Tom Erlandson topped the tacklers with eight stops
as he shifted toward Oakland's strong side. It was unorthodox,
with three tackles or defensive ends in that five-man front.

Then came the Jets in Miami, with Joe Namath back at QB
after recovering from an injury. It was a close one, with the Jets
taking it, 19–14, although Miami may have played its best of that
first season. The Dolphins came from behind the nineteen points
to score two touchdowns in the fourth quarter, but they were
undone by errors—twelve of the visitors' points were set up by two
interceptions and a safety.

Norton started this game poorly and gave way to Wood, but he
returned to collaborate with Bo Roberson and Kocourek to get the
first Miami touchdown. Later, Miami safety Pete Jacquess hauled
in a Namath pass to go twenty-seven yards for the second, with
Mingo converting. But the Jets got back down to business, and
Miami was through.

It was even more so in the succeeding game, when Buffalo's
physically overwhelming Bills—defending champions of the league
—gave the Dolphins the beating of their lives, with the middle of
the Miami line pulverized and slashed again and again by big,
heavy backs who rummaged around among Wilson's linebackers,
looking for fresh meat. The score, 58–24, remains the largest
ever run up against the Dolphins, but Sid Gillman almost topped
it in the first of two West Coast games after the grim proceedings in
Buffalo's dank stadium.

This time, Gillman's San Diego club didn't have even the mercy
shown Wilson's fledglings in the preseason opener; but at least
George had the moribund satisfaction of seeing his old rival fail
to top the Buffalo count, by a fat four points. Alworth and as-

sociates did a job on Miami, 54–10, but they didn't go ahead until the third period and Tensi got four late TDs with his tosses. The Dolphins' secondary simply broke down in the last stages of it.

Even the brave old tigers who had been thumped before were disheartened by the grisly turn of their fortunes. Wilson, he of the uncompromising competitive spirit, held himself together but was obviously a man in turmoil. The quarterback situation was only part of the mounting burdens, for now the defenses George had concocted to give his offense a chance were no more effective than the offenses themselves. As happens in all games where the emotional pitch of the participants is so large a factor, Bob Lundy's training room looked like the wheat field at Gettysburg. It was a time for finding who was friend and who was foe, especially at the ticket window.

Although he was among the wounded, brave young George Wilson reported able to work against Oakland, and the senior Wilson started him. "The kid has a lot of guts . . . if he thinks he can play with that ankle he hurt at San Diego, he'll play," his father said. The Raiders, coming off losses to San Diego and Kansas City, were eager for a kill.

This meeting occurred in the new Oakland-Alameda County Stadium. Tom Flores was the opening QB for the Raiders—he was to be traded later to Buffalo for another quarterback fellow named Daryl Lamonica—and he found the Dolphins no less contentious than the Raiders' Cotton Davidson had found them in the first game of the season. The Raiders blitzed constantly, but young Wilson's job in the face of this rush earned the praise of Johnny Rauch, the Oakland coach. Unfortunately, the Dolphins' Front Four couldn't rush Flores much, and Oakland passes were the difference in the 21–10 Raider victory.

The best quarterback we had the first season was George Wilson, Jr. . . . He wasn't built too strong but he had the heart of a lion and he had a good mind for football . . . He wasn't as wise in the game as Dick Wood but he always had something when the time came.

—Auer

But now, on the sixteenth of October 1966, the mouse bit the cat, the kid beat up the bully, etc. . . . Miami finally won its first game.

It occurred at the expense of Denver, 24–7, and came at a moment when the coach and his braves were about ready to take a header off a pier into Biscayne Bay. There were 23,393 in attendance at the Orange Bowl when the Broncos (1–4) appeared. Injuries to Emanuel, Eddie Wilson, and Frank Jackson in the exhibition loss to Denver still were a plague to the Miami club.

The defense did it for the Dolphins after nine straight drubbings in the nine chances, with four interceptions in the second half breaking the game wide open. When it was over, George Wilson, Jr. ran toward the mass of Denver players and sought out Tobin Rote, the gallant old (thirty-eight) Texan who came out of retirement to beef up Denver's thin quarterbacking troupe. Rote had a poor day in Miami, but Wilson's attention was a tribute to the past, when Rote was a star for the Lions and Coach George Wilson's kid carried his helmet to the bench.

Dick Westmoreland intercepted two passes, with Erlandson and Willie West snatching the others. Two led to touchdowns.

A couple of days later, while the earth trembled from their strides, Cookie Gilchrist and Earl Faison joined the Dolphins— formidable, powerful men of great reputation who instantly gave a spiritual lift to a squad charged up considerably after the Denver victory. There was only one trouble about the coming of this pair: They were, in the final analysis, over the hill.

Both were among football's top figures when Cookie led Buffalo to the championship of the AFL and Faison was a great defensive end for San Diego. But time and the lush life had done them little good since. They were worth plenty of ink and airtime by reporters, however, and their presence indicated Robbie was willing to go for big bread to get players.

Faison played little for the Dolphins and ended his career with a complaint about his back, for which he sued the club to little avail. Gilchrist, a genuine superstar during his great years, was too heavy at 259, but he ran with the ball seventy-two times and was second to Auer in yardage with 262 for the season. Reporters were awed by his off-field personality more than by his work in shoulder pads while in Miami.

Bill Braucher, of the Miami *Herald,* recalls a luncheon with Cookie during which Gilchrist had some strong words for the eleven-o'clock curfew imposed by Coach Wilson and "a clunker of a car" Robbie had given him to meet a contract stipulation. Cookie thought the Robbie car had square wheels or something.

"So I wrote it," Braucher says, "and the next day Cookie was apoplectic. He ranted and cursed and vowed that not even a rope around his neck would ever induce him to submit to another interview.

"But it appeared exactly the way you told it, Cookie," Braucher responded. "Look. Here are the notes, word for word."

"I know, I know," Cookie came back. "That's what hurts. It's all so true. But now I got Robbie mad at me again!"

Before their parleying finished, Cookie quit screaming for a Cadillac—he admitted a Chrysler Imperial would do well enough.

Dealing with such a spirited citizen was another load for the overburdened Wilson, but George buckled down and led his troops to their second victory.

Young Wilson's sore shoulder was responding to treatment and he was named the starter when the team arrived in Houston to meet the Oilers, who had just dumped the Jets and Namath, 24–0. Miami's winning margin of 20–13 wasn't without its pain, however. Rick Norton, for example, passed thirteen yards to Gilchrist for the Dolphins' second touchdown and had his jaw broken in two places by John Baker. In retrospect, this cruel blow was the end of Rick's career. He never was to have such a clear chance at the first-string job.

Wilson, too, was eliminated for a time when he rehurt the shoulder. It was he who passed to Bo Roberson for the opening TD and gave way to Norton. Meanwhile, Houston's George Blanda —later to have an amazing career with Oakland—was being severely treated by Miami's line. The Dolphins in the pits badgered Blanda constantly; although the Oilers had averaged thirty points per game to this point, they were nowhere that day. Willie West intercepted three Blanda throws and Westmoreland another, to cap it all.

Now came a week off, and no team needed one so sorely—and the pun is intended. Thin to begin with, the Dolphins were beaten to pulp, but at last they felt competitive in the AFL. The rest of the way, they were considered to be at least a respectable football team, despite the way Buffalo treated them in their next out.

The Dolphins had outscored the Bills in the last forty minutes of their first game (the 58–24 horror) as Wilson, Jr. passed for three TDs. He tried again in the Miami game as 37,177 fans rooted hard—this was the first season's largest crowd, by the way —but nothing worked against the defending AFL champions. They even stopped Cookie cold when he tried to smash for a score from the two. Wilson's three interceptions were one more than he had thrown all year and matched his completions in thirteen tries. Perhaps George could have survived later pressure if he had remained on the bench with his sore shoulder that day.

Now came another series of bitter defeats, at Kansas City, at New York, at Boston, and at Denver. The Dolphins were staggering and roadworn when that month finished.

Then they blew a glittering chance.

The Chiefs came into Miami with four straight victories—this was the Kansas City team that later played Vince Lombardi's Green Bay Packers even for the first half of the first Super Bowl game— and the Dolphins' quarterbacks threw six interceptions. Still, they twice took the lead from the gifted Chiefs, and only a Len Dawson fling to Chris Burford in the last seconds saved it for Hank Stram's outfit. Fewer than eighteen thousand fans paid to see that one, and it almost developed into the upset of the year. Kansas City nipped their less skillful tormentors, 19–18, with the late TD.

A lamentable thing in this game: Howard Twilley, the receiver, suffered a broken cheekbone at the hands of Freddie Williamson, he who called himself The Hammer. Twilley, in characteristic fashion, resumed his career after considerable suffering.

In the middle of that losing streak, Coach Wilson called John

Stofa back to the main squad from a minor-league team, the Lakeland, Florida Brahmans, and Stofa—the only healthy passer in South Florida, it seemed—was to have a day like no other for any Dolphin quarterback yet. Not even the splendid works of Bob Griese have matched the sixty minutes Stofa gave the 20,045 spectators in the Orange Bowl as he threw four touchdown passes that licked Houston, 29–28, and finished the season winging.

As if part of the script for this hairy affair, Auer caught a Stofa toss for a touchdown that tied up the count at 28–28. Gene Mingo —a curiously inconsistent fellow with considerable leg—kicked the conversion with thirty-eight seconds on the clock, and Stofa's role of "Cinderella Man" for the Dolphins was nailed down forever.

This gave the Dolphins a third victory in fourteen league contests, tieing an expansion team record then held by Minnesota and Atlanta. It also gave Stofa a reputation for keeping his gun hand dry even in the most pressing situations. No matter how many of the Oilers sought his pelt at once, the tall, pleasant man who had endured so much for this game he loves just stood there and threw the football after starting the battle only because Dick Wood's arm went lame in the warmup.

With young Wilson's future obviously unclear, with Wood's knees telling him to quit and Norton's face bashed lopsided by Baker in the earlier Houston game, there was a place for John Stofa with the Dolphins.

He spent the winter in the warm glow of his grand achievements against Houston, with the knowledge that he was the first-string quarterback and that any who would take the job would have to come get it. John later was to give no sign that the winter draft of Bob Griese bothered him. He at last was master of his own destiny.

I think it got down to the point where Robbie didn't want to have the combination of father and son because reporters would say I was playing my son. . . . If I had to cut my son, I would have cut him, I traded him when I didn't want to because the front office was talking too much and didn't want

him there. . . . As far as I'm concerned, I still think my son
was railroaded out of pro football.

—G. Wilson

But, as we shall see, this was not to be. Stofa would have been
the greatest of Greek dramatists had he lived on the side of the
Acropolis in the Golden Age of Athens. His autobiography would
have been enough for the heavyweight title there.

Auer's fourteen-yard catch of a good pass by Stofa was accomplished with a spectacular leap, and Joe—the Coral Gables
boy—closed the season as he opened it, on a wave of applause.

THE SECOND YEAR: SEASON OF 1967

Ma Bell made thousands on Joe Thomas and George Wilson during
the off-season as they desperately called other organizations, trying to juggle the Dolphins' roster before another campaign. In some
areas they were successful but, in most, it was a matter of bitter
waiting before a blue chip could be found in the trades other teams
were willing to make.

The 1967 winter draft of college stars (see the Appendix) produced excellent results and continues to do so. Among those signed
were Bob Griese, Jack Clancy, Jim Riley, Larry Seiple, and John
Richardson, but Griese was not the instant star his later play
might suggest. He was always a promising performer, but Stofa
was very much on top of the situation when camp opened at St.
Andrew's, Boca Raton.

Stofa's competition was wealthy, but he had the job. Competing
for it was Norton, the $300,000 second-year man; Griese, the
$150,000 rookie, and Jon Brittenum, a $60,000 Arkansas whiz
obtained via the "redshirt draft" of 1966. He, too, was a rookie
and soon went out on a trade. All three had no-cut contracts.

Stofa's contract when he joined the Dolphins in 1966 after the
quarterback group became almost uniformly lame gave him a bonus
of $3500 and an annual payday of $13,000 but no protection from

The Turk—the mythical assassin who cuts players from pro football rosters. Nor did he improve this situation for the '67 season, except that he was paid $15,500 and had a bonus proviso, reported to be worth $5000 if he played more than fifty percent of the time. He never received that five grand, of course.

At twenty-five, Stofa was as mature as he would get, with experience at the University of Buffalo and three Florida minor-league teams—Daytona, Orlando, and Lakeland—before sticking with the Dolphins. Along the way, he also was with the Steelers briefly. He was a genuine journeyman quarterback who had bettered himself. In 1964, he made $75 a game at Daytona and taught at Lopez High. In 1965, he moved up to $100 per game at Orlando—a wage equal to that of many stars of the National Football League before World War II but peanuts now. In thirty-four starts as a minor-league pro in the next two seasons, John would never appear in a losing game; he threw thirty-nine touchdown passes in that span.

In the startling performance against Houston, Stofa completed twenty-nine of fifty-seven passes that ran up 425 yards, with those four touchdowns already mentioned. Coach Wilson would have been the star performer at a necktie party if he had insinuated that anybody else would be his quarterback at the start of training in 1967.

George Wilson, Jr. was traded between seasons to Denver, which also got back Cookie Gilchrist with Earl Faison, and Ernie Park, for running back Abner Haynes, linebacker Jerry Hopkins, and defensive end Danny LaRose, plus a draft pick. Haynes and Hopkins were to be of considerable help in the approaching season, while Gilchrist and Faison didn't do much for Denver. Young Wilson fervently wanted a chance to help the Broncos, but Coach Lou Saban shrugged him off within a few days of the opening of training camp.

Bitterly disappointed, George went on to the Cincinnati camp and suffered a like fate there. He soon gave up his dream and seems to have lived happily ever after. His father was outspoken about the cavalier dismissal at Denver, but otherwise kept his own counsel;

George, Jr. had accomplished far more for the Dolphins in 1966 than anyone could predict from his prior record, and he conducted himself with honor.

The greatest advance for the 1967 Dolphins was in confidence, for now they figured they could play any team, anywhere, with a fat chance of winning.

Their preseason indicated as much, too, for they jumped out to victories over Denver and Buffalo before losing to San Diego, Atlanta, and New Orleans by a total of seven points, not counting a TD given Atlanta in the last few seconds when a fourth-down maneuver failed to get a new series started, deep in the Dolphins' territory.

As camp progressed, Wilson and his staff turned toward the rookies and other young players, peeling off the marginal veterans when possible. When the regular season opened, the Dolphins were a different team from the one that reported to Boca Raton two months previously.

Among those unimpassioned veterans who departed during this paring procedure were Billy Joe, Bo Roberson, Laverne Torczon, Dave Kocourek, Ross O'Hanley, and Alphonse Dotson. Kocourek was to play for Oakland's Super Bowl team before retirement, and some of the others continued active for a time. With the Dolphins, however, the thrust was for youth, the team averaging 25.2 years in age and 2.8 years in experience when the campaign opened. Half of the forty-man squad were rookies (eleven) or sophomores (nine).

Three new veterans—tackle Ray Jacobs, linebackers John Bramlett and Jerry Hopkins—appeared in Wilson's defensive troupe after trades. There was some trace of depth for the first time.

Willie West, the free safety who had done so well in 1966, suffered a shoulder injury in the preseason that required surgery and was lost for most of the season, and tackle Tom Nomina had to have knee surgery. These developments hurt the club.

In the secondary, Tom Beier, a former University of Miami standby, won the strong safety job over Bob Neff, with Jimmy Warren and Westmoreland retaining their cornerback positions.

Petrella, who remains a valuable Dolphin as a utility man in the secondary, held the free safety job usually occupied by West.

A big running back and offensive line help were sought daily, but such trades weren't available to Joe Thomas. The team was termed "explosive but thin," a true evaluation. There was no safety margin; every injury was a grave one.

A fast veteran, Haynes was a sound running back headed for the sunset years and he certainly blended better with the Dolphins' needs than those he replaced. He and Auer would alternate at running back, with Sam Price the fullback in Wilson's attack. Sam appeared more effective as the power-and-block guy than as the primary ball carrier.

In the preseason, Stofa hit for a .457 average and was not consistent, reminding watchers that he was the same passer who went 0–10 against Denver and then threw four TDs against Houston later in the same 1966 season. The rookie, Griese, looked to advantage in the New Orleans preseason game, but it was Stofa who got the call for the season's opener with Denver this time.

On the first play from scrimmage, Big John let fly a forty-five-yard pass to Auer from the Miami forty-one; he then hit Twilley for six and ran the last eight yards to a touchdown himself, giving the Dolphins a 7–0 lead after only one minute, forty-one seconds . . . an explosive beginning, indeed, before twenty-nine thousand hometown fans in the Orange Bowl.

Two minutes later, Stofa was carried off with a twisted knee and a severely fractured ankle and, from that moment until now there has been no serious doubt that Bob Griese is the Dolphins' quarterback.

After Miami fans sighed in despair, Bob passed successfully twelve of nineteen times for 193 yards and two touchdowns. He hit six for seven attempts as the Dolphins drove eighty yards in the second quarter to a score, and he gave a sure hand all the way. The Dolphins tromped Denver, 35–21, as the new star was born.

This proved a deceptive success for the Miami players. They

had found a quarterback, but they still were not equal to the quality control necessary to hang tough with the big fellows each week.

Kansas City beat them severely—worse than the 24–0 score— in the second game, and only the extraordinary work of the rookie punter, Larry Seiple, got the gate shut even occasionally. Seiple's forty-eight-yard average on five kicks established him as a first- string performer for the Miami club, and he has remained so ever since.

Griese was banged in the head early in the fourth period but, considering the superiority of the Chiefs, he had a good day, with eleven hits in twenty-two tries and two interceptions. He was sacked five times and survived other rushes only with mad dashes to safety. Buck Buchanan was his particular nemesis.

Now came hard times at Shea Stadium and one of the most artistic attacks it has been the Dolphins' misfortune to encounter and a game in which Griese hurt his shoulder.

Joe Namath beat them 29–7, with 415 yards passing and seven- teen first downs by air for the Jets, in addition to the three of the four TDs on the board. Wilson admitted after this demonstration that Namath's setup and ball release was the quickest he had ever seen. Told of this high compliment by the veteran football man, Namath responded: "If I set up quicker than any quarterback Coach Wilson has ever seen, it's because I'm the most frightened quarterback he has ever seen!"

By a cruel jest in the schedule, a second game with Kansas City came next, and it was even worse than the first . . . the final, 41–0, made it a laugher for the Chiefs.

Griese did not play because of the shoulder. Norton threw thirty-four times, with a respectable fifteen completions, but he was intercepted four times, while Wilson gave his offensive line credit for better work than against the Chiefs in Miami.

This was one of the low points of the Dolphins' existence, in retrospect, for they had scored only seven points in three games, while yielding ninety-four.

But the turning point was still down the road, for the Patriots battered them, 41–10, before the Jets and then Buffalo, San Diego, and Oakland took turns flailing Wilson's weary and dispirited troops. Altogether, the stretch of defeats reached eight games, the enemy scoring 258 points to the Dolphins' sixty-one, and a Dolphin without a limp was a curiosity seldom seen.

Wilson's stolid loyalty to his players was unshaken, as events proved later, but the poor man was under brutal pressure; his most ingenious defenses crumbled under continuous shocks. Jests at their expense were almost tougher on the Dolphins than what happened on the scoreboards of the AFL. At Boston, for example, a youngster whacked Babe Parilli on the back in delight at the old boy's performance in the rout of Miami and Babe cried: "That's the hardest we've been hit all day. . . ." There was more truth than wisecrack in the response, for Babe passed for five touchdowns that afternoon, while Miami's Norton was harried at every turn by the Pats' rush line.

The Jets were no more kindly and, after a half, Rick packed it in. Griese's shoulder was restored by now, and the rookie threw seventeen completions in twenty-one tosses (81 percent) on the muddy field of the Orange Bowl. But it was too late, Namath had retired at the half with thirteen hits in fifteen tries and a 24–0 lead that eventually brought a 33–14 count. Norton's four completions in seventeen throws soured the air around the expensive second year man, dissipating good will earned against Boston.

In snow flurries at Buffalo, the Bills slashed and hammered the Dolphins' ground defenses without letup and won, 35–13, and then came a second shutout, 24–0, at San Diego, to be followed by a 31–17 pounding at Oakland. These were hard times the Dolphins who joined the squad in the last two years haven't known, yet a notably tough and resilient cadre of Miami fans kept the faith; organizations like the strangely assorted group of businessmen known as the "Dolphins Veeps" maintained a vigil that should be a model for others. Wilson and the Dolphins not only had friends, they had admirers. These weren't always reasonable or judicious people, but they were believers, and they sustained the Dolphins.

At both San Diego and Oakland, the defense largely contained the other team until the last quarter, but the breakdowns then were almost audible, they were so definite. In the latter game, Billy Cannon caught three touchdown passes, a rare day, indeed, for the onetime fireball from LSU. Griese's seventeen hits in twenty-nine throws and 229 yards was a standout performance, too. The Front Four clouted Daryl Lamonica six times but lost anyhow.

When the team returned from that ten-day hideout in California, Miami's response was heartening: some 27,050 people showed up for the second Buffalo game, in the Orange Bowl, although the eight consecutive losses usually had been spectacular drubbings.

After all that pain and another fifty-nine minutes of frustration, the Dolphins got the thing turned around.

They jumped out to a 10–0 lead, but the Bills were protecting a 14–10 comeback when—with sixty-nine seconds to play—Griese found himself on the Bills' thirty-one-yard line, with fourth down and eighteen yards to go, after being decked three straight times.

Behind unusually good protection from a usually permissive front line, the quarterback drifted back to the forty, looking and bobbing. Finally, Bob saw Howard Twilley cut to the middle after faking a sideline pattern, and the strike was caught right under the goal posts—an electrifying ending to those long weeks of woe and trouble.

It was a near thing but it was beautiful, in the eyes of the team's bedraggled faithful, as they reveled in the 17–14 victory.

Westmoreland picked off three of the four interceptions Miami enjoyed at the expense of Buffalo's Jack Kemp. The five-year corner man said later that it was the "best day I ever had" and it could not have come at a more welcome moment for the Dolphins. Auer, who had netted one yard in the month coming into this game, came off the bench for the last twenty minutes and put Miami back into the ball game, with the result noted above.

The year before, Houston had surrendered two of Miami's three victories, and this neighborliness was almost repeated now, but the hard running of Hoyle Granger was too strong. A late field goal by Booth Lusteg wasn't enough, and the Dolphins lost, 17–14.

Perhaps there have been more satisfying experiences for the Miami team than the next game but, for those who have stood by on the sideline and watched the flowering of this South Florida institution, the second battle with San Diego has no equal.

It wrapped up all the wounds left by the Chargers and everybody else in that humbling campaign, even heaping retribution on Sid Gillman in the way George Wilson had told him he would be paid back for their first encounter, the preseason initial out for the Dolphins in 1966.

The 41–24 explosion included a record number of points for Miami, Griese leading the way with fifteen completions of twenty-eight attempts. The Chargers had the additional embarrassment of knowing that their former patsies had eliminated San Diego's last hope of title contention in the Western Division of the AFL. Oakland won it, instead, and later came to Miami for the second Super Bowl game against Green Bay. San Diego, among other things, saw Dolphins take in five interceptions—a scalding experience for the Chargers and their highly volatile air game devised by Gillman, with Hadl and Alworth the principal weapons.

The rookie, Griese, accounted for two touchdowns and scored another as the lead changed hands four times in his duel with Hadl. Griese was much the better that day. Gillman admitted later "Wilson has done a great job" and the Miami fans agreed, especially the job George had done on Gillman.

In the fickle manner so familiar to football observers of long standing, the Dolphins—who had been crunched by Boston, 41–10, earlier—now were favored over the Patriots. And it was justified, for the Dolphins were completely sound and tough as they dispatched the visitors, 41–32, in a wild game in the local bowl. Miami scored four touchdowns in five and a half minutes of the second period, but nobody left the park as the action continued. Griese and another rookie, Jack Clancy, connected for five catches and three touchdowns. Clancy moved up to third in the league pass-reception race off this good work.

When the final game was played, the Oilers gave Griese a particularly hard evening, intercepting five of his passes as the brilliant rookie flattened out at the tail end of a season that had brought him national recognition. Before that somber comeuppance, Griese had thrown 122 passes without an interception, an AFL record, and the final score, 41–10, did little to cheer up the Dolphins.

Wilson indicated he would continue to emphasize youth for the next season and no secret was made that prominent Dolphins— Auer, Jackson, etc.—would be dealt off, if possible.

> *We drafted fourth in 1967. . . . Baltimore started off with Bubba Smith and the Vikings took Clint Jones. . . . Now I was sweating; San Francisco had third choice and I figured they wanted a quarterback. Florida's Steve Spurrier and Purdue's Bob Griese were sitting there. . . . The Forty-Niners saved me by taking Spurrier. He was the Heisman Trophy winner and very popular in Miami; and I suppose I would have had to leave our office by helicopter if I had chosen Griese over Steve, but I intended to do it if the Forty-Niners had gone for someone else.*
>
> *—Joe Thomas*

6

The Wilson Years II

SEASON OF 1968

In their first two seasons, the Dolphins had won seven—a fourth of their twenty-eight league games—and solved several nettlesome questions, the most important of which was the critical quarterback position.

Griese was a permanent monument there. In the winter, Stofa was shipped to Cincinnati, where he had a chance to become Paul Brown's first quarterback with the new Bengals. That he didn't stick with Brown is a matter of fact, but just why not is a matter of conjecture, including a report that Stofa tried to outguess his leader with a play call once and that was the end of mutual understanding. The Dolphins picked him back up for little more than a handshake but, when he first went to Cincinnati, Miami got two draft choices belonging to the new club, one after each of the first and second rounds—a dandy deal. The first of these brought Doug Crusan, soon a starting offensive tackle, and the second Jim Cox, a likely tight end until he cracked a knee.

The 1968 draft (see the Appendix) was a signal success, accounting for Larry Csonka, Jim Kiick, Dick Anderson, and Randy Edmunds, with Crusan all useful and, in several instances, superior football players. As we shall see, Csonka enjoyed only flashes of his later form, for he soon suffered a severe head injury that cast doubt on any sort of football career. Kiick wasn't quickly successful, either. He didn't have the instantly recognizable physical assets of Csonka, nor did he have great speed or remarkable agility. It took some time for Jim's enormous heart and hypersensitive instinct for doing the right thing to gain him the recognition he deserved.

Anderson was a fixture from the day he suited up in the deep secondary, and if any of the coaches had doubts about him, they weren't expressed aloud.

At least in cost per pound, Manny Fernandez was the biggest bargain of the 1968 flesh deals. From the first day of rough work at the Boca Raton camp, Wilson liked the quickness and tearing power of the former Utah player. His presence lent an air of reserve strength to the front defensive line that, while not perfectly true for that season, gave a strong, broad base upon which to build. Bill Stanfill and Bob Heinz would round it out a year later.

Wilson felt 1968 could be a year of constant improvement and maybe more than that . . . Griese's 50.2 percent completion record, with the sixty-seven receptions of Jack Clancy, a record for AFL rookies, promised long-range scoring punch; Csonka's presence meant power, and another strong runner was Stan Mitchell. The Dolphins consistently played well on defense now, and Wilson was content with his prospects. Again, young players got the call over marginal veterans.

One nagging worry was the lack of public appeal. Their first two seasons developed a uniform average of twenty-seven thousand spectators for games in the Orange Bowl, certainly no great reason to take heart for the future. Prices for equipment, travel, staff, and other needs were soaring—but this was the business of Robbie and his partners. Wilson had enough money at hand to meet his requirements in fielding a team. Some games were moved to Saturday nights, and a stronger promotional campaign was developed, but these produced no marked improvement in fan interest.

One of the thrusts for Thomas was toward a larger team. The 1967 bunch was the smallest in pro football—a situation tolerable only if superior quickness was available. It wasn't. The Dolphins were bringing in both size and quickness among the newcomers, but the blending of these with the average run of veterans would take time.

Tom Nomina, a veteran defensive end, was out all the previous season but was back and healthy. Jim Riley and John Richardson had a year's experience and figured to improve. The defensive line and offensive backfield would prove stronger. A constant worry was the situation at middle linebacker, where McDaniel and Emanuel hardly knew from one series to another who would be playing the position. Both were willing, but neither offered the example nor the savvy so essential for leadership from this key position.

Randy Edmunds, No. 8 draft from Georgia Tech, earned the opening job at left linebacker; Fernandez at tackle and Anderson at safety were the other rookies who made the defensive unit. Crusan was in there at an offensive tackle when the Dolphins opened their exhibition season against Buffalo—in Rochester, of all places. It ended in a 28–28 standoff when Miami Rookie Jim Keyes blew a field goal from seventeen yards out in the last seconds. The Dolphins had overcome a fourteen-point head start by Buffalo to get even.

Mitchell, a 220-pound running back, was a strongman of the offense then; Dick Anderson's three interceptions solidified his position in the organization. Otherwise, Wilson figured the game was just a lost exercise.

Griese was seventeen for twenty-six in the next game, a sparkling 23–7 victory over Philadelphia—if sparkle was possible on the same field with the Eagles in those days. Jack Clancy caught ten passes for 125 yards and one touchdown in this first Dolphins' victory over a team from the National Football League.

Another missed field goal—by Booth Lustig from the thirty—in the last fifteen seconds cost a slight victory over Boston in the next game, the Pats winning, 19–17, as Wilson experimented with rookies and different combinations of veterans. Then came the first meeting between the Dolphins and Baltimore and—though harsh words and bitterness all lay in the future—it was a natural from the outset.

The powerful Colts—later to get their comeuppance from the Jets in the same stadium in the Super Bowl game at the end of this season—were too fast and talented for Miami and won, 22–13, before 68,125 spectators. It confirmed Robbie's suspicion that there was gold by the barrel in his franchise, but it was costly proof: The Dolphins' biggest crowd to that time saw Clancy pop a knee and Westmoreland crack a collarbone.

Jack Clancy's career has not reached the same productive state since that wretched injury. The brilliant receiver was to return after an operation, but the edge seemed to be taken off his speed. After the 1969 season, Jack was to be traded to Green Bay (for Marv Fleming) and—in 1971—was cut by the Packers and then Atlanta's Falcons. Don Shula picked him up then as a taxi-squad member of the Dolphins. Clancy's story is classic in its frustrations and its pathos—the exceptional athlete begins his career with instant acceptance and widespread acclaim and then, with one crunch, his life is pulled inside out by the mischance of an injury . . . an injury not severe enough to make him quit, but one severe enough to influence his performance, at least in the judgment of the experts.

Westmoreland's wound was even more painful than Jack's, perhaps, but it was only a matter of weeks before Dick was able to return to the lineup.

Baltimore's Terry Cole raced fifty-nine yards for a third-period TD that proved the difference in the score . . . and, in 1971, Cole would be a member of the Miami taxi squad alongside Jack Clancy. Pro football is a small but violent world, indeed.

An interception in the fourth quarter of this game was the first thrown by Griese in 101 summertime passes. Noonan was an outstanding catcher for him, and Karl was producing points, too. One-eighth of his catches resulted in touchdowns.

In the fifth, and last, of the preseason affairs, lost fumbles were a problem, but Griese kept a firm hand on the offense otherwise and the Falcons were beaten, 19–13, before the uneven but generally satisfactory 1968 league season got under way. The preseason net was 2–2–1.

In rapid succession, the first three opponents of the league schedule jumped to quick leads and—when the Dolphins tried to catch up—they shot down the Miami air force.

In the opening game against Houston, Griese heard boos for the first time in Miami although, as usual, his critics set a higher standard for him than for themselves. He threw three interceptions that cost the Dolphins one or two TDs and led directly to one for the Oilers, while Bob dodged beefy linemen who boiled around him like barracuda in a shrimp bed. In twenty minutes the Oilers wrapped it up, 17–3, although a fumble by Csonka at the Oilers' one in the third period stopped a probable turnaround. Griese said it was his own worst game.

Bob hardly felt any relief the next week, when Daryl Lamonica cut the Dolphins to giblets with four touchdown passes in the first half for a 33–14 lead. The Oakland quarterback's total yardage was 344, with the Dolphins' pass defenses broken apart. And the toll of injury to regulars continued.

Before their third league game, against the superior Kansas City Chiefs, the Miami club had lost seven regulars . . . and, in a way, these were lucky to be out of harm's way. The Chiefs smashed the Dolphins 48–3, and didn't even use Curtis McClinton or Mike Garrett, their two best running backs. Wilson came away groaning that he had tried everything he knew—play-action, screens, maximum-protection blocking . . . "They just overpowered us, just stomped us into the grass," the coach was honest in his lamentations.

Griese's two strikes in seventeen throws was a new low for him. Wilson called in Norton in the second half. Rick passed for nine of nineteen. His three interceptions were even more depressing than Griese's two . . . and Norton suffered a fractured hand in this exercise in futility.

But in one of those intriguing reversals of form that they showed so often in their early years—and still drop in the hopper occasionally—the hard-pressed Dolphins turned around and dumped Houston, 24–7, in the Astrodome, with their Hoosier quarterback coming through with six completions in twelve throws, one touchdown, and no interceptions. (The reader is admonished that the continued recitation of the passing statistics is intentional in these accounts, for there is a constant relationship between the figures and the degree of success the Dolphins' offensive troupe, especially the line, achieved in a given game.)

Jim Kiick and Larry Csonka had played previously in the same backfield but not so effectively as they did that night in Houston. In a preview of their salad days of the future, Kiick churned out 104 yards in twenty-six carries—"he's a helluva football player," Wilson declared of the rookie out of New Jersey by Wyoming— and Csonka ran as often for eighty-two yards. The Dolphins that night at last were a ball-control team, with the defense intercepting four passes and covering three fumbles in a startling reworking of the usual script.

There was a jarring return to reality the next week, however, as Buffalo—considered now a team Miami should handle with no great problem—tied the Dolphins with fifteen seconds remaining, 14–14, with a two-point conversion. For this, Ed Rutkowski passed to Gary McDermott, who had just scored the touchdown on a fling from another teammate.

Csonka's chimes were rung in this game, and it was later found that he had a dangerous injury. But the huge fullback refused all help and walked to the ambulance, mumbling, "I walked in here and I'm going to walk out," and who was to say him nay? Larry went out of the stadium sitting straight up in the ambulance, in defiance of Dr. Herbert Virgin, who had ordered him laid out flat. Virgin reported that the big guy was seriously injured, "he passed out on the bench, he had a temporary loss of memory, and he still doesn't know what's happening."

His skull would be tapped and felt by all manner of experts; in time Csonka would play in an hydraulically padded helmet— small pouches of oily fluids protected his dome from the crashing impact of iron-hard plastic when he rammed people. But then Larry willed it otherwise and he no longer employs the gurgling hat, although some of the other Dolphins use it now.

A 24–22 scrape by Cincinnati was worrisome for a while, even after the Dolphins took a 24–16 lead in the last period. Mitchell handled a speedball pass from Griese—his third touchdown fling —for the edge, but Dewey Warren's throw to Bob Trumpy got the Bengals back up a couple of minutes later. Dick Anderson had allowed that catch, but the safety darted up to bat aside the two-point conversion pass try, and another tie was avoided.

Since they were 2–3–1 at this point and Denver was next, there was some sense in the optimistic air that prevailed when the plane took off for the mountains, where the Broncos were having another of their gray seasons. As always seemed to happen for the Dolphins of that era, however, they couldn't stand prosperity. It all went blooey, even though they jumped off to a 10–0 lead in the first quarter, after which Marlin Briscoe, a sawed-off quarterback in those days, drove them bananas. He ran for two touchdowns and set up a third, while Floyd Little carried for 126 yards.

Wahoo McDaniel and Bob Bruggers had an even harder time than the other Dolphins out there in the clouds. They ran afoul of the local gendarmes outside a popular watering hole at nine in the evening before the game. George Wilson, already on record with both men, bailed them out but waived and cut them from his squad, an angry man. The loss of the two linebackers was important in the game, as it turned out, but Wilson had shown a sternness that met general approval. Frank Emanuel was belted heavily and retired, with Ed Weisacosky coming in to relieve him. Briscoe caught the switch to the recently acquired Weisacosky and ripped the middle on a quarterback sneak that put Denver ahead to stay.

The next week, Griese had one of his sparklers, with twenty of twenty-seven passes on target and three TDs—and still didn't win. The Dolphins' defense was porous when it counted, and San Diego finished an exhausting game the winner by 34–28. This was the sixth victory for the Chargers of that season and, in some respects, they were fortunate; there were minutes when it wasn't at all a sure thing. Csonka rumbled back into action in this one and was doing fine until a Charger with more desire than reason ran headlong into the onrushing Larry just before the half. Poor Csonka was led off to the sideline to kneel there for the rest of the game, his head injury causing real alarm among the informed minority.

One informant later said that Csonka bled from an ear on at least one occasion—apparently indicating important skull damage (see below). It is entirely in the character of the giant runner that he should ignore such a symptom and will himself well—perhaps with quiet prayers in the night that he might be restored and play football better than ever, winning more and losing less and, eventually, to stand at the pinnacle of the pile with Jim Kiick and his other friends and talk about how to stay there. A man such as Csonka is not a usual man at all.

At this stage of the 1968 season, however, it appeared very likely, indeed, that Csonka's budding career was finished or at least so restricted that he would be a marginal player. The very idea of this gnawed at him, and Larry was not much fun to be around, although he tried to be cheerful.

What bugged Csonka, among other things, was the idea that "A little shrimp of a San Diego cornerback" hurt his head by being in the way of it. In time, he was told this second injury was confined to a ruptured eardrum that took a long time to heal.

After Zonk recovered, Griese described the way the larger man came down after a run: "He attacks the earth. . . ." It wasn't far wrong, either; Csonka has changed little in style, although he does seem to keep his noggin from boring into the ground more often than not now.

For their fourth consecutive game on the road, the Dolphins were slight favorites over Buffalo, even without their fullback. The early play indicated that the oddsmakers were out of their minds. Buffalo ran up a seventeen-point lead in the second period before Griese could get much out of his offense. After the halftime interlude—during which George Wilson "raised some hell for sure"—Griese leaned even heavier on Kiick than previously, and Jim was to rush for 111 yards. Griese's scramble covered the last thirteen yards of a third-quarter move to Miami's first score. In another five minutes, he hit Karl Noonan with a beauty that the tall blade of a man hustled across, and then the steady Kiick dodged and bulled behind Norm Evans for a TD that gave Miami the decision, 21–17. Denizens of Buffalo's old stadium flailed their padded arms on their padded chests in fury and took off their stocking caps to scratch their heads about it. But there it was, 21–17, Miami.

The situation might suggest—after such a splendid recovery at Buffalo—that the Dolphins now were on the rise at last, with Cincinnati's youngsters coming to the Orange Bowl for a hiding. But the grim punishment that Paul Brown's people inflicted upon the Wilson troops caused George to say in complete sincerity, "This was the worst day ever for us."

It was a justifiable indictment. A sample: Miami's ground defenses gave way for three touchdowns in the last quarter as the Bengals came from behind a second time and pounded home a 38–21 upset that had even Joe Robbie speechless when it was over. Right or wrong, the impression of the Dolphins after this game was that of candy people who couldn't stand heat or steady wear and tear. Wilson was beyond dismay, and his handsome face told the misery that he was in.

Another factor was meaningful only at the box office: All but two of the Dolphins' six losses had occurred in the Orange Bowl, but none of their three victories. This also was Brown's first victory in six regular-season or postseason games against teams coached by George Wilson—and that's the kind of thing a man remembers most in the swirling world of professional football. Wilson felt disgraced by the whole performance. He was no Laughing George in the next days, as the Dolphins got ready for Boston in Fenway Park.

For some weird reason, they were great there in front of a hostile crowd, clubbing the Patriots by 34–10, with Griese hitting Noonan twice and Csonka—back in there—once for TDs. Dick Anderson played his first game at free safety that afternoon and raced back ninety-five yards with a fourth-quarter interception that gave the Dolphins a seventeen-point lead and wiped out a good try by the Pats. A charley horse had interfered with Anderson's work a couple of weeks previously, but he had not been playing well, either, when he was benched at Buffalo—the first time since junior high school that the mountain man hadn't been a starter. It hurt him deeply, and the Boston performance retrieved his pride.

The good things he did at free safety in that game led Dick down the wrong path for a time, however. In the following season, he would be kept in the free safety job, and his career flattened out. But when he moved back to his old position, strong safety, in 1970, his success was never in doubt.

Their next stop, Shea Stadium, did the Dolphins no good at all. Two citizens wise in the passing game, Babe Parilli and Don Maynard, whipsawed the secondary without mercy. Maynard outstripped Jimmy Warren relentlessy, taking three Parilli throws for touchdowns and setting records otherwise with seven receptions for 160 yards. Griese had a fine game, and Kiick—perhaps inspired by the spoor of his native New Jersey across the waters— had his usual good performance on the Jets' home grounds. He ran and received passes for more than 100 yards. It was paunchy old Babe, who relieved Namath in the second half, who shot down Miami's dream of restoring its second-place ambitions. Babe had himself a picnic, reminding experienced Miami watchers of the icy day in Lexington when he personally thrashed Andy Gustafson's good University of Miami team for Kentucky.

The final count at Shea was 35–17, with the defense in a shambles again. At one point, Maynard asked Warren, "Are you sick?" Jimmy only shook his head. But the last two games would be at home, where the weather, at least, was accommodating.

So was Boston in its Miami appearance. The Pats turned up toes, 38–7, for Miami's fifth victory and third place in the American Football League's Eastern Division . . . but this was the first time the Dolphins had won in the Orange Bowl that season, and the smallest assembly of the home season (24,242) witnessed it. Csonka trucked in for two touchdowns and Griese passed for two, and their fans were content . . . but Griese's knee was bruised.

For the record, Wilson refused to discuss his contract situation with the press at that time, with the Jets still to be met at the end of his third season on a three-year original contract.

Norton started at quarterback against the Jets but could manage only six completions in seventeen throws, with only fifty-nine yards and one interception, before he broke a finger. Kim Hammond, the former Florida State quarterback later traded to Boston in the Nick Buoniconti deal, hit nine in seventeen for sixty-six yards and one interception. Namath and Parilli enjoyed the freedom of Miami's secondary in this 31–7 drubbing of the Dolphins; it's unlikely Miami would have scored at all in this game, except for an interference penalty against the Jets that allowed Csonka to bust over from the one.

In summary, the 1968 season wound up 5–8–1, with those five victories the most accomplished yet in the Dolphins' young years. As time passed, they were to appear a monumental success and, ignoring the eight losses, Dolphins fans gradually assumed the posture that their chaps had come very close to breaking loose for at least a title game in their league.

The truth is, however, that they suffered several severe beatings and almost came unstuck, recovering their poise only through the will power and stubbornness of George Wilson.

Shortly after the season wound down, Wilson was given a one-year agreement by Robbie. It called for the same thirty-five thousand dollars for which George had come down from Washington originally.

SEASON OF 1969

In their six years of trading bodies, five key deals stand out in memory when the present Dolphins' squad and success are analyzed. Two of these occurred during the winter preceding the 1969 season.

Kim Hammond, linebacker John Bramlett, and a fifth-round draft choice were sent to Boston for the stubby figure of Nick Buoniconti, the smallest of middle linebackers and, at that time, coming off a season when he had serious knee troubles. Obviously, the Patriots thought the former Notre Dame All-American was near the end of his career at twenty-eight. Five times an all-league choice, Buoniconti left his own special imprint on every game in which he participated.

Nick's knee was to hold up without any problem whatever, and Boston regretted the swap almost immediately. Bramlett was to play well for them many times, but Hammond was a factor only briefly, and Miami—its defense now able to jell at last around the middle linebacker position—instantly was improved. At no more than five-eleven in height—if that—Buoniconti soon would be under his listed weight of 220 and, toward the end of the 1971 season, for example, Nick scaled 209 and looked more like a running back than the guy who bags them.

An excellent rundown of Nick's value to the Dolphins is found in the remarks of Terry Bradshaw, Pittsburgh's quarterback, who told the Miami *News* after the 1971 game: "He's the thing about Miami's defense that's tougher than Baltimore's to beat. . . . The Baltimore secondary is better. The Miami boys are young—good but young. They make mistakes like we make mistakes.

"The Miami linebackers are good. They play you different. Drop back on first down, give you five yards, and then on third down get up in there with you. Then they don't give anything.

"The way Buoniconti runs that team, he's really tough. He's so quick. . . . I'd rather face Mike Curtis, of Baltimore. Curtis is an animal. He's got a little more animal instinct. But Buoniconti is harder to figure. You don't know where he's gonna be or what he's gonna do. You have to outthink him, and then you have to beat him, and he's quick as a cat.

"I got tired using my brain against his. I'd rather get hit hard a couple of times than have to go against a man like that on every play."

Shakespeare could not have developed the character and value of Nick Buoniconti to the Dolphins' defense better than that. Combative and sly, Nick is impressive only when the play starts; until then, he usually stands around, resting on one foot with the other crossed over, waiting for the other team to start something. More often than anyone else on the Dolphins' defensive team, he finishes it.

Wilson and Joe Thomas were hugely relieved when they found Nick sound on his arrival in the 1969 summer camp.

In another move hardly noticed at the time, the Dolphins sent Mack Lamb, a defensive back of average talents, to San Diego for a human tank—the vastly overweight yet powerful Larry Little. Signed by the Chargers three years before from Bethune-Cookman as a free agent, the onetime player for Booker T. Washington High in Miami was to get solid recognition in his first year with the Dolphins, although carrying 285 pounds on a frame of only six feet, one inch. He had a knee problem for part of 1969 but eventually outgamed it.

Little's presence gave some blocking capability the Dolphins' front needed terribly, but it would be another year—and twenty-five pounds of blubber off—before he would become the blocking terror of the league.

These two trades, for Buoniconti and Little, were to be of prime significance in the future of the Dolphins. We shall account later for the moves that brought Warfield, Fleming, and Scott and completed the skeleton of the team that quickly became football's most exciting group of people.

The 1969 draft of college players was highly successful, too. Bill Stanfill, Bob Heinz, Mercury Morris, Norm McBride, Karl

Kremser, Jesse Powell, and Lloyd Mumphord were among those picked off by Thomas and were of quick benefit to the club. With the exception of Morris, almost the entire emphasis of this draft was among defensive players: line, linebackers, and secondary. Morris was all offense, of course. In his school career at West Texas State, Merc gained more ground than any man in college history—covering 3388 yards for an NCAA career record.

In their first three seasons of play, Dallas had won nine games, Minnesota ten, and the Dolphins twelve . . . a fact of the situation that reinforced Wilson's belief that steady progress had been made with his Miami team and that it would become a winner soon.

Unfortunately for his peace of mind and coaching career, however, this was not to be an immediate thing. His 1969 Dolphins would have some golden moments, but they were mere glints in the gloom, for everything bad that one might have thought up in a nightmare happened to Wilson's team that year. But it looked otherwise before the campaign opened.

With Griese steadily coming on and Noonan scoring eleven touchdowns—these tied Warren Wells for the league record— after Clancy's injury in 1968, and Twilley recovered from his multiple wounds, a passing attack was assured. Csonka's skull appeared to be back on straight and Kiick had proved an extraordinary talent—he was in the top ten of both rushers and receivers in the AFL, the only one with this recognition—and the line figured to be measurably improved. Morris offered an outside threat not present previously. John Stofa was signed again as a free agent and Barry Pryor, a fast running back, came by the same route.

In the preseason, the Dolphins were to lose five games before winning one at Birmingham. The first found Minnesota's Bud Grant examining his veterans for flaws in the first match, at Tampa, and finding few as he lashed Wilson's team, 45–10; the Dolphins experimented with their young people in this one and took an awful beating. The Bears came to Miami then and dumped their hosts, 16–10; Philadelphia won, 14–10, while Cincinnati was better, 28–21, before Baltimore did in the Dolphins, 23–10. That last one cost Jack Clancy another knee injury.

Finally, at Birmingham, the flow was reversed and Wilson's team dumped Boston, 13–0, in the sixth game. This was the first time Miami had played six exhibitions—or "preseason games," as club officials whimsically insist they be called—and they had a far-reaching effect. Several players and Coach Wilson—he most of all—were outspoken in their criticism of the long preliminary season, saying it wasted the energies of players and vastly increased the chances for injuries. No doubt these were facts, but outside observers noted a perceptible change in the attitude of the team members as the criticism was repeated throughout July and August . . . short tempers abounded, no doubt nourished by constant defeats no less than the length of the preseason schedule, for which players are paid only a trifle above expenses. The implication was that Robbie and his companions at the cash box were trying to gather gold on the cheap.

At odds with this reasoning, however, was the money position of the Dolphins now compared to all previous seasons. In May 1969, as we note elsewhere in this volume (see the Appendix), five new limited partners from the Miami area were brought into the ownership, the First National Bank of Miami undertook 100 percent support of these men, and Robbie could breathe easily for the first time in his tumultuous career as the franchise's leading figure. All the new partners were wealthy. Some were rich.

These investors—Harper Sibley, Jr., Earl Smalley, James W. McLamore, Frank J. Callahan, and Wilbur Morrison—were instant links to areas of the community the Dolphins could use and did not have access to previously. Morris S. Burk and James Davis soon were added, as were the partners in the law firm of Frates, Fay, Floyd, and Pearson . . . all men of substance and keen football fans. The ownership structure as established in 1969 remains largely unchanged to the present, except for the entry of Don Shula, early in 1970.

For the season of 1969, the preseason was only the foretaste of bitter things to come.

In addition to Clancy, tackles Norm Evans and Jim Urbanek, guards Larry Little and Joe Mirto, tight end Jim Cox, and defensive back Bob Neff all suffered knee injuries in the preseason. Evans and Little were able to avoid operations, but all the others went under the knife, and it is worth noting that none of the group, save Clancy, is even with the club now. Clancy, as mentioned earlier, was signed on for the taxi squad in the fall of 1971. Griese also missed time in these weeks with a sore shoulder. Norton's play as his sub did little to make Wilson think more of him.

In the opener at Cincinnati, rhubarb flourished when the Cincinnati defensive team very leisurely strolled back to take positions with twenty-five seconds to play after a Griese pass for forty-nine yards to Gene Milton, good to the Bengals' twenty-two. Wilson stormed up and down the sideline, shouting that the clock should have been stopped while the teams settled into position. Referee Ben Dreeth shook his head, declaring "It's too late," and walked away. Paul Brown said there was no big mystery about what the Bengals did—he and others from the sideline yelled to their players to take their time. They did and won, 27–21, while Wilson and the Dolphins fumed. They were to do more of this in geometric progression as the season progressed—it was almost funny the way the Dolphins slipped back two every time they made a foot forward.

A perfect example of this can be found in the next game, eleven seconds from the finish, when George Blanda crept out from the sideline without stepping on his beard once and sent a forty-six-yard field goal spinning true through the posts, winning for Oakland 20–17, although Miami had outplayed the Raiders almost every foot of the way.

Hoyle Granger, Houston's strong running back, practically got off his sickbed to lead the Oilers over Miami the next weekend. Well he might; in the five previous times he had played against the Dolphins, Granger ran up 440 yards and felt that he owned them. And he had another good day this time in the Astrodome. But what fried Wilson most was the miserable runback of kicks: the Dolphins accepted six kickoffs while being destroyed, 22–10, and didn't bring one of them beyond their own twenty-two. The Oilers limited Griese to two pass completions in the second half, when the Miami lead of ten points was overrun . . . the kind of breakdown Wilson felt deepest. That second half also cost Stan Mitchell a shoulder separation, while Karl Kremser's field-goal tries wandered off course—a dismal piece of business.

The next week, however, the Dolphins distinguished themselves against Oakland once more. The Raiders, winners twenty-eight times in their last thirty-one games and best in the league in Wilson's estimation, were lucky to escape with a 20–20 tie in the Orange Bowl. "Oakland shouldn't have even been in the ball game tonight," George growled in the dressing room. "There was no doubt in my mind we'd win it—we had good defense, good play-calling, good passing from Griese and field-goal kicking from Kremser—you name it, we had it."

The Dophins did have all these things but so did Oakland, while breaking the elbow of Howard Twilley so thoroughly there was serious doubt if the receiver ever would play again. Csonka appeared in this game—the first time in some weeks, since another head problem during the preseason—and had the discombooberating experience of running head foremost into Kiick on a busted play. The clash of craniums could be heard all over the big bowl as the two pals sailed into each other . . . but Csonka still got twelve yards on the play. Asked about it later, Griese said it was a regular part of the playbook. "It's called Two Backs Crashing into Each Other Play—that's the way I call it in the huddle." This almost deadpan.

Against San Diego, Griese hit eighteen of thirty-one but had two interceptions, while Hadl hit Greg Garrison for a pair of long touchdown strikes that won for the Chargers, 21–14, eventually. The Miami defense was noticeably stronger in these early games than in the 1968 season but still couldn't make big plays when they could count most . . . an interception was welcome, but the catcher was knocked down immediately; if a pass rush was effective—and that didn't happen often—the passer was still able to get to his safety-valve or screen receiver . . . that sort of thing.

It can be a nerve-wracking experience at any time to face off against Kansas City even for the pregame warmup, yet the Dolphins spotted the Chiefs seventeen points in the first half and came within a hair of catching them later. Cornerbacks Emmett Thomas and Jim Marsalis both hit Dolphins' receiver Gene Milton, the ball flew off to one side, and Thomas intercepted on the final play of a game that had the Chiefs hanging on the ropes at the end of it. . . . This was their fifth victory in six starts, but they could take very little satisfaction from the 17–10 affair. "We're scaring daylights out of people, but scares don't count, damnit!" Wilson kicked a chair mildly as he said it in the clubhouse. His Dolphins were 0–5–1 but had been in every one until the gun. . . . George was drying up before the eyes of reporters covering his club, the defeats were eating on him that fiercely.

At last, good old Buffalo came to the rescue.

The Bills broke the famine by rolling over and not fighting back much in the Orange Bowl, and it is worth noting that 39,837 Miami fans attended, despite all the misery their team had endured previously. When Doug Crusan and the grizzled center of the Dolphins, Tom Goode, carried Wilson off the field after the 24–6 victory, the coach got a mite dizzy from the altitude, unaccustomed as he was to it.

Nick Buoniconti led a defense that at last held an enemy to no touchdowns, a first in Dolphins' history. It would be the season of 1971 before another team (Boston) was held entirely scoreless by the Dolphins. Jack Kemp, Bills' quarterback, said of Nick: "He's still the best middle linebacker in the AFL. He's always making just the move you think means a blitz—and sometimes it does."

The Bills, with O. J. Simpson healthy and on the grounds, were held to fifty-seven yards' rushing for the day—grand work, indeed. Simpson logged twelve yards in ten carries . . . hardly the figures expected of the best prospective running back since Gale Sayers fell on evil days with his bad knees.

In a recitation of this kind, it is difficult to occasionally pause and pay proper respect to, or take sufficient note of, a great game of football. One must continue the course and pace of the narrative, touching only the high spots and peaks of the action surging below. But let us pause, if you will, to consider the closest thing to a memorable game the young Dolphins experienced: the 34–31 victory of the Jets over Miami on the second day of November 1969. . . .

Significant in many ways, this one also dealt Jack Clancy a crippling blow after the onetime brilliant youngster was recovering from knee wounds. His right knee gave way, tearing the posterior cruciate ligament; now he would face an operation on that knee. Problems from the earlier operation on his left knee weren't completely overcome . . . Jack was in for it. He had just caught six passes for seventy-nine yards, the kind of thing the old Clancy might do. His second major injury was a tragedy for the young fellow.

Kiick, as always, did well in Shea Stadium, with 106 yards, although he had a dislocated knuckle in his right hand and twisted muscles in his upper left arm.

John Elliott blocked a punt of Larry Seiple's and (the only other such indignity for Larry occurred in the 1971 game at Shea, when Paul Crane did the dirty deed), but Griese had four touchdown passes for a career high, and there were other salutary things about the surging fight, remembering that this was the Jets team that had won the Super Bowl game in Miami the previous January.

A New York interception of a Griese throw in the last moments wiped out a fat chance the Dolphins had to pull one of the year's top upsets. It was a misty, miserable day there in Shea, but not a creature moved toward the exits until the gun sounded . . . it was that kind of a game, and the Dolphins took heart from it. Only the eighteen points produced by Namath, Maynard, George Sauer, and company in the fourth quarter saved their hides that day.

(During the next week, Cincinnati sold John Stofa to the Lions. But the quarterback only stopped by Detroit for one day, saying later he couldn't see his future with them or the kind of money they offered in the present. In less than a month, John was back on the Miami roster.)

The weather in Boston on the following weekend was infinitely more wretched than even that in New York. An icy rain had the field at Boston College a bog, and the 8374 souls who braved the elements deserved Purple Hearts—especially since their beloved Pats took it on the chops again.

But not by much this time. Naturally, Csonka had a great day—he was in his element, in the slime and cold and misery—and carried sixteen times for 121 yards and took no prisoners when blocking. Among his deeds was a fifty-four-yard touchdown run . . . magnificent. Strangely, Norton was at his best in this unlikely situation, throwing seven completions in nine passes when he came on in relief of Griese, who went down with an injured right knee. It was called a bruise, but it kept him out the rest of the season.

Buoniconti also bumped a knee and Mumphord an ankle in this game.

The Pats came on strong in the fading minutes and, when Mike Taliaferro passed to Bill Rademacher for a touchdown with forty seconds to play, they had a chance to win. The two-point conversion try failed on a pass from Taliaferro toward Carl Garrett, but Clive Rush and his Pats at least went for it. "With the kind of season we're having, a tie would do us no good—we needed to win," said the disappointed Rush afterward. The Dolphins could use the victory, too, although it turned out to be only a 17–16 scraper. Bill Stanfill had the enormous satisfaction that day of intercepting a pass and stumbling seventeen yards to a touchdown through the goo and the astonished Boston players, who found Bill even larger than Csonka and a terrifying figure in the gloomy afternoon.

A third weekend in a deep-freeze—this one at Buffalo—was too much for the Dolphins, who gave the natives up there a day of joy when they were thrashed, 28–3, while O. J. Simpson had one of his good afternoons, galloping seventy-three yards with the opening kickoff and scoring a pair of touchdowns with Jack Kemp passes. The Dolphins' only move was a twenty-one-yard field goal by Kremser in the first quarter. Norton led the Dolphins within the Bills' ten-yard line three times, only to be grounded in each case by Buffalo rushers, who trapped him for large losses.

Another time, his pass toward Larry Seiple—wide open in the end zone—hit a crossbar of the goal post. Yet, Norton accounted for 281 yards, with twenty completions in forty-one passes. Sacked eight times, Norton lost eighty-three yards. Had he not been so stiffly conservative near the goal line, it's quite possible Rick might have retrieved his fading career that afternoon. With Griese out with his sore knee, the future lay before Norton as the Dolphins went into their last four games of their worst season on record.

Against Houston in Miami, Norton was little short of awful. Sympathetic watchers could find nothing in his performance to justify arguments in his behalf . . . the bare statistics prove it. He completed only seven of twenty-six passes and was intercepted five times—and the seven completions were good for only forty-three yards. The 32–7 loss to the Oilers was just another thrashing, except for the ways the Dolphins achieved it. They did almost nothing right, and Robbie finally blew his stack.

"This is the most disastrous thing that's happened to our team in its history," exploded the managing partner to Bill Bondurant of the Fort Lauderdale *News*. "We have finally ground to a halt. This is the culmination of our season, losing all the close games to the top teams early in the year—then, when we come to the easy part of the schedule, we are unable to cope because of key injuries. There's no way for us to go but up. . . ."

Griese sat on the bench through the dismaying spectacle with his knee in a cast, while Miami's offense failed to score a touchdown. Stanfill intercepted again, this one from Pete Beathard, and again rambled seventeen for a score.

Behind Norton, Wilson had a youngster named Tommy Boutwell activated, but he promised no real help. Indeed, Wilson left him on the kamikaze squads, the specialty teams where survivors should be awarded the Combat Infantryman's Badge. Fans took out their displeasure by booing Norton at every opportunity— they were hoarse when the sun went down.

Even the gutty but not very skillful Boston Patriots were avenged the next weekend, 38–23, in a game at Tampa that went far toward making the Pats a favorite target of would-be promoters who wanted a pro team for the Gulf Coast city. Bill Sullivan and other owners of the Pats considered it soberly until their own new stadium was built and the team's name was changed to the New England Patriots.

In the course of that game, Wilson was unhappy with Mercury Morris and his ball-handling after a punt—Mercury circled back into the end zone, seeking freedom, and was nailed for a safety—but Morris held his ground, saying he'd do the same thing again. The coach and Norton also had conflicting reports about who called a pass play early in the fourth quarter when Miami was on its own one-yard line after Fernandez covered a Boston fumble. The Dolphins led at the time, 23–22. On second down in that perilous area, Norton threw toward Noonan, but Larry Carwell snatched it down and ran back to the Miami three. Jim Nance then broke over for the touchdown that gave the Pats the steam to win. Later, Norton was to say that the pass call came from the Miami bench; Wilson said Norton called it himself. In any case, the statistics were more of the old story: 115 yards for Norton on twelve completions, with three interceptions.

In a parenthetical happening in Tampa Stadium, the Miami coach lost his temper over the appearance of Bill Peterson in the press box, for the then coach at Florida State (later Rice, now of the Houston Oilers) was most prominently mentioned among possible successors to Wilson if Robbie opted for a coaching change in the coming weeks. "Peterson isn't good enough to coach in pro ball—he's not good enough to get my job." Wilson snapped to reporters. Peterson denied any such ambitions, of course, and said he had sped to Tampa from Houston (where his team was beaten the night before) to watch Kim Hammond and Ron Sellers perform for the Pats. . . . The incident quickly was lost in the pressure of events, but was revealing. Wilson was alert to the chance that he would not have his contract renewed; Robbie kept his own counsel and had no comment to reporters about the future of Wilson with the Dolphins.

The coach rallied his team one more time, in any case, winning a wild game from Denver, 27–24, in the Orange Bowl. But the pleasure over this result was obliterated by the severe heart attack suffered by Les Bingaman a couple of minutes before the end of the action. The massive former Detroit star collapsed at the Dolphins bench and was reported to have actually died on the spot but revived with a shot of adrenalin administered by Dr. Virgin.

For some days, the big assistant coach lingered near death but recovered for a time and was to live until the following year. His collapse was another burden for Wilson, whose great years with the Lions and the eventful, early times with the Dolphins were shared with Bingo, as friends called him.

In that Denver game—in the span of fourteen minutes—Norton passed for two touchdowns, equaling his four-year production up to that time. He completed fourteen of twenty-three and handled the stormy rushes of Kiick and Csonka with no flaws. It was too late for him and the Dolphins, but it gave him a high point to remember.

Now came the last game of that unhappy year, against the Jets in the Miami bowl, where Namath had a remarkable success in just a few minutes and retired, turning over the job to Babe Parilli, who feasted at the Dolphins' expense as he had previously in New York. In the first period, Namath passed for TDs to Bake Turner and Matt Snell and left for the day. Parilli passed over Warren to Turner for another score and, generally, did as he pleased.

Norton's final appearance for the Dolphins in a regular-season game hardly could have been more depressing.

Interceptions of two throws by Rick gave Namath field position for his two TD flings; Norton completed only three of fifteen passes in the first half for thirty-nine yards. A crescendo of boos encouraged Wilson to make a change—and here came Stofa again.

John responded to this new opportunity with the Dolphins by completing fourteen of twenty-three passes for 144 yards and had the offense inside the Jets' ten three times but got only Csonka's touchdown to show for it. Stofa had come to the Dolphins again two weeks prior to the final, 27–9, loss, and was in a solid position to back up Griese in 1970. Norton, obviously, was trade bait, but his big contract was a burden few teams could stand, considering his chances to be helpful.

The Dolphins' most disappointing season in at least their first six years of life thus ended with three victories, ten losses, and one tie. Many of the individual losses could be explained, but this made them no easier to live with. Injuries, large and small, were constant and decisive. Without Griese, the Dolphins were not themselves; even with him in 1969 they weren't anything to brag about.

Wilson and other club leaders had been openly and fervently optimistic before the wars began that summer . . . now they were reminded of that enthusiasm in the face of the disasters of autumn.

The coach was careful to express himself positively in all statements about his future with the team and of the team's future with him. . . .

7

Change in Command . . . or, How to Jar Football

The 27–9 loss to the Jets that finished the 1969 season occurred on December 14. The next week, the author announced on television that George Wilson's contract would not be renewed, that he would be replaced as head coach. This information was authentic. Another station got more excited than this report warranted and said a few minutes later that Wilson had been fired. This was not true.

It would be February 18 before Wilson would be told that his contract would not be renewed—certainly a less cutting blow than abrupt suspension of an active contract—but open conjecture by the media during the Christmas period was hard on Wilson's family. As January matured, the coach felt relieved. He decided that the earlier reports were wrong and that Robbie would offer a new, one-year agreement as he had the previous winter. However, Robbie was busy otherwise.

First, he turned back over a track long since cold—toward Ara Parseghian, of Notre Dame. Always an admirer of Parseghian's cut and style, Robbie had offered him the job originally, but the young leader of the Fighting Irish stubbornly refused to consider the switch. Bill Peterson, who had developed an attractive football program at Florida State University, also came back into the picture.

Pete was considered, but never offered the job, at the outset of the franchise. Later, after the 1968 season, Robbie had serious talks with him, but several factors entered the situation as time wore on, including Peterson's natural reluctance to leave FSU when another year there would make him eligible for substantial tenure and retirement benefits; meanwhile, Robbie's attention was constantly being diverted by his squabble with Bud Keland. This fight for control of the club finally was decided in Robbie's favor by Commissioner Rozelle early in 1969, but the chance to explore a possible coaching change was confused by the intense battle with Keland.

Peterson sparred verbally with Robbie, but there still was enough doubt in Robbie's mind to restrain him from going all out for the FSU coach. Indeed, he still had considerable confidence that Wilson could continue to improve his results with the club and, after a brief hesitation, he decided to go with Wilson for another year.

Better than most, Robbie knew Wilson's backbreaking burdens as the 1969 season progressed. Injuries to almost every regular player—especially that of Griese—made improvement in the record impossible that season. But Robbie came to believe that the over-all health of the organization called for a change on the field.

This time, he talked again with Parseghian, and again nothing came of it. Although he had devised a plan where his new coach could earn his way into a considerable ownership position in the Dolphins, Robbie had no luck prying Parseghian out of South

CHANGE IN COMMAND   99

Bend. There were signs that Peterson very definitely was interested now, but Robbie decided not to bring him into the picture and did not talk with him this time.

Shortly before Christmas, a mutual friend suggested that Paul (Bear) Bryant might be interested. After all, he had won the national championship at Alabama, and the prospect of bringing a young team forward in the reorganized National Football League easily might be attractive to the tall Arkansas ridgerunner.

Bear and Mary Harmon Byrant spent two weeks on vacation in Miami during the Christmas period. Robbie talked daily with the coach and, for the first time, Bryant realized that the kind of money the Dolphins were offering was backed up by a substantial chance to own a piece of the action . . . a novel arrangement, in some respects, but developed by Robbie with the assistance of experts from the Price Waterhouse accounting firm. Later, Robbie flew to Birmingham and met there with Bryant's financial adviser, who told the coach it was a golden opportunity.

Robbie thought he had a deal but had an understanding with Bryant that the University of Alabama must be satisfied with the quality of Bear's successor. As Bryant says elsewhere in these pages, he brought John McKay into the picture, and the people at Alabama were favorably disposed toward the Southern California coach. But he turned them down, and Bryant remained at Tuscaloosa.

When this decision was reached, January was far advanced and the Dolphins either had to make a decision to retain Wilson or move quickly in another direction.

Robbie put out feelers without results for some days and decided to wait until after the draft at the end of the month before moving toward a final conclusion. On the last night of the draft, immediately after the picking of college stars ceased, he began a process that resulted in arguments and recriminations that continue to the present and can be expected to do so for as many years as the principals survive . . . but, for the Dolphins, that process brought Don Shula.

I was telling myself nobody had ever done both—that is, nobody had ever won national championships of both the colleges and the pros. . . . But—I hate to admit this—I reckon I was using this as an unconscious excuse, because when the Dolphins talked to my tax adviser he came back and told me it would take an awful long time for me to make that kind of money in college ball or anything else. I talked with our president, Dr. David Matthews, and the board was mighty nice about it and tried to talk me out of it—they told me to look around and see if I could come up with somebody acceptable to take over . . . only one man was offered the job, John McKay, of Southern Cal, and he turned it down. . . . He was the only one of the capable ones that I thought might make a change.

—Bear Bryant

The results speak for themselves.

Shula's departure from Baltimore brought a minimum of comment from the Colts' front office initially. Later, it heated up and soon blew into a typhoon of denunciation that eventually brought Commissioner Rozelle's decision that Robbie had acted beyond the bounds of NFL rules in negotiations with Shula and must pay for this by delivering Miami's first-round choice of the following draft to Baltimore. That's how the Colts got Don McCauley.

Rosenbloom and Robbie have conflicting stories of the circumstances and timing of these negotiations, to say the least. Shula gave his own rundown soon after the storm blew up, but since then he has kept silent, enduring a persistent shower of insults and innuendoes from Carroll Rosenbloom and enjoying them not at all.

Robbie has claimed that the name of Shula first entered his own conversation when he and Edwin Pope, sports editor of the Miami *Herald,* talked in the Dolphins' downtown office on the last day of the draft, which was held in New York with a web of communication lines to the member teams, as usual. Pope had a whiff of the Bear Bryant story and braced Robbie with it. Robbie countered that negotiations with Bryant had failed but that he had not given up the search for a major figure in the coaching trade and that his next interest was Don Shula, if Don was available.

Pope responded that Bill Braucher, who covers the Dolphins for the *Herald,* was a classmate of Shula's at John Carroll University, in Cleveland, and knew him well enough to find out if Shula had any interest at all in the Dolphins.

That night, Pope, Braucher, and Robbie met at the Palm Bay Club, after the draft was completed, and Braucher attempted to call Shula at his home in Baltimore to learn if conversations were even feasible. He was told by Mrs. Shula that Don had gone to dinner from the Colts' office with some of the office personnel when the drafting finished. The meeting at the club broke up with Braucher agreeing to contact Shula the next day.

The next morning, Braucher told Robbie that Shula had returned his call and appeared interested in the coaching position. Braucher reported that he told Shula a talk with Robbie was possible only if he (Shula) obtained permission from the Baltimore leadership. Shula called Robbie a short time later and said that his understanding of Braucher's remarks included the chance for possible purchase of part of the Dolphins, since this was offered Bryant. Robbie says he told Shula this possibly could be done but that they could talk no further until Shula got permission from the Colts for a dicker with Robbie (this according to NFL rules). Shula accepted this and broke off the conversation.

A day or two later, according to this version, Shula called Robbie and said that he had talked with Steve Rosenbloom, then assistant to the president of the Colts (his father, Carroll Rosenbloom) and that young Rosenbloom stated he would not stand in the way if Shula could advance himself with an ownership option. The elder Rosenbloom was vacationing in the Far East at the time.

Considering this sufficient coordination with Shula's current employer to meet NFL regulations, Robbie went to Washington for a meeting there with Shula at the Marriott Hotel. From the outset of their first conversation there, Robbie has said, Shula ap-

peared to want the job. Preliminary points for negotiation were
outlined to the coach, and it was agreed that another meeting,
the following week, would take place in Miami. With this, Shula
returned to Baltimore, where he informed Steve Rosenbloom of the
situation. The following week, Shula and his cheerful and attractive
wife, Dorothy, were met at the Miami airport by Elizabeth Robbie,
whose spouse figured he'd best not be seen with Shula until a deal
was made. Mrs. Robbie took the Shulas to the Jockey Club
apartment Robbie had rented for them and returned to her own
home, while the Shulas went to the dining room of the club.

Hiding any prominent person in this room is slightly more
difficult than stuffing a St. Bernard in a shoebox . . . it is a vortex
of the jet set and—in certain situations—some others.

The latter that night included the rather unlikely *quiniella*
of the late Vince Lombardi, boss of the Washington Redskins,
and Elinor Kaine, the gifted lady writer about pro football and
possessor of a news nose of formidable sniffpower. The pair of great
coaches also attracted the house photographer, of course, but Shula
begged off from any pictures with a lame excuse—a move he later
regretted, for the unsuspecting Lombardi was to lose his life to
cancer the following August, two days before his team met the
Dolphins in a Tampa preseason game.

Miss Kaine accepted the Shulas' comments about how nice it
was to be vacationing in Miami in January . . . like other reporters not party to the secret negotiations between Robbie and
Shula, she had no reason to suspect that Shula was thinking of
leaving Baltimore. The incident in the dining room closed with
the coaches chatting a little about football and the upcoming
league meeting.

The next day, Robbie and Shula got down to meaningful conversations about tax matters and other details of the proposition
the Dolphins had in mind. Shula departed Miami with sheafs of
papers for his Baltimore lawyer, Dave Gordon, who continued in
the conversations until the signing the next week. Peter T. Fay, a
Dolphins' partner, then a Miami lawyer and now a federal judge,
dealt for the Dolphins with Gordon, and their negotiating included

time in Baltimore and on the plane coming to Miami, and continued until four o'clock in the afternoon of February 18. According to Robbie, when he and Shula finally shook hands on the agreement, he called Steve Rosenbloom in Baltimore and they discussed a proposed press release Shula had shown Steve before leaving Baltimore. Robbie says young Rosenbloom and Don Klosterman, the new general manager of the Colts, suggested changes in the release and that Shula adopted them. Robbie says they agreed in that telephone call that the press would get the release at seven o'clock that night.

Carroll Rosenbloom was en route home from his Far East trip, and Robbie called him in Hawaii. Carroll told him: "It's too late to talk to you about anything. . . . I'll say whatever I have to say to the commissioner." Then he broke off the connection.

Robbie then called Rozelle, who was in a meeting, a circumstance that complicated matters because a press conference was then being called for seven o'clock at the Jockey Club and George Wilson still had to be informed of the change.

A half hour later, Robbie called again and Jim Kensil, assistant to the commissioner, got on the phone and heard his tale. With that, Robbie made a series of rapid moves, including racing home to change clothes and to see George Wilson there.

Wilson, a fighter who knows you lose some if you go to the pits often enough, was bitterly disappointed but took the savage blow in good grace. It probably was especially galling to him that he would be eased out for one of his former assistants, Don Shula; in any case, George went to his own home and was not available to reporters until the next day.

Robbie reached the Jockey Club a minute or so before the press conference opened. When Shula appeared on the patio in the cool air of a perfect winter's night in Miami, it confirmed a rumor that had started only moments previously among the gathering newsmen. The group listened in tense silence as the most successful coach in pro football showed up at Robbie's side. They knew it was a stroke of huge proportions and would be the winter's biggest football story . . . but it would not finish with the handout from

Charlie Callahan that duplicated those being given other reporters in Baltimore at the same hour.

For the first day, it appeared that the coach's departure would be accepted with regret but no great passion in Baltimore, except by some newsmen who appreciated his gifts and methods of dealing with them . . . but then all hell broke loose.

In a succession of declarations, Klosterman said Robbie's actions in hiring Shula were "tampering," a heinous crime in the highly volatile personal relationships of the NFL establishment. When Carroll Rosenbloom laid into Robbie before Commissioner Rozelle, the rupture became permanent.

The elder Rosenbloom declared—and has repeated many times since—that the deal between Robbie and Shula was in the works before the draft of players at the end of January, more than three weeks before the announcement was made in Miami that Shula was transferring . . . the inference being that Shula had done poorly in the draft, that his mind was on other things. Too, that the shift to Miami occurred with ten days remaining on the interconference trading period and that Shula's absence thus wrongfully hurt the Colts.

Shula was stunned by this response. Outsiders cannot know his relationship with the Rosenblooms during his Baltimore years, but his pride was hurt deeply by the attacks upon him by his former employer. "I've done nothing wrong, I informed Steve of everything I did and kept him abreast of the whole situation as it developed," Shula insisted.

Eventually, Rozelle took action favorable to the Baltimore owner when he declared that Miami's first choice in the 1971 draft would go to the Colts. Later, however, Rozelle fined the senior Rosenbloom five thousand dollars for his continuing vendetta against his former employee. The wounded egos in this byplay to the main drama guarantee that no permanent rapprochement is possible. Their teams, in one season, became rivals no less thirsty for the blood of the other than the oldest and most bitter enemies in pro football.

Shula's financial arrangements with the Dolphins include benefits that some insiders claim exceed the fantastic array of goodies Edward Bennett Williams arranged for George Allen when he succeeded to the Redskins job after the 1970 season. Shula is a vice president of the Dolphins (as he was of the Colts), and his salary is in excess of the reported seventy thousand dollars he received from Rosenbloom; he also is hired on a revolving contract arrangement similar to the one he had in Baltimore. It is automatically renewed each season.

What brought him to Miami was the ownership opportunity. Early estimates placed his piece of the club at 2 to 3 percent. The truth at this writing is that Shula owns more than 10 percent— about the same as the chunk owned by Harper Sibley, like Shula a limited partner—and Shula probably could cash out today and walk off with a profit approaching five hundred thousand dollars.

". . . I'm not a miracle man. . . ." Don told his audience at that first press conference in Miami. Perhaps not, but he has kept his average of victories up to the point where he must be considered at least a football genius.

(1) It wasn't a good day for Don Shula at Foxboro, scorewise or sartorially.... Doug Crusan (77) can't believe the hat.

(2) RIGHT On the night of the Bears' game, Larry Csonka weighed 238 pounds, and there was more flab on the ball than on the giant fullback.

(3) Sunrise and sunset: young Jim Mandich with veteran Bob DeMarco.

(4) Tackle Norm Evans, the surviving member of the Dolphins' original "stocking" draft from other AFL teams early in 1966.

(5) BELOW   Don Shula (*right*) with offensive line coach Monte Clark.

(6) Garo Yepremian waits to do his field-goal thing. He isn't loaded down with heavy pads like most of the Dolphins.

(7) Cookie Gilchrist was a fullback of great reputation, great wealth, and great girth when he got around to playing for the Dolphins occasionally in 1966.

(8) Jim Kiick, he of the soft voice and shy smile and murderous instincts, the "Butch Cassidy" to Larry Csonka's "Sundance Kid" . . . a New Jersey schoolboy who went to the high plains of Wyoming for football purposes. It is presumed this is where Jim decided one must tie down one's hair or he could lose it to the natives.

(9) Larry Csonka having a hard day at the office.

(10) Jake Scott's world is one of racing images and shattering crashes, usually involving Jake's own chassis. Quiet and easygoing, the Virginian via Georgia wears No. 13 and hears no footsteps.

(11) Big man and quick man ... Larry Little (66), voted the best offensive lineman in the AFC by other players, leads Mercury Morris on an off-tackle slash.

(12) Paul Warfield, football's most feared receiver.

(13) Garo Yepremian, the little tiemaker with the scoring touch. He follows Ben Agajanian as an Armenian with a telling toe.

(14) Jim Kiick's shirtmaker is a happy man.

(15) John Stofa (*left*) and Frank Jackson, a Dolphins passing combination of the first year, long before Bob Griese hooked up with Paul Warfield to give the Miami club one of football's most deadly weapons.

(16) BELOW Marv Fleming, is one of football's best blockers among tight ends. The onetime Green Bay star blossomed in 1971 as a pass receiver for the Dolphins.

8

Shula

It is extremely unlikely that any team in history was stamped so quickly and thoroughly with the personality and drives of a new coach. The Miami Dolphins of 1970 were the mirrored image of Don Shula, then a forty-one-year-old of slightly under six feet, with a good stand of hair and a jawline firm enough to enhance the tableau on Mount Rushmore.

Although it is possible that the Dolphins were ready for the disciplines, mental and physical, so characteristic of Shula, it also is probable that the coach—having turned out pro football's best record over his seven years at Baltimore—was ready for a fresh field and a new experience.

The latter we'll consider presently but, for the moment, let us consider Donald Francis Shula, person. . . .

There was a dinner party at the Miami Club, a seat of the local Establishment, in October of 1970. The host, Bill Frates, slung it in honor of his younger law partner, Peter T. Fay, who would be invested as a federal judge the following morning. The attorneys, owners of minor holdings in the Dolphins, were friends of the Shulas, who sat at the table with the Fays.

During the course of the dinner, a guest to the right of Mrs. Shula asked this cheerful, intelligent lady if a party in midweek wasn't somewhat unusual for Don during a football season.

"I'll say it is," she chuckled. "This is the first time we've been out socially, at any time of any week during a football season, since Don became a head coach, eight years ago!"

This would seem to make Shula a monastic type, an ascetic little given to conversation or the comforts that come with an income in six figures and the friends a successful coach attracts. But such hardly is the case. Between seasons, his day always include a while in the office. But the visitor who sees Shula in his sprawling, beautifully decorated home in the Miami Lakes area usually talks to him through a tangle of arms and legs as his five children wander up and down and around him. Ever so often, he'll send one packing off for talking a little much, but the offender will return in a minute or two, silently crawling over the parental landscape while Don gabs with his company.

As a golfer, he is infinitely more the carpenter than the cabinet maker, doggedly chopping away at the Miami Lakes and other courses near his home. But it would be foolish to expect that Don Shula would anticipate playing a certain course or hone his game to the perfection he demands in his work. To him, golf apparently serves as a quiet time for noodling problems, for picking at his own mind and deciding things. A good man at the nineteenth hole and usually a talkative one with friends, Shula's changing mood is signaled when he falls silent and—while apparently listening to the small talk around him—his thoughts are far away. But only the mind is abrupt. Don Shula's breeding absolutely prohibits

him from being either sour or rude to anyone around him at a
social gathering, but he is master of the swift handshake at quick-
step. If he weren't, he'd never get through a doorway in Miami.

To Shula, the football season is a special time of year, like
Christmas is for kids . . . he steams up to an awful pitch before
it arrives and seems a little lost when it's over. He talks football
by the hour and seems to enjoy it; unlike many men, those who
never want to talk "shop," Shula's attitude is one of pleasure, so
long as the speaker isn't a full-time bore bent upon spreading
his own brand of unthink. Indeed, Shula's strongest friends are
those he met along the way in the game, at Baltimore, Detroit,
Cleveland, and before. He'll talk the ears off their skulls when
his work is done. But these, too, know when to recognize the
gradual slowdown of his conversation and the sudden realization
that Don's mind is elsewhere, Out Yonder someplace, noodling
away.

It's a natural thing that he is what he is today; every indicator
along the way pointed toward a lifetime interest in sport, even to
the point of making his living at it. But there was little to suggest
the heights of success that he would reach. Nor is it likely a psy-
chiatrist or other kind of a head-feeler could have foreseen the
man's consuming interest in improvement of self and his work
long after he arrived at a plateau of attainment high enough to
satisfy the most ambitious. Nor would his teammates have guessed
he would retain a quiet faith that brings Don Shula into a Roman
Catholic chapel almost daily. Long conversations with him indicate
no grand design, no pattern-cutting as a boy that drove him a
certain way or chained him to an ideal; rather, he is a man of
short-haul targets, attainable goals, yet challenges that demand
every ounce of his concentration.

Because he is this way and not given to wild dreams that
compel him toward impossible summits, Don Shula probably will
reach his late years with all his marbles and most of his bounce,
although the passage won't be easy.

A friend, in talking about his own career, once told Shula of
his regrets that he took a certain job some years previously.

"Why would you have regrets?" the coach almost snarled out in a surprising response. "If you can't make up your mind to live with a decision, you don't have mind enough to make it up about anything . . . . and you can never lead other people while you're looking back."

From the tangled web of a career whose threads are so intricately interlaced with others of equally positive personality, this answer by Shula is the kernel of his approach to life: Make decisions . . . live with them . . . lead.

"When I think about what's happened over the years, I realize how important football and athletics have been in my life," Shula reflects now in his slightly nasal, sometimes sleepy manner of speaking when at ease. "I wouldn't have had the opportunity to go to college. There were too many obstacles, except through sports."

These obstacles included the demands of a large family and a thin purse for an earnest, working man with scant education, but the pride usually found with a Hungarian accent. Don's father, Dan, was foreman of a work group at a nursery near Painesville, Ohio, in Lake County. When Don was a baby, his dad earned twelve dollars a week. This was during the Great Depression. Soon after, Mr. Shula was forced to take another job. The force came in the form of triplets; since three older children—Don was the third, after a brother and sister—already had made his payday a borderline matter, Shula left the nursery and got a job on a fishing boat in Lake Erie for the more handsome figure of twenty dollars per week.

"Dad had come to this country from Hungary at the age of six and—while Mom was born here—she was from a Hungarian family too. Neither of them had much formal education—Dad through the sixth grade, my mother through the eighth—but they had things they believed in.

"I always was sure there would be food on the table and that my clothes would be clean. The old-timers felt those things were of primary importance to them as people—food for their children and clean houses with clean clothes. They weren't bad things to try for, either," Don says now, without dwelling on the subject.

As the Shula children grew, they split into several directions and probably weren't close in the ways some of their friends' families were. But they were active and kept in touch with each other; Joe, the eldest, soon went into the service during World War II, and the older sister had her own circle of friends, while young Don went across the street. That's where the games were, on a playground, and there he lived his young life.

All the young bucks from the small town centered their activities there sometime during the year. The difference was that Don Shula was there at every season, taking violent exercise and schooling himself in ways only another athlete could understand. His most substantial gain from all this flailing about was not muscle for his chunky body but a tremendous desire to compete with other boys—at whatever game or race was possible. This soon was to mushroom when he reached grade school and, for the first time, he entered competitive team games.

The first of these occurred in the sixth grade, at St. Mary's Catholic School, in Painesville, where Joe Jenkins was the football coach. Joe arranged for his seven-man team to meet outsiders prior to Harvey High's games, at Recreation Park, on Friday nights. Shula played halfback but, on the night of their biggest game of the season, disaster struck.

Don usually borrowed a pair of shoulder pads from a cousin, and Mrs. Shula wouldn't let him play without them. On the night in question, the cousin unthinkingly loaned them to one of Don's teammates. Mrs. Shula told Don she was sorry, but he couldn't play.

Heartbroken, he bummed a ride to the park anyway and was standing outside the gate when Jenkins appeared and asked Don why he wasn't suited up. Shula sobbed as he explained the loss of the shoulder pads, whereupon Coach Jenkins found the lad who had borrowed them—he was a second-stringer—and gave them to Shula, who went on to have a pretty good night.

There is no record that twelve-year-old Don Shula argued against the lifting of the pads from the other boy, but it is characteristic that Joe Jenkins is still a big man in his life. "He had played ball with my older brother and was an exceptional coach. We've been solid friends ever since then and we had a great time last year when he came down for a visit." Soon there were other coaches, in junior and then senior high schools.

As all aging players will recall, the advancement or graduation, if you will, from junior to senior high athletics is one of enormous importance to a boy. At that point, young Shula had some standing with his coach, who selected the little (115 pounds) reserve to join the eleven starters on the junior high squad to work with the high school varsity before each of the varsity's last three games. In one of the scrimmages here, Shula sailed into a runner. Some sort of metal object on the runner's uniform split the nose of the tackler, and it bled furiously. Somebody slapped a Band-Aid on it, but the rip was still a mess when Shula faced his mother that night. She hit the ceiling and forbade him to play again. It was Doomsday, the ragged end. . . .

At the beginning of the following year, the coach learned of this prohibition and talked long and hard with the chunky halfback. Shula listened and then brought himself to a hard decision: He would sign the necessary card himself, instead of taking it home for a signature. The subterfuge worked, but it was a near thing many times, for Mrs. Shula was extremely curious why her son couldn't make it home on the regular bus after school. Finally, Don busted loose with the truth and begged his mother to go to a game where he could play that night. Both parents turned out, and—by the happiest of chances—Don had a good night. He ran a punt back for seventy-five yards and a touchdown, then banged over for another; the senior Shulas never gave him any more static. They went to every game and howled like everybody else does in that part of Ohio, the most feverish area of that football-crazy state. They remained fans for the rest of his playing career, but Shula recalls the mandate after the nose injury as the low point of his existence to this day. There's a scar on his sniffer to remind him with every shave.

And so life went forward, substantially measured by football seasons, with an occasional high point in a baseball or basketball game, interspersed with track meets. Shula dated girls enough to have one on his elbow for the big proms and dances, but not much in between. His grades were high-average, nothing special. His existence was highlighted by moments of victory in games after hard, exhausting efforts; he could churn the hundred-yard dash in ten seconds, and had sound experience as an all-round athlete. In normal times, this would have brought him college scholarship offers in bunches, but 1947 hardly was normal.

Veterans of World War II were pouring out of service, and many had spent their careers there on teams equal to the best from the colleges. There was little reason why a college coach would fritter away a scholarship on an untried kid from Harvey High School when he could get a seasoned veteran already proved out. It was a tough period for all but the most famous high school stars, unless their parents had the money to pay the college freight. The Shula family had no such resources. Don decided to work for a year and then try to pay his own way through college.

Again, a coach had a decisive effect upon his life.

Howard Bothman learned Shula's plan and talked him out of it, knowing full well that the boy's chances of continuing in school were practically nil, once he laid out for a year and entangled himself with distractions on the "outside." Bothman advised Shula to take a partial scholarship to John Carroll University, a comparatively small school in Cleveland, and play well enough to earn a full scholarship after that freshman year.

In the end, this is what happened, and Shula's path—although he had wobbled a trifle—remained true to the ambitions that now had him by the ears. Above all else, he wanted to play football as a winner. And it appears he was willing to pay the price. Before he entered John Carroll, he packed twenty more pounds onto the 165 he carried in high school. Young Dolphins who don't quite believe that weight-lifting can do that to a fellow have little luck arguing the point with Shula today. By the time his precollege summer was finished, he was fully developed and physically able to meet the challenge of college football. This critical factor is lost on some observers of the game who predict great things for graduating high school stars, although the lads often simply aren't strong enough to play the game and to absorb the grinding punishment found on every college practice field; what happens in weekend games to the survivors often is a welcome relief.

More important than the above-average speed and "good hands" Shula had developed at Harvey High, Painesville, was an agility constantly improved by participation in other games; all the hours playing basketball, baseball, and running dashes in track were profit now, although Mrs. Shula may have thought more highly of some household chores that went untended.

Expenses for the first year were cut to the bare bone. Shula was in a car pool with five other boys, and they traveled thirty miles to John Carroll University daily. He soon formed a lasting friendship with Carl Taseff, a tousle-haired member of the varsity backfield troupe. Carl had entered John Carroll a semester prior to Shula, but they were the same age and their temperaments blended so well that their mutual admiration continues to this day. Taseff was one of the early assistants hired by Shula when he took the Miami job in 1970, and Carl does the scouting of enemy teams for Don's club and works with the backs. No such relationship seemed possible in 1947, however, for both were scrambling for recognition in a city that seethed with interest in other football players and other teams.

The focus of attention was the Cleveland Browns, of course, for the great Paul Brown, the consummate teacher and frosty leader who already had enjoyed resounding success at Massillon (Ohio) High and then Ohio State, had created a masterpiece that would chase the Rams out of Cleveland and all the way to Los Angeles. The All-America Conference didn't amount to much in the long view of American sport over the generations, but it did make the Browns possible, and this was a major contribution. The crisply drilled and enormously talented Browns brought new dimensions into pro football; their precise, demanding leader opened approaches never considered by his predecessors.

Paul Brown also was to become the largest influence upon the career of Don Shula, by example rather than personal tutoring.

Coach Herb Eisele, of John Carroll, was a worthy preliminary influence, however, and apparently he had no lack of ability. Shula's high estimate of Eisele is backed by his record, for it included a victory over a powerful Syracuse team that included Jim Ringo and others later notable in pro ball. That 16–14 victory over the Orange was accomplished before an astonished hometown crowd in Cleveland and, in retrospect, we can see plainly how precisely factors must fall in place in the careers of outstanding men. . . . What if Paul Brown had not gone to that night game in Cleveland's Municipal Stadium or, probably no less decisive, what might have happened to Don Shula if he had been a junior that night instead of a senior, playing both offensive and defensive halfback? A three-year regular for Eisele, Shula was not the flashiest player on the John Carroll club but, at least that once, the whole outfit must have looked like champions.

As a direct result of that game, Shula was picked ninth by the Browns in the winter drafting session of the National Football League. He was flabbergasted and admits it.

"I couldn't see Brown wasting a ninth-round draft choice on a defensive back from John Carroll, when he could have picked me up as a free agent," Shula says now. "But I was drafted and Carl Taseff was too, in Round 16 or 17, and I was a very happy boy. But I had some decisions to make.

"I had the chance to go to Canton (Ohio) Lincoln High and be an assistant coach, while teaching mathematics and physical education, making four-thousand dollars a year. This was solid work and a decent income for a young fellow just leaving college in 1951 . . . but the idea of playing football got to me too strongly."

Shula and his friend Taseff got up early the morning they had been told to be in the Browns' office. They tied their ties a few dozen times, scrubbed their shoes on the back of their pants legs to make them shine on the way downtown, and they talked about how it would be to meet Paul Brown for the first time. They also wondered aloud how the great coach would act when they appeared.

When the moment came, he acted very briskly and politely.

Paul Brown shook hands with the two halfbacks—Taseff the runner, Shula the cornerback—and said "Hello." Simultaneously, he
pushed contracts across the desk and said, "Sign these."

The contracts said five thousand dollars each, with no mention
of a bonus. None was mentioned by the players. There was no
debate. Shula, a man renowned now for his cool, was shaking
with excitement at this great chance. He and Taseff signed without
a word. Until trades would them part, they were Cleveland Browns.

It can be said the significant occasion hardly slowed Paul Brown
in his busy day, however. The coach shook hands with his freshly
minted rookies when they handed back their contracts and stood
still for a moment while a photographer from the Cleveland
Plain Dealer snapped a picture of two local players joining the
big club. That was all. Brown turned back to his desk, and the
bedazzled Shula and Taseff were fortunate enough to find the
door. The whole meeting had taken no more than two minutes;
Canton Lincoln had lost out. The major in sociology and minor in
mathematics—even the masters he got the next year in physical
education—were to become secondary tools to Don Shula for the
rest of his lifetime.

He had passed his twenty-first birthday a few days previously,
and he was to be the youngest player on any NFL squad in that
season of 1951. But he had to make it first.

From the moment he and Taseff joined the other fledglings
at the Browns' camp in Bowling Green, Ohio, they were facing
monumental odds against more than a night or two at the place.
National Football League squads were limited then to thirty-three
players each (as opposed to the present forty), and there were
only twelve teams, even after the shakeup that occurred with the
demise of the All-America Conference.

The original Baltimore Colts and Buffalo Bisons were among
the casualties, and this freed dozens of players worth consideration
by Brown and other NFL coaches. Today, marginal players usually
can find work with one of the twenty-six teams of the NFL—the
forty-player limit is further promise of at least a trial—but things
were harder when Shula broke into the league. Old-timers admit

that today's players are bigger and faster, but seldom will they grant them the physical toughness and endurance of their predecessors of the 1950s and before. There were fewer substitutions, smaller squads, etc. In any event, young Shula knew he was in for it. He and Taseff grimly went to work.

A veteran, Chick Jagade, and another rookie, Ace Loomis, were Shula's main competitors for steady employment as the camp ground toward its finish. Blanton Collier, later to succeed Brown as head coach of the Browns, had the defensive backfield responsibility then and he was strictly a man-for-man exponent, with a five-three-three alignment; the deep secondary was responsible for three receivers: the tight end and two outside receivers, now called wideouts. At times, the cornerback would switch with the safetyman, with the two deciding if they would play strictly man-for-man or play inside-out on the two receivers coming down. It was hairy enough, but not nearly so sophisticated as deep defenders find pass defense today, with its zones, half-zones, and such, in addition to the man-for-man and combinations of all these.

Collier gave the young Shula credit for quick absorption and poured the work to him. Herb Eisele's teaching at John Carroll came in good stead, too. Eisele and his staff roosted in the stands at Browns' games on Sunday afternoons and, on Monday, installed the lastest wrinkles of the pro club. Shula had played the pass defenses favored by Paul Brown every day he was on the John Carroll University practice field. This was no small factor in the situation, perhaps, when the last preseason game loomed. The Rams were the opposition and, when he appeared in the dressing room at Cleveland's Municipal Stadium, Paul Brown wasted no words.

"Don, I'm going to start you tonight," the coach said to him quietly. "If you play well, you'll make the football team. If you don't, you won't."

Shula's reaction might be called typical of him: "This had the virtue of laying the possibilities right out in front of you—there was no lack of clarity . . . but I was pretty shaky for a couple of minutes."

Finally, the young aspirant told himself to quit worrying, that he could do nothing about influencing Brown's mind by what he did or said off the field. "I decided to give it my best shot and try the hardest I'd ever tried . . . and let the chips fall. With a teacher's certificate, there still might be a job around somewhere."

Perhaps such speeches to himself worked off the tension. In the game against the Rams that started a few minutes later, Shula intercepted two passes and did a good job of housekeeping in his part of the pasture. He felt pleased when it was over and was cheered to some degree by Brown's terse statement in the dressing room: "You played a good game. You've got your foot in the door." But did this mean the "band" (or taxi) squad? Shula simply didn't know.

Brown had his own method of telling players if they were to remain with the team or to look for another jersey in a foreign town; again, this had the virtue of clarity.

He told each of the players who could be called doubtful quantities to show up at the team office on Monday or Tuesday morning. When all hands appeared as instructed, Paul Brown handed an envelope to each man. Inside was a note. It this case, seven players were handed the dread missives, some saying "Sorry, you didn't make it . . . ," others saying "You've made our football team and the next meeting is ten o'clock Wednesday morning," or whenever he had scheduled it.

Shula was among the fortunates who received the "good" envelopes, and he showed up early for the meeting at League Park, practice ground of the Browns. Some of the assistant coaches tried to help the losers get over their shock and, in his own way, Paul Brown made all things right for some of his unlucky correspondents. Walt Michaels and Ace Loomis both found that Brown had arranged jobs for them with the Green Bay Packers. Before the next season, both were back with the Browns. Paul traded for them to meet his particular needs. By such actions all of the Browns' draftees and free agents were taught to believe that the great coach did not hold against them their failure to make his

squad on the first time around, a significant facet in the complex
personality of this unusual genius.

Don Shula, at twenty-one, the youngest member of a National
Football League squad, was the only rookie who made the Browns'
squad at the time of the original cutdowns. Later in the autumn,
an injury to Dopey Phelps gave Carl Taseff an opportunity to
move up from the taxi squad—the "band" squad, as Brown and
his former players describe the ready-reserve of hungry aspirants.
The friends were united once more.

The first season was a constant and furious battle, it seemed.
The Browns were targets for the older clubs of the NFL, and—
spurred by envy and the inevitable fear of pushy neighbors—
the old boys went at them even more violently than they went at
each other. Shula survived. He had reason to suppose that his
second season would be less productive of anxiety, but this was
not to be. His National Guard infantry unit was called to active
duty—the Korean War was at its height—and the young cornerback and his pal packed off to Louisiana shortly after the 1951
football season ended.

Soon after induction into the Army, Shula was offered a chance
for Officer's Training School, but told the officer who suggested it
that he wanted out at the first possible moment. So he remained a
doughfoot but soon found a cushy berth—he and Carl Taseff were
assigned to coach the Camp Polk football team. There is no record
of brilliant achievement in that first chance to teach the game,
but it had the enormous virtue of keeping the two friends in
running shape and constantly oriented toward football; the latter
often is the largest loss for an athlete called to military service. His
physical condition remains sound, but the tasks he is assigned
haven't even a vague relation to the way he makes his bread on
the "outside." The damage done will vary with the individual
and his experiences, but it is quite real.

Even more damaging—as it can be to the careers of nonathletes
—is extended assignment overseas, whether in combat or not.
Again much depends upon the individual.

In any case, the luck of the Shula-Taseff duo held again:

The Korean War suddenly ended and their unit was deactivated, almost in a matter of hours.

Shula was told on a Friday morning that he would be eligible for relief from active duty the following Friday. He put in a call to Paul Brown and was practically gnawing the mouthpiece of the receiver when the coach answered. Shula told Brown what he and Taseff had been doing at Camp Polk, and the coach interrupted him to say that Don should catch a plane immediately and join the team—that Tommy James had just pulled a muscle in practice and that Shula could move immediately onto the roster.

Minutes after his discharge from service, Shula was on the way to Cleveland by plane. A few hours later, he was practicing with the Browns on Saturday and—on the following day—played against the Philadelphia Eagles.

"The Eagles were wild-eyed when they saw me show up," Shula admits. "They knew I'd been out and that I probably wasn't ready for full duty, but James' injury forced it. . . . Bobby Thompson was the Eagles' quarterback, and he directed traffic my way all afternoon."

Jumping on the "cripple" worked for the Eagles. Shula didn't have much of a day and had to leave the fray after a collision with Art Pollard cost the Cleveland cornerback two teeth and a ripped lip that required fourteen stitches. Bobby Walston, the Philadelphia receiver Shula was supposed to be responsible for, enjoyed himself hugely. Brown apparently shrugged off the failures before the collision, for he kept Shula at the job for the remainder of that season. When Detroit defeated the Cleveland club by one point in the NFL's championship game, however, Shula's career under Brown was at an end, although neither knew it then.

In the off-season, in April, when he was working on his masters degree at Western Reserve University, Shula was having lunch in the cafeteria when he opened a newspaper to find his own picture among several at the top of a sports page . . . he was part of a trade to Baltimore that involved a total of fifteen players, with the Browns giving ten bodies or draft choices and the Colts surrendering five players or draft choices. It was one of the bigger trades of that era and one of the most important, not because of Shula's presence but because of the records many of those fifteen players established later with the Cleveland and Baltimore teams.

In 1953, the Colts were just being regenerated, with Carroll Rosenbloom the owner—a reluctant one, according to his own admission—and the new club needed bodies. The late Don Kellet, the Colts' general manager who engineered the deals that were to make Baltimore such a formidable force in football in less than a decade, arranged the trade with Paul Brown. Among other things, this trade gave the then Baltimore coach, Keith Molesworth, three-fourths of the defensive backfield that would play together for four years: Shula, Bert Rechichar, and Carl Taseff. Weeb Ewbank was to come to the Colts and succeed Molesworth from Paul Brown's staff of assistants the following season, and the good times would begin to roll for the Colts.

Incidentally, a classic tale of the chances and mischances of life can be found in that move by Ewbank, who would lead the Colts and later the New York Jets to the pinnacle of professional football: Kellet actually was trying to reach Blanton Collier over the telephone when he called Cleveland after the 1953 season, but Collier was working with Brown at the Senior Bowl game. Instead, Kellet wound up talking with Ewbank and their conversation led to a visit and, soon after, Ewbank's employment as Baltimore's head coach. . . . If Collier had been physically present in Cleveland that morning, he very likely would never have paused for a time in Lexington, to be head coach of the University of Kentucky, nor is it likely that he would eventually succeed Brown, at Cleveland. It is worth a small footnote in this abbreviated study of Don Shula's formative years that he early was aware of the aforementioned chances and mischances in every man's passage through life; this is evident from his own determination that his "professional" playing days should be ended after seven years of action and that he should get along with coaching or, as he labels it, "my life's work."

Shula stayed with Baltimore through the season of 1956, when he had a disappointing fall, and went with the Colts to camp the following summer; he learned early in that camp of the club's desire to deal him off. Instead, another trade brought cornerback Henry Moore from the New York Giants, and Moore soon was getting more attention from the coaches than was Shula. One day Don came to the dressing room and found his locker empty.

Cut just before the opening of the regular season, Shula was under the brutal pressure so well known to certain pro football players at the start of each season. . . . Other squads were set, he had not sought other work, and he must seek a way out of the dilemma through his own devices.

He was one of the lucky ones. Shula learned the Redskins were looking for a cornerman and he got in touch with Joe Kuharich, who gave him a chance with the Washington club. Shula made the team but was determined never to find himself in such a bind again. After the 1957 season, he gave up all idea of playing—"three teams in seven years is a pretty strong indication that you might be better off in something else," was his thought on the matter —and he went hunting work as a coach.

His luck held. Dick Forrest, a former assistant to Red Blaik at Army, was the new head man at Virginia, and Shula spent one season with him before joining Blanton Collier at Kentucky. But the yen to work back into the pro game caught him, and Shula— now getting a measure of reputation as a good student of the game and an able teacher—had to pick among chances. Pop Ivey invited Don to join him with the St. Louis Cardinals, but George Wilson was said to be looking for a young defensive backfield coach with pro experience. Shula called Wilson, they met and liked each other immediately, and a three-year association started soon after.

The Detroit Lions under George Wilson ranked with the greatest defensive clubs ever to appear in the National Football League. The late Les Bingaman was the defensive line coach; Shula worked with the linebackers and defensive secondary, and their results were outstanding. The harmonious relationship among the coaches no

doubt was a large, contributing factor; one of football's memorable
games saw the Lions' defense shred a Green Bay offense that had
brought all others to their knees. The resulting acclaim for Detroit's
defense originated with football's own experts, rather than fan
fervor, and Shula was among those given credit by these people
for an extraordinary job.

His name rose to the top at precisely the right moment. The
Baltimore Colts were making a coaching change—Weeb Ewbank,
dumped by Carroll Rosenbloom, went to the New York Jets, there
to rise to the heights once more—and Wilson recommended Shula
to Rosenbloom. George recalls that he suggested to Shula that he
have a "revolving" contract, where he would automatically be
renewed after each season for a stipulated number of years. If
the Colts wished to make a change, he would have plenty of time
to find another job while still busy at Baltimore. It was a shrewd
idea. When Shula moved to Miami, such a contract still protected him at Baltimore on a five-year revolving basis.

The Shula Era at Baltimore began after the 1962 season and
was to prove far more successful than the young coach dreamed.
In his seven seasons there, the Colts had seventy-one victories,
lost twenty-three games, and had four ties for a .755 percentage.
In the seven seasons, the kid who loved to play games in Painesville
was named Coach of the Year three times—and racked up the
same honor from *The Sporting News* after his brilliant first year
at Miami in 1970. He was named again after 1971.

In these years of leadership in the most constantly violent of
team games there is a thread of continuity, although there is no
one accomplishment that sets him apart from other practitioners.
This continuity is found in his method of bringing a football team
together. Although he creates a team of intensely motivated and
dedicated men—Shula did this in Baltimore, too—he is not given
to emotional harangues in the Knute Rockne or Jimmy Conzelman
pattern. Rather, he might be described as the teacher talking to
graduate students, since he learned to govern a temper that earned
him the nickname "Captain Redneck" as a player. On the practice field he sometimes shouts, often speaks bluntly, and occasionally

shows temper; but this is to jar the student back into the subject at hand, or so it seems to the observer.

"Everything I do is based on classroom teaching. Paul Brown was a pretty good man to learn under, a great teacher," Shula says now. "He's more responsible than any other person for bringing teaching into coaching—the idea of the play-book, for example . . . the presentation in the classroom, then work on the field, then review after review, using movies and all other devices available to you now. Paul Brown was up front among those who brought organized programs of teaching to football.

"I've utilized a lot of lessons I learned in studying teaching methods as a student in college. We're going to a lot of expense to expand our classroom situation at Biscayne College, and we'll employ every kind of teaching aid that makes sense.

"Vince Lombardi—more than the inspirational leader, although he had great gifts in that direction—was a teacher above all other things. He taught in a New Jersey high school after he graduated from Fordham and he later was under Red Blaik at Army. Blaik and West Point represent the highest development of teaching techniques for men learning things they can use profitably in stress situations.

"Lombardi was the best kind of teacher, for he demanded discipline and gained it while imparting knowledge to the men he was teaching. To know how to do something but not having the discipline to do it at the proper moment makes the knowledge itself a waste of time. . . ."

It's possible that Shula's most constant problem is disciplining his own fierce spirit. This can be traced to his earliest beginnings; when a very young fellow, Don would visit his grandparents, who lived a block or two away, and would spend hours there, playing a game from the old country called "Five Hundred," a kind of rummy. Everything was fine until he lost, when Don would throw the cards aside and run home, crying in rage.

Watching him turn purple after his club loses to one he knows to be inferior, we can believe that there still is rage in him, but

Shula usually controls it well enough to pass for a man of iron will.

We have game plans, thorough ones. . . . But when the plan isn't working, there's no reason to stay with it. The job then is to locate the breakdown and do something about it while your decisions can have some effect. It's a helluva lot better to do it in the game, rather than wait until the movies on Monday.
—*Shula*

More than most, Shula believes that the coach on the sideline can influence what happens on the field. He holds himself responsible for it. Reporters who scramble to get to him after a loss, eager to hear him whimper or load up his players with blame, are met with no excuses. Shula gives the mechanical reasons why things came unwired and when, but he considers himself the one man able to change the course of the Dolphins during a football game and—when that course proves erratic—he doesn't look to a substitute to absorb the bricks.

This hardly means that Don Shula enjoys barbed questions or loaded gaffs from reporters. Like other able men, especially those in sports, Shula under pressure can become impatient very quickly with newsmen who constantly employ clumsy or obvious questions and confirm after every game that they've never learned what it's all about, no matter the area of conversation—players, game strategy, or the aspects controlled by coaches. But it is accurate to say that Don Shula is strong enough and confident enough to admit where blame should fall, though this brings his own pelt under fire—a trait not found often, even among the most successful.

Captain Nice can blow his stack but, when dealing with newsmen, it usually is a controlled explosion, definitely recognizable to those tuned onto his wavelength. When Shula answers a question with a question—"Why would you think that, when the receiver obviously was slowed down at the line of scrimmage?" might be an example—he's nettled with the original.

Asked recently what he would like to be remembered for, when his coaching days are finished, Shula's response was quick and typical of him:

"In Baltimore, I was able to bring to prominence the fact that the 'special teams' could contribute toward winning or losing a football game. In the years there, the 'nonentities' of our squad decided many, many games. We made the kickoff team, the punt-receiving team, and the rest of the special groups something special in the eyes of fans. I think this was a contribution."

Shula went so far as to name one of his leading belligerents captain of the Colts' special teams. The next weekend, this worthy, Alex Hawkins, appeared for the midfield coin toss with Johnny Unitas, captain of the offensive team, and Gino Marchetti, captain of the defensive group. When Unitas introduced Hawkins to the referee, the official responded with a line that borders on the most memorable in the history of football:

"Captain Who?"

Shula loves to tell that one, but his interest in and respect for the special teams under his command are genuine.

9

The Turnaround Season
of 1970

From the moment he stepped to the microphone there on the pool deck of the Jockey Club, Don Shula's enormous problem was time.

First, however, he had to meet with George Wilson and—as best he could—lessen the impact of the blow to the proud older man, who previously had given him such a large chance to expand his own horizons as a professional coach.

It was a difficult moment for both on the morning after the announcement when they met at the Dolphins' office on Biscayne Boulevard. There were handshakes and smiles for the cameras, both men saying and doing the things they could to make the other less uncomfortable. But their conversation behind closed doors was private and, at this writing, was the last between them, although their homes are only a mile or so apart and they attend the same church in Miami's northwestern suburbs.

Wilson's disappointment was obvious and, especially to those who know his code, understandable. He was upset with Robbie that he was not informed at the end of the 1969 season that he would not be signed again—his contract ran until March 1970—but something else nettled him even more: Wilson felt that Shula could have reached him with a telephone call during the two weeks Shula and Robbie were dickering for the Baltimore coach to succeed Wilson. (George claims there were twenty-two days.) Locked into a situation where he could afford no leaks of his conversation with the Miami club president, Shula didn't make the call. He has paid public tribute to Wilson's influences on his own career—Shula was an assistant to Wilson at Detroit when Wilson recommended him to Rosenbloom, who hired Shula as Baltimore's head coach—and Shula commented afterward that Wilson's attitude toward him after the Miami change was very generous. But the coolness became a glacier when Wilson blurted to Charlie Nobles of the Miami *News,* five days before Super Bowl VI: "A coach named Joe Doakes could have done what Shula did with the Dolphins—a ready-made team." It was a complete loss of control. Shula immediately interviewed them: Tom Keane, a teammate of Shula's in the Baltimore secondary years before, and Les Bingaman, with whom Shula coached at Detroit, were rehired. Contracts of the others were not renewed. Shula's agreement with the Colts that he would not approach any assistant coaches there until a new chief was named also influenced his staff moves . . . but a coincidence played right into his hands.

Bill Arnsparger, Shula's defensive line coach at Baltimore for five seasons, had departed the Colts on February 3, a month after Don Klosterman became general manager of the Baltimore club and two weeks before Shula came to Miami. The announcement said Arnsparger was leaving the Colts to "accept a tremendous opportunity in business." Some doubt was cast on that phrasing when Bill joined Shula in Miami within a week after Shula's arrival; when he named the Kentuckian his defensive coordinator and linebacker coach, Shula moved the ailing Bingaman to the front office and a scouting assignment. Big Les lost his battle, however; he died in less than a year from complications arising from the heart attack that felled him on the sideline during the last game of the 1969 season.

Arnsparger, a brilliant football man of considerable achievement, immediately blended perfectly with Shula's needs; a quiet man and complicated personality, Arnsparger is seldom sought by reporters. Theirs is the larger loss. Once the defensive game plan is decided Shula leaves it with Arnsparger and concentrates on offensive tactics.

From George Allen's Los Angeles staff, Shula summoned Howard Schnellenberger, who had served Blanton Collier with Shula and Arnsparger at Kentucky ten years previously. Schnellenberger would be the Dolphins' offensive coordinator and receivers coach. Mike Scarry, whose playing experience included seasons in both the NFL and the extinct All-America Conference, had a long coaching and personnel scouting record for NFL teams; he would be Shula's defensive line coach. Carl Taseff, a chum of Shula's on teams discussed elsewhere, was hired for the offensive backfield responsibility, and Monte Clark came in from active play with the Cleveland Browns to be the offensive line coach. These, with Keane remaining for the secondary, formed Shula's original staff at Miami, with Bob Lundy (trainer) and Danny Dowe (equipment) held over and completing the field group.

It's doubtful if one of them got more than a half-sandwich for lunch in the first six months after shaking hands with the new head coach. Long, grinding days opened with eight-o'clock meetings and finished well after sundown or hours after that. Miamians who called to invite the new man to speak to clubs or lunch at some prestigious place downtown were brusquely told that there was no chance. They've made little headway to this day, as a matter of fact. Shula has the rather basic notion that the football season is for nothing else and that the off-season is for getting ready for the season. Those who cast their lot with him go the same route.

Arnsparger's philosophy on defense and approach to defensive problems was much the same as Shula's from the outset, of course, after their huge successes at Baltimore. Schnellenberger's offensive ideas included those he learned under Allen, at Los Angeles, and under Bear Bryant, for Schnellenberger was Alabama's offensive chief for several seasons before joining the Rams. As the Dolphins' new offensive playbook evolved, the big assistant coach admitted that it had a little of everything—"we didn't overlook a source"— but the basis of the whole attack was ball control.

It has not changed since.

Shadowing all of Shula's preparations and schemes was the nagging memory of the NFL's major reorganization and the way the new season of 1970 would throw his developing Dolphins against the veteran Colts three times—first in the preseason and then one game in each city during the AFC's Eastern Division play. This had to dominate many of Shula's quiet hours. The actual switch of the Colts, Cleveland Browns, and Pittsburgh Steelers to the AFC had occurred on February 1, 1970. When the first test came against Baltimore in August, Shula was ready . . . but it was a near thing.

> *The coach who lets things slide in practice will find they slide in a game. . . . You play like you practice. If it's well done earlier in the week, the chances are excellent that it'll be well done when the whistle blows.*
>
> —*Shula*

While his freshly assembled assistants pored over films, grading and evaluating players during the cool months and early summer, Shula spread himself thin. Included in the spread was time devoted to establishing a permanent base at Biscayne College, a Catholic four-year institution on Miami's northern perimeter. With only 450 students, Biscayne has no built-in need for extensive athletic hardware, but it has considerable unused acreage. Joe Robbie's early association with Biscayne led to the strong alliance that since has proved profitable for both the professional football team and the college; two football fields and a large dressing room were built originally. Today, Baltimore Orioles' farm clubs are using extensive baseball facilities created in another joint venture with the young school . . . but that was for the future when Shula laid out his needs to the college authorities.

"Coming up with a coaching staff that could do an objective job of teaching during the first season was foremost in my mind, and we came out quite well," Shula recalled, months later. "You delegate authority and let these men pretty well run their own shows and you, as the head coach, supervise what's happening. After seven years at Baltimore, things happened automatically on our staff. . . . That hardly was true at Miami early, for Arnsparger was the only one who had worked closely with me in recent times.

"There were other, obvious pressures. I knew a little bit about the Dolphins after having coached against them for preseason games twice previously. At Baltimore, when we knew we were moving over to the American Conference from the NFL structure, we started studying the teams who would be our new, primary opposition—Miami, Boston, Buffalo, and New York. We studied the Miami personnel.

"First, we noticed they really didn't have a lot of convictions about their people in the offensive line. They shook them up quite a lot and switched their people around a lot in the preseason. When they finally settled on some people, they didn't do a very good job of blocking for the passer. . . . We felt the Dolphin team we played in the 1968 preseason was much stronger than the one we met in the 1969 preseason. Griese, for one, looked a lot better in that first ball game than he did in the second."

Shula had doubts about Griese's knee, the one injured midway in the 1969 season. The quarterback still was young enough (twenty-five) to recover from a knee operation with little chance of impeding his career, if the surgery were required. If it were not necessary, however, no man in his right senses would want a "preventive" operation—knee surgery is a daily occurrence somewhere in American's football subculture but it is not the most exact of sciences, even at the most expert hands. In the case of Griese, he had been advised both ways by surgeons with wide experience. In the face of this split opinion, Bob decided against the operation in the late season of 1969.

"When I came down, the first thing I did was investigate this [knee] situation," Shula said. "I'd been told before coming to Miami that George Wilson had tested Griese on the field after he had taken the necessary measures to strengthen the knee and that Bob did everything asked of him then, with Wilson and [trainer] Bob Lundy and Dr. Herbert Virgin all present. It certainly looked like surgery wouldn't be necessary. But I'll admit there was a nagging doubt in my mind. . . . Obviously, Coach Wilson, Joe Thomas, and the others thought Griese was all right, otherwise they never would have pulled the deal for Warfield. . . ."

The coup that brought Warfield from Cleveland occurred on January 27, almost a month before Shula's arrival. Thomas sensed how determined the Browns were to get a quarterback via Miami's pick on the first round of the draft and, for days, he said only Warfield was acceptable in trade. The Browns offered the Dolphins many other deals, but Thomas hung fast. Finally, a few hours before the first-round picks began, Cleveland gave up their great receiver for Miami's first choice. Thus, the Browns got quarterback Mike Phipps, who had been a whiz at Purdue—but the Dolphins got Warfield, who had been a whiz in the NFL. . . . A prime point in all this is that the Dolphins would not have passed up the chance to get a prime young quarterback even for Warfield, if there was doubt about Griese's knee.

This thought comforted Shula until he could see for himself that Griese was telling it straight when he said the joint was all right.

A comprehensive test of Griese and many another questionable asset was not possible until late April, when forty-seven players, most of them Dolphins veterans, went through a one-day shakedown at the University of Miami practice field. One week later, another such look was taken at the rookies; the new coaching staff was much better able to judge where it stood after these workouts.

"It was apparent to me that Griese not only handled himself

very well physically but he also met all the mental requirements for a cracking good quarterback. . . . Putting in a new system is a lot tougher than most people realize. When you take a system you're familiar with and try to instill it into a group of athletes accustomed to something else totally different in names and formations, numbering systems, the way pass or run plays are called— all of it—and you ask them to learn this in a stress situation, it increases the difficulties enormously.

"You can sit a group of people down and teach them these things by normal methods, but when the outcome of a ball game depends upon it and you haven't been able to sit them down as you would like, it compounds the problem and it takes intense concentration by everyone concerned.

"Our coaches—with the exception of a couple—had the same problem: to adapt their thinking to mine and the new system in a spread of time that didn't match the size of the problem. . . ."

Shula and his newcomers wasted little of that time in debate.

There was to be even more pressure on the new coach and his people than they realized when they studied the calendar, for this was to be the year of the strike of veteran players—or, in another metaphor—the mass holdout of veterans. Only the one-day camp of spring saved Shula from seeing his veterans for the first time when they finally reported, five days before the first preseason game against Pittsburgh at Jacksonville. That brief look at the University of Miami campus established weights at which the players would report—or suffer in the purse—and it had a heavy influence on Shula's decisions about who would play which position.

On the field at the university, he tried to pick up little things that would help the decisions when real coaching began. "Their attitude in that indoctrination session—all through the whole year —was tremendous. They did everything, without question, that I asked them to do. I think they did this because they realized that they hadn't won and they were interested in winning.

"Usually when you get a group of athletes together, they want to win. If you can guide them along the right paths, you can make winning that much easier for them.

"You have more friends when you're a winner than when you're a loser."

Shula has been called hard, abrasive, etc., as were other winners before him. He admits it when he starts tearing weight off players.

"Two instances where I think this helped our team in 1970: Larry Little, who I thought was far too heavy, shed a lot of weight —about thirty pounds from the time I saw him in the indoctrination sessions until he started practice in July. In the first practices, he couldn't finish one. He'd get sick and couldn't take the heat. Finally, when he got in shape, he became one of the leaders in our offensive line. And look at Larry Csonka.

"Of course, I'd had a lot of respect for Larry as a college player at Syracuse but he'd had problems as a pro, with head injuries and things that kept him from performing. I asked Csonka to get down to what he weighed in college, 235 pounds. He's a big man and it was tough, but he did it—that's what I'm talking about, that kind of response.

"Later, I was to discover I had some fine athletes going for us, but we had to strengthen our offensive line."

A day or two before the first engagement with outsiders—against Pittsburgh at Jacksonville—Shula said, "Our early camp training was unlike anything that's ever been experienced in football. Improvisation, the timetable has been shotgunned, we've worked with rookies harder than ever before . . . everything is different this time."

As noted elsewhere, in the weeks before the veterans appeared, the rookies who came through—Kolen, Swift, Scott, Foley, Ginn, Johnson, Langer, Kuechenberg—were an integral part of Shula's plans, whether he calmly sat down and reasoned them to be such or not. They were ready to play; the veterans were only half-ready for Pittsburgh.

There was some thought by Abe Fletcher, promoter of the fray at the Gator Bowl, to cancel the Miami-Pittsburgh game. Robbie and the Steeler brass agreed to wait until the Monday prior to the game before a final decision; even the pull of Shula's first appearance as Miami's coach was not enough to get a decent gate if the vets didn't play. As already noted, this fear was not realized.

In the game, the Dolphins looked like they had been playing together for years—one of their more remarkable feats, actually. Only 13,407 fans were watching through the rain as they tore into the Steelers and held Terry Bradshaw to nine completions in nineteen throws and went on to win, 16–10, with Shula sticking to his plan of testing four quarterbacks—Griese, Norton, Stofa, and Rookie Jesse Kay—to discover that Griese was the one who could move his team. Stofa was fairly successful, but the other two were not.

From this game forward, Jake Scott was a star, handling the slimy ball as if it were covered with sandpaper and roaming the outfield as if he'd always played free safety instead of flanker, running back, and what have you.

Kremser and the intriguing mite from Cyprus, Garo Yepremian, started their war of flying footballs in this game, Kremser kicking two field goals and Garo one. Neither missed. Their struggle would continue for all the weeks of the preseason, with Yepremian slipping to the taxi squad only to rise after the opening league game and go on to lead the National Football League in ratio of hits with twenty-two of twenty-nine field-goal tries for a 75.7 percentage, scoring ninety-seven points to lead the team. Most important, he was to successfully kick eleven of fifteen field-goal tries that began between the forty and forty-nine yard lines, with forty-seven yards his longest.

Griese's five completions in seven passes thrown pleased Shula, but Norton's dreary one-for-five and two interceptions cost him his career with the Dolphins.

Shula was to say afterward that he wished Norton had been with him as a rookie but that it was too late, the team simply didn't have time for the expensive bonus player to get rewired and easy in his mind. He would go next to Cincinnati as a free agent for a tryout, thence to Green Bay, and out of football early in the 1971 season.

A hint of the future came in the next preseason game, the home opener against Cincinnati, when 60,460 spectators paid their gold to see the revitalized Dolphins lick the Bengals, 20–10. Attendance for the home exhibitions was no less satisfactory, with 58,745 for San Francisco; 76,712 for Baltimore and 50,259 for Atlanta. The difference in attendance in the preseasons of 1969 and 1970 (with one more game) at home was over 100,000.

Shula was paid for before he even started coaching for keeps.

Griese passes to Kiick and Warfield scored early touchdowns against the Bengals, and it was largely downhill after that in this first test of the new Poly-Turf artificial grass in the Orange Bowl Stadium. The players liked it, for the most part, with a loud dissent from Jake Scott. "I've never liked this kind of stuff, but I guess it's here to stay," Scott gloomily responded to reporters. "I'll just have to keep my armpads on and pull my stockings clean up to my knees, no matter how hot it is out there. Otherwise, you get all kinds of rub burns from that stuff."

Shula's stratagem of making roommates of players whose cooperation was vital to the team already had begun to work. . . . Griese and Warfield were a combination whose hookup would provide lightning as Kiick and Csonka in the same backfield provided thunder. Intelligent and reserved by nature, Griese and Warfield got along well from the outset, apparently, and spent training camp hours talking and scheming out their timing and suggesting ways of making their weapon work against all defenses.

The Dolphins had had no such weapon—a deep receiver capable of turning back downfield and then blowing for the end zone—and the presence of this new one was of the utmost importance. "A feared passing combination establishes a pressure point, a place where you can hurt a defense—something you can do consistently," Coach Schnellenberger told Al Levine of the Miami *News*. "It'll open up a lot of things for your offense, including the running game."

Warfield admired the quickness of Griese's arm, saying he delivered the ball much quicker than any passer Paul had dealt with during his years in Cleveland—Frank Ryan, Jim Ninowski, Bill Nelsen—and he had to turn his own head quicker to follow the flight of Griese's ball.

The pair contributed again to the unprecedented third straight victory of the preseason, this one over San Francisco's strong team, 17–7, in a battle that included a resounding victory for the Miami defensive line and their support troops: the Forty-Niners were kept from scoring in four straight plays, beginning at the Miami two-yard line. When they finished, the stunned San Francisco runners still were two feet from a touchdown. When Griese passed to Warfield and Paul sped away to a fifty-yard touchdown run on the first play of the fourth quarter, the ensuing furor was compared by some to the happiness of Miami fans following Joe Auer's memorable return of the opening kickoff in Miami's first game. This was the first of the long-range bombings for which the pair is famous.

The 76,712 people (a Dolphin record to that time) who appeared in the bowl the following week to see what all the noise was about hardly could be expected to believe the propaganda that "the feud between the Colts and Dolphins only is felt in the front offices." Not when it was over, anyhow. Even that first meeting after Shula's transfer had a lot of electricity in it and today it has more so, for these are the strongest teams in the Eastern Division of the AFC.

One superheated chronicler called the Dolphins' 23–10 decision over the Colts "The revenge of Dr. Frankenstein"—over his monster, the Colts—and certainly a night of sweet peace for Don Shula followed it. With a scant three games under him, the Dolphins unceremoniously dumped the most prestigious team in football, a couple of whose players had said rough things about their former coach in the weeks coming up to the game. Others quietly visited the Shula home during their weekend visit, while most of the Colts kept their mouths shut and said only innocuous things when asked opinions of Shula. . . . Listeners in football togs have long ears, and conversation is a way of life in some tribes. . . .

It would be another year before Bubba Smith would call Shula "a damned good coach" publicly. Prior to playing against the Dolphins in 1970, the giant defensive end said he wanted to beat the Dolphins so he could beat Shula, that he didn't like the man, etc.

Shula admitted privately that he was harsh with Bubba when the Michigan State star joined the Colts. "I was tougher on him than I've ever been on a player," Shula told the author. "The reason was simple: Bubba was a great athlete who was too fat. When the blubber came off, he became one of the finest players in the game—but it was hard on him and he resented it."

In the game that August Sunday in the Orange Bowl, Smith's luck was ordinary. Norm Evans scuffled with him incessantly, trying to keep the monster from wrenching the head off Griese. But Bubba wasn't the only Colt who got his comeuppance that afternoon.

The Dolphins wrapped it up with ten points in each of the second and third quarters, with the touchdowns coming on a pass from Griese to Larry Seiple, playing tight end, and from Jim Kiick's blast at tackle in the third period. Kremser's field goals shortly after each TD completed the Dolphins' scoring. When Tim Foley slipped on the artificial turf while trying to turn to block an Earl Morrall fling toward Ed Hinton, the Colts had a fifty-eight-yard score in the third period. Otherwise, Baltimore was kept at arm's length, save for Jim O'Brien's field goal.

(On the morning of this game, Paul Warfield signed a three-year contract with the Dolphins, employing the same agent who later served Kiick and Csonka in their 1971 negotiations. Paul's annual wages are in the seventy-thousand-dollar bracket, with performance clauses that can run it substantially above this. He isn't the highest paid of the Dolphins, however. Bob Griese gets more.)

Reminded on a television program that a certain Baltimore team official had admitted that Shula won a lot of games with the Colts but "lost the big ones," the coach was asked if he considered the lick over Baltimore a big game. "First, I'd take exception to that first statement," he shot back. "We won a lot of big games, too, during the years with Baltimore. We did lose the Super Bowl game to the Jets, and nobody regretted that more than I did. As for this Baltimore game last Sunday—yes, it was a big game." The straightforward manner of Shula, even when irritated with a question as he was that day, cannot be better illustrated than with this response.

In Tampa, the Dolphins found themselves the subjects of considerable curiosity after beating the Colts and three other teams impressively in the preseason. But the death of Vince Lombardi on Thursday cast a pall over the meeting with Lombardi's Washington Redskins. The great coach—victim of a most virulent form of cancer that almost literally exploded within him—would be buried in New York and his team would play the Dolphins, then fly to services in Washington before Vince would be laid to rest. Bill Austin, Lombardi's longtime assistant at Green Bay and Washington, served as the interim coach. Later, Bill was Washington's head coach for the 1970 season, and then was replaced by George Allen.

That night in Tampa, the 'Skins were able to convert Miami mistakes to their own advantage, and Sonny Jergenson was superb as he went all the way and won it, 26–21, with a ten-point fourth period. The Washington team dedicated the game to their fallen leader, and all of football mourned his loss.

This was the first preseason affair a Shula team had lost in twelve games and the first time Washington ever defeated one of his teams, after seven years of trying. But Shula didn't fret over this; what did bother him was a peculiar flattening out of his offensive team's efforts in the second half. Griese suddenly had poor luck, throwing off target or short, and other particulars of the game alerted Shula to possible weaknesses that hadn't been indicated earlier. Bob completed only two of twelve passes in the second half.

The preseason was completed the following week against Atlanta, with Bob Berry throwing a fourth-down pass to tight end Jim Mitchell that gave the Dolphins their second lump, 20–17. There were thirty-four seconds left on the clock when Mitchell crashed over. It was a very physical game, as those involving Atlanta always are, and the Dolphins were bruised for the season's opener. Altogether, the preliminary games could be counted successes—even the last two—since they gave the youngsters being blended into the defensive unit a chance to play together and test themselves against older hands.

For the most part, they passed the tests. But the opener in Boston found failures in unexpected places.

Miami's front line had allowed enemy tacklers to hit Dolphins' quarterbacks fifty-three times in 1969 . . . and the Patriots sacked Griese and Stofa eight times in this game. The percentage of increase was dramatic besides costing the Dolphins eighty yards in losses—the best day's work a Boston Front Four and associates ever enjoyed. Griese completed ten of twenty-seven throws, with two interceptions and no touchdowns. Stofa, who came on for him late, completed three of five in the poorly played game.

The Dolphins started out well enough, moving quickly to a touchdown, and led, 14–3, in the second period but not for long. Daryl Johnson intercepted Griese early in the third quarter, and things got hairy quickly after this. It was a long ride home for the Dolphins after the 27–14 drubbing dealt them by a team that was spirited and not without skills but that prospered on Miami mistakes more than its own efforts.

Shula never is a bundle of joy after any defeat, but he was more so after this one . . . his first effort with his new team was second-rate, and he was stung by it.

Kremser missed an important twenty-two-yard field goal in that fracas, and Shula took Garo Yepremian along to Houston the following Saturday. The coach then had the two specialists practice their kicks in the Astrodome, after which he put Kremser on the "move" list and activated Garo, the amiable little tiemaker. Garo was stunned by this sudden elevation from the taxi squad but didn't object and, the next day, he scored with goals of thirty-one and forty-two yards against the Oilers. Kremser, who had seemed so important to the team the season before, was finished as a Dolphin, with that one miss in his only try of 1970.

Griese, after perhaps his worst performance the week before, now had one of his best, and Jim Kiick joined with Csonka to show marked improvement in the running game, the Dolphins knocking off the favored Oilers, 20–10. A goal-line stand by Miami de-

fenders after the Oilers had a first down at the one forced Houston
to retire with only a field goal after a strong attack early in the
game—a stand that seemed to rejuvenate every man on the squad.
Manny Fernandez, John Richardson, and Nick Buoniconti were
the toughest of a good lot in that exemplary defense. Shula was
delighted with this show of strength, for Houston is no patsy down
front.

Oakland came into the Orange Bowl then and, for the first time
in their series of furious encounters, the Dolphins won. It was no
massacre, but the 20–13 victory was a highlight in the Miami
players' lives, for they had tried so very hard against Oakland
before and come close, only to fail. The bright and brittle Al
Davis, Oakland's managing partner, said of the Dolphins that Saturday night: "That Warfield is making a contender of this team. . . .
He gives them a threat they never had before." Davis had no more
than said it before Warfield pulled in three passes from Griese good
for 120 yards and two touchdowns, while Al Davis ricocheted
around the press box, grinding his teeth. The margin could have
been much more than the one touchdown, however, and another
biggie found out about the new Miami team a few days later. . . .

There was not an inch of Shea Stadium without at least a foot
in it when the Jets made their first appearance of the 1970 season
there against the Dolphins. As usual, Weeb Ewbank had a list of
wounded the length of his forearm, but he had Joe Namath
available, and Emerson Boozer was up and about, and these two
can be enough for any one team to meet over any sixty minutes.
Mistakes and the absence of stars had led to three straight losses
for the Jets, however.

Miami's 20–6 victory was not complete vengeance for his loss
to the Jets in the 1969 Super Bowl, but Shula enjoyed it completely, his usually stony expression on the sideline giving way to a
quiet smile late in the last quarter. . . . Until then, he had to
remember the rattlesnake's speed in the arm of Namath, who was
served poorly several times—including two bombs—when receivers
dropped his passes. Joe was flagged by the Miami Front Four and
limped considerably toward the end of the game. Defense was

the key to this victory, with the Jets kept from making a first down in the second half until the last minute of the fourth period, while Griese hit fourteen of twenty-four throws for 224 yards, including scoring passes to Warfield in the opening minutes and to Twilley later. Namath was only seventeen for forty, being intercepted three times. . . . When Ewbank said that Miami was the best his club had faced that season, the veteran was not paying lip service to any old friends. The Dolphins looked now like they could lick anybody.

This included Buffalo, of course, and Griese manipulated his running backs with two good passes to march the length of the field in the cold, dank Buffalo stadium and score quickly. In a few minutes Miami had the Bills by the windpipe, as Garo put all his rubbery little body behind a forty-six-yard field goal, then another from forty-two yards out before Dennis Shaw put the Bills on the board with a pass to Miami's nemesis when he was quarterbacking, Marlin Briscoe, now a fast receiver. The same combination worked for another score later, but the Dolphins by this time were over the ridge and gone, with Garo topping his day with other field goals of forty-seven and thirty yards. The 33–14 final was a comfortable cap to a four-game winning streak and the first awareness by the rest of the country that Don Shula might be whomping up something special down under the palms.

Now came the reckoning: what remains the most complete defeat of Shula's team since he appeared in Miami.

Cleveland's Browns played an almost errorless game and tied the Dolphins into hopeless knots before a solid sellout of 75,313 fans in the Orange Bowl. Blanton Collier's people were so much the better team in every way this day that their later failure was hard for Miamians to believe. The score of 28–0 was puzzling only because it should have been more. Bill Nelsen, for example, hit twenty of twenty-six passes for 229 yards and one touchdown, with Mike Phipps three-for-three when he came on in relief. Kelly, Scott, Morrison, and Minniear were the runners who ruptured Miami defenses when they felt the need. Griese's passes got him only forty-two yards, and he was creamed three times. Grim.

Flabbergasted, Shula tried to talk his club back to normalcy before the first of two regular-season matches with the Colts, this one in Baltimore.

It would be a kind of homecoming for Shula, who confided to friends that he really didn't know what to expect from Colts fans up there in "The Asylum on Thirty-third Street." When the time came and Don walked onto the field, he received a standing ovation from his old rooters, and again—although the score was a merciless 35–0 against him—they stood and cheered furiously when the former Baltimore player and coach walked out. On the second stroll, Don would have preferred a plank over the side of a ship, probably, for his Dolphins plainly were embarrassed in Baltimore.

However, despite the score, they weren't beaten badly.

Indeed, the statistics were in their favor. But the Colts broke open the battle with long strikes when Miami's special teams—a particular interest of Shula's, as described in detail earlier—broke down on key plays.

Rookie safety Ron Gardin grabbed a short punt by Larry Seiple on the dead run—Ron already was through the first wave of Miami kamikaze tacklers when he caught the ball—and streaked eighty yards up the middle for the first of the five Baltimore touchdowns. Mike Curtis intercepted a Griese pass in Dolphin country for the next chance, with Norm Bulaich busting across late in the second quarter. Jim Duncan accepted Garo's kickoff to start the third quarter at his own one and hauled it ninety-nine yards for a TD that got under Shula's skin more than all the others; in his brand of football, such a runback does not occur. Not only is it forbidden, it is impossible—yet there was Duncan laughing and slapping hands with teammates. Johnny Unitas passed to Ed Hinton for another and the situation unraveled completely for Miami, although the Dolphins gained 383 yards to 239 for the Colts.

Oddly, Mercury Morris was at his racing best that day, with 68 yards on passes, 145 on six returns of kickoffs, and 89 on runs from scrimmage: but, for the second time in eight days, Griese was relieved by Stofa at quarterback.

Shula's name did not appear in the program in Baltimore's Me-

morial Stadium, and Carroll Rosenbloom couldn't resist the tempta-
tion to salt the wounds of his former coach. The Colts' owner told
reporters: "George Wilson and Joe Thomas put together a terrific
[Miami] team. I can't believe my eyes. I thought they would be
better coached. There's not a coach in the league who wouldn't
like to have this material. . . . Look at the receivers—Warfield and
Willie Richardson. Richardson was All-Pro last year. . . . Look at
Kiick and Csonka, they're both terrific.

"You remember the Super Bowl game?" the Colts' owner pressed
forward. "The Baltimore team was the finest I've ever seen—but
the next year we played one good ball game all year. We went
8–5–1 and should have lost every game we played. . . ."

When Shula was read these statements, the grim Miami coach
flushed as he answered: "I haven't answered him before. I won't
answer him now. It's too far along now. . . . By the same token,
I'm not going to walk out of a room or off a field because he walks
on it."

The insult ate into his guts, and Rosenbloom would rue it.

Compared to the quality of its play against Cleveland, Miami
wasn't that bad against Baltimore; yet the thirty-five points amassed
by the Colts were second only to the forty-one of Kansas City, back
in 1967, against all Dolphins teams in regular-season play.

But the bottom was not yet. It was reached forty-five minutes
into the game on the next Sunday, in Philadelphia, where the
Eagles blanked the Dolphins until Yepremian kicked a twenty-four-
yard field goal that made the score 24–3!

Never has Griese's world been in such a tangle as it was then.
The unaccountable slump of the last three weeks would have completely unnerved most high-strung artists—Griese certainly is one of
these—but the blond quarterback didn't indicate any such feelings,
not even when John Stofa took over from him and led the team
to two touchdowns in the last period.

The great effort on John's part fell short, of course, but it at
least proved to the Dolphins that they were neither impotent nor
unready, merely that they had not been minding their lessons and
sticking to the job as they knew it. Taking a hiding in Philadelphia

is no more pleasant than it is anywhere else, but the 24–17 margin was infinitely preferred to the skunkings dealt Miami by Cleveland and Baltimore.

Griese had been running the team for four years. Bob didn't panic, although he admitted he had been unable to get the strong offensive unit cranked up for three games. A local newsman joined the hare-and-hounds chase of Griese by critics who suddenly became all-knowing but, above all, vocal. This unfortunate fellow listed a couple of hundred public figures and athletes, declaring all of these were better quarterbacks than Griese. Even George Plimpton (*Paper Lion*) made this catalog of misfits. . . . One would have to think that the author of that article broke his typing finger once a week for the rest of the 1970 football season. It certainly did him no favor.

Shula had to consider relieving Bob of the starter's responsibility. He admitted later that he toyed with the idea. "But the final decision wasn't difficult at all," claims the coach. "Here we had a man of proved physical capability, one of the brightest minds in football and leadership qualities that can be recognized at a glance —Bob needed the backup of confidence we could give him. He got it. We've never regretted it for a moment."

This was high praise, indeed, for this is the first time a Shula team had ever lost three in a row.

Griese started the next Sunday against New Orleans in the Orange Bowl, although against Philadelphia he was successful only six times in fourteen throws, with three interceptions and three sacks, while Stofa was five-for-fourteen, with no interceptions and two touchdowns.

The expression of confidence paid off handsomely.

The 21–10 victory over the Saints was directly accountable to expert, top-quality quarterbacking; Griese hit fifteen of nineteen passes for 225 yards, with all eight of his second-half throws right in the hopper. Too, the Dolphins came from behind to win it, and Shula looked years younger when the thing was over. "I wasn't aware of my statistics, but if it took that kind of completion stats, I'm happy we got it done—I'm just happy to win," the quarterback said quietly, no more excited than he was when fresh from the pasture after a sour performance. "I had a lot of help out there."

Indeed, he had help. Among other examples, Jim Kiick's fifty-six-yard dash set up a score—"I knew something was wrong when the guards started passing me in traffic," Jim snorted—and the Dolphins were altogether themselves once more. Three times, the Saints were denied when they tried runs on third down with short yardage: when the Saints were leading, 10–7, in the second period, rookie linebacker Doug Swift blasted Tom Barrington both times the New Orleans running back tried to get first downs. After Miami took a 14–10 lead, Manny Fernandez and cornerback Curtis Johnson stopped Jim Otis cold on the one-yard line.

A new attitude was found in camp with Tuesday's customary morning assembly. There was reason aplenty.

From a thousand miles away, the Dolphins heard footsteps. The Colts were coming.

When they reached the Orange Bowl, Shula had his people ready.

Griese went ten for sixteen, including a fifty-one-yard work of art to Karl Noonan—Warfield was dealt a cracked rib by Rick Volk in the second quarter—and he threw no interceptions as the Dolphins took a full measure of revenge for their earlier embarrassment, 34–17. Unitas also was himself, throwing successfully twenty-two times in thirty-six attempts, but John had two interceptions and never was able to establish the balance between the run and the pass that Griese contrived for Miami. Baltimore Coach Don McCafferty admitted the Dolphins were the better team that day—this was the Colts team that went on to edge Dallas in the Super Bowl on the same field later that season—but there is no record of quotes from Carroll Rosenbloom, the Baltimore owner.

The most spectacular piece of business in this intriguing game was Jake Scott's swift runback of a David Lee punt for seventy-seven yards and the first touchdown of the afternoon—a proper response to the one by Ron Gardin in the first game. This one unsettled the Colts no less than Gardin's rattled the Dolphins in the first match.

Griese's performance was touched up by another happening: He cut through the middle of Baltimore's defense on a quarterback draw for fifteen yards and the second touchdown. Then he whisked a touchdown pass to Warfield when Seiple covered Duncan's fumble of the kickoff. His long one to Noonan hammered home the victory.

Shula was delighted—some might say surprised—but he didn't heap coals on the already smoldering Colts and their chiefs.

The game ball was presented to the widow of Les Bingaman, who died on the Thursday night prior to that battle.

Critical as this game was, the one following was called the key to the season by Shula.

"In 1970, we needed the solid play, rather than going wide with reverses and gimmick-type plays that they used a lot a couple of years before. We were able to develop this solidity because of the presence of Fleming and our gifted backs running behind Little.

"With Fleming we could sweep around either end or go off tackle, for Marv is a big man able to go against big people and whip them. This is why the offense developed—it was kind of a natural thing that reached its prime in the Monday night game against Atlanta, where he went up against a big, tough, physical football team that was thought to be capable of ramming the ball down your throat, and we just did a turnabout. . . .

"We took the ball and rammed it down their throats, and after that game we sensed we were capable of moving the football against *anybody*. This was one of the milestones of the season," says Shula. "This is where we got our style offensively. Defensively, we came up with some big plays.

"Now we were the kind of football team you like to be associated with—the kind that takes advantage of every situation presented offensively or defensively or in a special-teams situation."

The 54,036 Atlanta fans sitting in their circular stadium and the millions watching on television hardly saw this flowering of the Dolphins . . . all they knew was that the Falcons couldn't cope with the thunderbolts that came at them. There was a world of difference, although the score was only 20–7 in Miami's favor.

On the opening kickoff return, the Dolphins blasted a path for Mercury Morris, who got up to the Miami forty-five. Two plays later, blockers wiped out the left side of the Falcons' defense and Morris got twenty-seven yards. The drive ended with a field goal, and Miami led the rest of the way. The Dolphins went on to get 217 yards rushing, twice as much as the average opponents had chopped out against Atlanta in ten games. Csonka ran for 108 hard yards and plunged for the clinching touchdown after Atlanta had closed in to 13–7 in the fourth quarter.

Big plays in the decisive drive that covered eighty yards and eight minutes included two third-down successes by Griese to keep the thing alive and a brutal, eighteen-yard carry by Csonka that sounded like a pair of Percherons on the front of a beer wagon. The big man did his thing, and has been doing it ever since.

If a sportswriter of the 1920s were the chronicler of the Dolphins now, he would say "The Hungarian Horde was born that night!" —and it would stand up.

Claude Humphrey, Atlanta's exceptional defensive end, said of Csonka: "You hit him and he hits you back and keeps making like a mechanical ditch-digger. . . ."

Next, and the fourth straight victory, the Dolphins smashed Boston's Patriots—they would be renamed the New England Patriots before another season—in an Orange Bowl romp, 37–20. The Dolphins had a 27–6 halftime lead and no problems at any time. Morris teed off on the poor Pats with a ninety-six-yard return of the opening kickoff for a touchdown—nobody catches Mercury once he is in high gear for forty yards—and Lloyd Mumphord blocked and then ran in with a Pats field goal try before Griese ever touched the ball. After Griese finally got to play, he had fourteen points worth of cushion. When Bob got his big backs to drumming on the Poly-Turf, one reporter described it to Shula as "a laugher."

"Me? With a face like this I've never had a laugher," the coach snorted.

Sniffing a playoff berth as the "wild card" in the American

Football Conference—that is, the conference team with the best record that is not a division winner—over seventy-five thousand Dolphins fans stuffed into their big bowl the next weekend to watch the Jets take another hiding, by a modest 16–10.

Miami's lone touchdown resulted from a Griese throw of twenty-three yards to Howard Twilley in the second period as The Claw continued his domination of the Jets secondary. Yepremian thumped field goals of forty, thirteen, and twenty-one yards that overcame a second-period touchdown pass from Al Woodall—Namath was hurt—to Ed Bell. A playoff chance was very real now, for their 9–4 record gave the Dolphins an inside track to the wild-card ticket.

A victory—even a tie—in the final against Buffalo would get them there, and the Dolphins were a hungry outfit. But they also were human, and Shula used all his skills to keep their minds on the Bills, whom they had cuffed, 33–14, in an earlier game. He was successful, for the Dolphins leaped out and clobbered Buffalo, 45–7, in a savage display that took them beyond Kansas City for the wild-card playoff position.

Miami made nineteen first downs to ten for Buffalo in gaining their sixth victory in a row, with Jim Kiick scoring three touchdowns and Csonka, Stan Mitchell, and Twilley one each. Yepremian, of course, drew blood with a forty-three-yard field goal. Worn and torn, the Bills scored after Miami had run up its highest point total in the five-year history of the club.

With a record of ten victories against four defeats, the Dolphins were the most successful of second-place winners in an AFC division and won the chance to meet Oakland—winner of the Western Division—in the elimination round of the playoffs.

It was an unfortunate site, for seldom has a field been so poorly prepared for a battle of giants as was Oakland-Alameda County Stadium the day after Christmas 1970.

"All that we've accomplished all season, everything we've worked so hard for is finished. Everything we built was left out there in the mud," a disconsolate Bob Griese told the Miami *Herald's* Bill Braucher when a pass from the quarterback to Willie Richardson for a touchdown signaled the end of a powerful comeback effort in the slime.

Rain of the previous days was the culprit, not those during this resounding battle. But the stadium—apparently sited by somebody who cut his classes in Primary Hydraulics—is located on ground that is below the level of the nearby bay. *Voilà*. The sun may shine, but water in that ground means water on that field. The game might have been better played in a Louisiana bayou.

The 20–13 decision over Oakland earlier in the season doubtless was a contributing factor to the solid confidence felt by the Dolphins. With Baltimore playing Cincinnati in the other bracket, Shula's group felt good about prospects of reaching the Super Bowl, a dizzying prospect, indeed. Warfield's presence—Paul was back for the first time since the tenth game—reinforced it.

And it was Warfield who got the Dolphins a lead that appeared the size of Stone Mountain in the second period. This followed the first of two lost fumbles by Oakland—both teams made enough critical mistakes to lose several games—at the Oakland nineteen. Bill Stanfill fell on it. Moments later, Warfield took a sixteen-yard toss from Griese on a curl pattern right under the crossbar. Yepremian, who had missed a first-quarter field goal try from the twenty-five, converted his first of two times.

Until late in the fourth period, the Dolphins couldn't put their offense together again, while Oakland came alive.

The Raiders marched sixty-two yards for their first score— shortly after Warfield got Miami on the board—and accomplished it with a twenty-two-yard post pattern from Daryl Lamonica to Fred Biletnikoff. But the disheartening thing about that drive was the way Lamonica pulled Oakland out of trouble with passes to Ray Chester and Bilentnikoff that gave it new life on third down and long yardage.

A second break came the Dolphins' way early in the third period when Oakland's Smith fumbled on the Miami two and, while the ball squirted from hands like a seed from a watermelon, Jake Scott finally overwhelmed it on the ten. Griese passed to Warfield for twenty-five to get out of the dangerous field position and Kiick, on a third-down play, picked off ten to the Miami forty-seven, and the Dolphins were rolling again.

But now Griese made his only mistake of the afternoon.

Willie Brown, responsible for covering the right zone (on Miami's left), found the ball flying straight toward him instead of toward Warfield behind him. Willie took it in and raced fifty yards for the go-ahead touchdown for the Raiders.

Aided by a pass-interference penalty early in the fourth period, the Dolphins progressed to the Oakland seventeen but, as he had in the forepart of the game, Yepremian missed the field goal opportunity, again with a curious spiral not at all characteristic of his normal kicks. He did not complain of Noonan's positioning of the ball, and there appeared to be no slippage because of the mud . . . Garo just missed. It was especially painful, since the Dolphins could be second-guessed for not going for a first down. At that moment, they were fourth down and three to go.

It was the last real opportunity.

Under no pressure from Miami's Front Four, Lamonica leisurely surveyed the bog before him and caught the flying figure of Sherman down the right sideline and let fly. . . . The ball was taken in full stride by the former college sprinter, and Sherman ran it the distance—eighty-two yards from the line of scrimmage and the difference at the end, for Blanda's kick made it 21–7. It was Sherman's first touchdown of the year.

Nine minutes and change were left on the clock.

It was enough, if the Dolphins could rally. In only eight plays—largely through the furious efforts of Kiick—the Dolphins were back down on Oakland's goal line, with Willie Richardson taking the eight-yard pass over Clint McCloughan and the conversion by Garo put the Miamians within tying distance—and a sudden-death decision—at least.

The combination of a determined Raider defense and field conditions grounded the dream, however. The Dolphins had averaged 149 yards per game with the league's best running attack. That day in Oakland, they only made 118 and five first downs with their rushes . . . Kiick was up to standard with 64 yards, but Csonka was good for only 23 yards, and Morris, 29.

In the four minutes remaining after their second touchdown, the Dolphins almost covered Garo's squib kickoff, but a Raider touched it last before the ball spun out of bounds, so it was given to Oakland.

Miami got the ball once more but deep in its own country and even then couldn't mount another major attack—thus, the end of hope.

Shula continued his strong opinions in support of his players and their accomplishments—as well he might—but the coach was disconsolate, for he had geared his thinking and that of his whole establishment to moving on against Baltimore for the final playoff game on the following Sunday.

"What do you do now when you had thought of nothing else but work on Tuesday? . . ." he asked a reporter, softly.

For one thing, the brilliant leader could enjoy the fruits of a largely fantastic first year at Miami. For the fourth time in eight years as a head coach in the National Football League, Shula was acclaimed "Coach of the Year" by *The Sporting News* and *Football Weekly*.

For the players, an endless round of good things began, with several becoming even better known through commercial promotions and off-season jobs in the South Florida community. As the mass of AFC statistics from the 1970 season was sifted, the Dolphins continued to show to advantage:

Griese had the best completion average (58 percent) among the throwers; Yepremian was third (with ninety-nine points) among the scorers; Jim Kiick was (again) in the top ten receivers and top ten rushers in the conference; Larry Csonka's 874 yards was second to Floyd Little's 901 among rushers; Mercury Morris was fourth in kickoff returns (he averaged twenty-nine yards in twenty-eight returns); Jake Scott was third in punt returns, averaging 10.7 yards in twenty-seven handles, while Dick Anderson was second in the AFC with eight interceptions. . . .

More than this, the Dolphins had found themselves and—as a

team—had a personality for the first time. The stamp was there that carried through the 1971 season: on offense, to keep the ball and pass only when necessary to break open a given situation; on defense, to prevent the cheap touchdown, the long pass or long run through use of the zone ploy in the secondary and increased pressure on the enemy quarterback by the Front Four, with a minimum employment of the blitz.

It was a good year. The ten victories, against four losses, was a full generation away from the 3–10–1 of 1969.

10

Preseason of 1971

If laid alongside each other, the problems and circumstances facing Don Shula at the start of his first and second preseason camps for the Dolphins at Biscayne College had little or no relationship. Even the physical facilities at the college were more comfortable and improved for the 1971 training season.

Instead of a 1970 preliminary roster heavily loaded with rookies and floaters from other teams, Shula in 1971 knew almost to a man who would be playing which positions for him in the campaign ahead. His ambition at the beginning of the second year was compounded of the success in 1970 and the obvious deterioration of great stars on other teams in the Eastern Division of the American Football Conference; Joe Namath's wrist and knee wounds hampered the Jets, who also had questions about the condition of Matt Snell's Achilles tendon and the retirement—apparently for spiritual reasons—of the brilliant receiver, George Sauer, Jr.; Baltimore, with Johnny Unitas not only old, but suffering from a tendon problem similar to that of Snell, and Earl Morrall in the twilight of his career, obviously had quarterback problems and uncertainties in other positions. Two victories in three games with the 1970 Super Bowl champions was a warm memory, too.

The Dolphins could win it all in the Eastern Division; this was there for everyone to see as the squads of huge, powerful men gathered at their camps in July. Twenty-two Dolphins rookies, eleven of them draft picks, and twenty of the younger veterans signed into the suburban training camp on July 11, a Sunday.

Shula's experience at Baltimore told him how to develop every reserve possible, for attrition among front-line troops is an accepted part of every season but a gut proposition for those teams making serious runs at division and league championships.

There was only one concern that ran counter to this determination: the proved benefit of continuous victories, in preseason no less than in league play, established by Shula at Baltimore and continued in the preseason of his first Miami campaign. Victory begets victories. Shula's Baltimore teams lost only four games in seven preseason summers. At Miami, the 1970 Dolphins won their first four unofficial games, then lost two.

It is not important that a fully detailed account of the 1971 preseason be included here, but it is germane to the Dolphins' story that we pick among the factors that bore upon it. The results of the games hardly were inspiring, and only the season unfolding could determine if Shula—long-range planner, calm analyst of strengths and weaknesses in groups of men—had won his substantial gamble.

He would build the reserve strength necessary for a championship try, even if it cost him some prestige and surges of unease among the fans who besieged Charlie Gesino's ticket office all through the spring and summer. The net included victories over Detroit and Washington, sandwiched between losses to Cincinnati,

Green Bay, and Minnesota. The last, a brutal beating, 24–0, was accomplished by a Viking team that was better than the Dolphins from first whistle to last . . . a signal that all was not quite right, at least, with a team that had excellence—or better—at every one of the "skill positions."

But Shula accomplished most of what he set out to do in the preseason. He gave his reserves time to find themselves and their level in combat, while his early conclusions about his first-stringers appeared justified. In the case of Otto Stowe, No. 1 draft choice and a taller version of the gifted Paul Warfield, he had a young receiver fast enough to penetrate enemy defenses quickly and brave enough to make payoff catches in that swatch of ground that terrifies even veteran receivers—that middle ground in the enemy secondary where wide receivers breaking to the inside can confidently expect to meet someone traveling at full speed on a collision course. This is the region of the clothesline tackle and other niceties that separate chillun and grownups. Warfield, the ballet master, is particularly effective in this part of the receiving zone, and Stowe indicated early that he would likely measure up here, too.

But, once again, an early injury to Mercury Morris—this time the swift running back banged up an ankle in the third game (against Green Bay)—and the chance to hone a "three-back" offense with Csonka and Kiick was lost. It already had been seriously impaired by the holdouts of the two bigger backs, who steadfastly refused to appear in camp until the Monday prior to the first game of the preseason, against Cincinnati.

Csonka's 874 yards rushing, second only to Floyd Little's 901 yards in the AFC, plus his brutish blocking for the passer and other runners, made his 1970 season by far his best; Kiick rushed for 658 yards and caught 42 passes (fourteen more than Warfield) for 497 more . . . the pals had talking points and hired themselves an agent to talk tough about them in contract negotiations with the Dolphins in the late spring of 1971.

"Butch Cassidy and the Sundance Kid"—Kiick and Csonka—denied they were pairing their contract demands in the fashion made notorious by Sandy Koufax and Don Drysdale, the Los Angeles Dodgers pitchers who once held out for more than one hundred thousand dollars each. In the practical sense, however, only the numbers were different, since the agent, Ed Keating, of Cleveland, refused to allow a settlement of one player's contract without the other being satisfied with terms of his own. Naturally, the figures never were revealed publicly, but both Kiick and Csonka wanted base pay of more than sixty thousand dollars. With performance bonuses, they could have approached one hundred thousand dollars. If the Dolphins got into the playoffs at season's end, the two running backs would be wealthy, if not rich. It was a heady prospect for the pair when the cat-and-mouse game with Joe Thomas opened. The Dolphins' offers were far short of their demands. Thomas insisted upon dealing with Keating on a basis of two separate agreements, rather than a package arrangement with only minor differences in wording between the contracts. The issues quickly became stalemated, with Joe Robbie in Europe.

The Dolphins' managing partner and his wife departed in early July for England and the convention there of the American Bar Association—a rather long-shot proposition in itself—and later visited Scandinavia. While he and Thomas, the personnel officer of the club, were often in telephone communication, Kiick and Csonka obviously were nettled that the top club official was not present for the talks.

Then, in the middle of the whole hoo-rah, Thomas fell ill and was sent to a Miami Beach hospital with a form of hepatitis resulting from heavy transfusions of blood in the previous winter after a serious heart operation. It was a dismal time for the Dolphins, as the days sped by, with Shula's frustrations showing and squad members carefully hedging their own conversations to avoid the chance of bitterness toward the holdouts.

Robbie's return from Europe was followed by long, hard sessions with Keating, sometimes with the players present. Between the meetings, the friends worked out as best they could while avoiding reporters, except on a couple of occasions when Keating saw advantages in such contacts. The largest issue raised by Thomas and then Robbie was the necessity for Csonka and Kiick to join the squad for workouts, signed or not, with negotiations continuing at camp. This was Shula's point in his public utterances, but the coach refrained from shouting it every day . . . it was a tense period for all hands.

Finally, on August 2, the Monday before the opening of the preseason schedule against Cincinnati in the Orange Bowl, Csonka and Kiick appeared at the Biscayne College training grounds. After talking with Shula, they met with reporters in bunches. Later, they put on their work clothes and sweated with the other players, whose satisfaction at this development was obvious.

The absence from camp was costly to Kiick and Csonka. The fourteen days of palaver at long range cost them twenty-eight hundred dollars each—at a rate of two hundred dollars each day imposed by the coach, with Shula not counting a Sunday when he gave the whole squad the day off. Apparently the club maintained the posture it first assumed on the fines, that they were not negotiable and that the players must pay them. However, they at least could afford the penalties.

Three-year contracts assuring each of the pair substantial raises were signed just before midnight, prior to the Cincinnati game. Both are in the fifty-thousand-dollar bracket. It is significant that the pens were put to paper in the hospital room of Joe Thomas; apparently Robbie, who had claimed throughout negotiations that Thomas had full power to deal with Keating, was determined that this fact should prevail, and the players appeared with their agent for the signing in the room of the ailing personnel chief.

From the first minutes they were available to him, Shula poured the work to the reluctant bully-boys, and they took it without a whimper. The amazing thing was that they were in prime physical condition—perhaps a trifle short-winded when compared to the young bucks who had been working three weeks in the broiling sun of the Biscayne College training camp, but well able to keep up and absorb the complex assignments Shula and Howard Schnellenberger, the offensive coordinator, had concocted for them.

In sum, the largest loss from the absence of Cassidy and Kid to the team in that formative period was in the timing and switch of assignments necessary to a successful employment of three backs— this pair with the elusive Mercury Morris. Three weeks later, when Larry and Jim were fully at home in the training routine, Morris had an ankle banged up in the Green Bay exhibition. Since this blending of talents was one of the keystones of Shula's increasingly sophisticated offense, its loss—even in this later time—cannot be estimated.

> *I first met Jim Kiick at the Chicago All-Star game. We went out and had a few beers together and got to be friends. . . . People look at Kiick and think they're looking at a sad-eyed cowboy from Wyoming. What they're looking at is a beat-up pool shark from New Jersey.*
>
> —*Csonka*

All three are resourceful carriers and pass receivers, with Kiick's all-round abilities a perfect fulcrum for the scissors effect of Csonka's enormous power and Mercury's flying heels. Csonka is one of football's best blockers, and Morris is a wraith of a runner, with the heart of a midtown bank robber. In 1970, Shula could see all this well enough, but too many other factors required attention for the mixing of skills to be emphasized. Now, in 1971, he wanted to hone it every day "so the other guys won't know that Mercury comes in just to carry the football." But, as the preseason progressed, the glittering prospect had to be set aside.

All three, when present and busy, had good results in the preseason. Shula had to content himself with this.

In two other directions, preseason games indicated a considerable strengthening of the linebacker troupe but no qualitative gain to speak of from the Front Four in the vital mission of beheading passers. In 1970, the Dolphins got to the throwers only sixteen times in fourteen league games, lowest in the AFC; in the six preseason games of the following summer, they managed only five wipeouts, a drop in a percentage that already was an open wound with the coaches.

It was obvious, however, that Bill Stanfill had returned to the form of 1969 when—as a rookie from Georgia who won the Outland Trophy as the nation's best college lineman in 1968—Bill decked opposition quarterbacks eight times. This dropped to six in 1970, when he was hampered by a foot and arm injuries at one time or another and, over-all, was far less effective than in his first season. His hurts had all disappeared when the six-five, 250-pounder returned to camp in the summer of 1971, and he was tough on everybody in sight. He had three of those five QB sackings in the preseason.

True, the Front Four was not exactly foursquare most of the way, for Manny Fernandez didn't appear until the fifth game, against Washington. His right shoulder, separated in the next-to-last game of 1970, against the Jets, was still a bother. The operation was successful but extensive, and even Fernandez couldn't swallow all that pain. His return evened out the combination—Stanfill, Fernandez, John Richardson, Jim Riley—and they finally were a unit only in parts of the last two warmup games.

Shula took some heart from the improvement of Jim Riley, one of those big people with gentle instincts. Mo Scarry's constant needling was having some effect, perhaps, but the big onetime Oklahoma star got the message with no static when Shula brought in a procession of defensive end candidates and tried them on the left (Riley's) side. Beautifully equipped physically, and mentally hep, Riley was too nice to people in his first three seasons with Miami, and Shula was getting edgy about it. Jim apparently realized the situation, and he bore down. He was no terrorist, but he consistently was tougher than previously as the long preseason schedule developed. This was a very positive gain.

Yet there was no indication that the Front Four unit was developing into a killer pack.

In the linebacker group, however, the Dolphins got larger dividends than expected, with a considerable assist from a considerate Cleveland club with the summer half gone.

The notable success of 1970 by the rookies, Mike Kolen and Doug Swift, who had blended so well with Nick Buoniconti, was compounded by the return to health of Ed Weisacosky, who missed the last eleven games of 1970 with a bum shoulder. The former University of Miami ace, a contentious citizen, and Randy Edmunds, a veteran whose injuries led him to the taxi squad in 1970, made a hard run at the first-string outside positions, but Bill Arnsparger had a larger worry: with Buoniconti thirty-one years old and the smallest middle linebacker in the NFL, it was time to give him some help. The ornery onetime Notre Dame All-American didn't ask for any, but he got it.

Kolen appeared to be a more natural middle backer than Swift—he's a harder hitter in a head-to-head meeting with the ball carrier—but Kolen's experience had been limited to the weakside job. In Shula's system, the middle man calls defensive signals, and while this is no great mental burden—all or most are inspired by semaphores from Coach Arnsparger on the sideline—it is a large responsibility. With mechanical changes natural to the switch from outside to the middle, the signal chore takes time to master. Although there is little doubt that Kolen—Auburn's "Captain Crunch" in the 1969 season—could get the hang of the middle spot in time, there might be no time. This was proved in the Detroit game of the preseason, when Buoniconti went out with a fracture of a small bone in his right hand. The red flag was up. But help came running from Cleveland.

Shula had been vastly impressed by the work of the Browns' middle man, Bob Matheson, in Cleveland's 28–0 pasting of the Dolphins in the previous season. "That fellow played a perfect game against us," the Miami coach admitted after breaking down the films. "I've never seen such a job by anybody in a game against one of my teams. . . ." He tried to make a deal during the winter, but Cleveland wasn't listening for anything less than a second-round draft choice and other goodies. The Dolphins backed off.

But Buoniconti's hand injury in August's game with Detroit created an entirely different situation. Shula called Cleveland Coach Nick Skorich, who had been debating between Matheson and Dale Lindsey anyhow, and they settled for Miami's second-round choice in 1972's draft. Matheson arrived from the Browns on Thursday and worked against Washington on Saturday night, while Shula's pleasure was plain to see. At six-four and 240, Matheson came in with four years of league play and no physical flaws—a trump by any measure. Buoniconti accepted his appearance in good grace, but the club had more linebackers now than it needed, and Shula quickly shook down the line.

Before he finished shaking, veterans Ted Davis, Edmunds, and Weisacosky and rookie Dennis Coleman were waived, with the last three picked up by New England. Jesse Powell's brilliant preseason and the appearance of the steady Matheson guaranteed not only quality but real depth at the position for the first time, with rookie Dale Farley on the taxi squad but a comer of great promise.

In all other areas there was a percentage increase in strength during the 1971 summer, although that in the offensive line couldn't very well be seen for bruises. Maxie Williams' back problems became chronic and he was put on the injured reserve list and would not be available until late in the autumn; Wayne Moore, the giant reserve, and Bob Kuechenberg also were banged up for part of the summer and Shula traded the good, second-string center, Carl Mauck, to San Diego for Tony Liscio, an offensive tackle who "retired" instead of making the switch. Liscio, formerly a Cowboy and who still resided in Dallas, eventually was prevailed upon by Tom Landry to return to action. His play was ferocious and he was of considerable help all the way to Super Bowl VI. It was an unsettling time for Monte Clark, who considered coming out of retirement at one point, when the situation became desperate because of injuries. But Cleveland still owned rights to Clark as a player, and Monte didn't suit up for the Dolphins. Kuechenberg's return shortly before the opener with Denver was a change in the flow, but Shula and Thomas—who recuperated from his illness at home after leaving the hospital—still were looking for offensive line help.

Meanwhile, George Mira, who had wandered from San Francisco to Philadelphia to Baltimore and then to Miami in his eight-year search for a starting job as a pro quarterback, was able to root John Stofa out of the backup job on the varsity roster shortly before the season opened. In the Washington preseason game, poor old Stofa opened at QB and was cracked down just when he had the team in gear. The hip-pointer John suffered then gave Mira the chance he needed so desperately; a sore arm had prevented early work in the preseason, and his three passes against Detroit were unsuccessful, including two wild throws. Against Washington, however, the former University of Miami matador was his old, exciting self—pitching to Jim Mandich for one fourteen-yard touchdown and to Otto Stowe for a beauty that Stowe hustled on down for a sixty-nine-yard TD. It was an exhilarating return to the friendly cavern where the Key West native set University of Miami attendance records in three years of varsity play as a collegian. Excepting two decisions over Vince Lombardi's Green Bay teams when he replaced an injured John Brodie and guided the '49ers, Mira's professional career had been distinguished largely by the size of his contract while performing in ordinary fashion—when, indeed, he got to perform at all. The Dolphins had rescued George from the Baltimore taxi squad the previous spring when a Miami columnist happened to mention that Mira was a free agent, his status at Baltimore having fallen into disrepair, although he still had a 5-year, $60,000 annual contract given him three seasons earlier by San Francisco when Mira played out his option and threatened departure.

It seemed to outsiders at the time that Shula and the Dolphins' brass perhaps were asking for problems from a Miami football public that recalled Mira's extraordinary facility for generating excitement in a ball game and that his presence on the squad easily might work against the grain of Shula's announced faith in Bob Griese. But the chance to embarrass Baltimore by snapping up Mira because of what seemed to be a housekeeping error in the Colts' front office was too great, especially with the uncertain condition of Unitas and Morrall and a clutch of other QBs named Clyde available to the defending champions.

After the Washington preseason game—in view of Stofa's painful but rather pedestrian injury—the move toward Mira also looked like good football sense. It should be noted, however, that the heat on Griese from the Mira cultists was perceptible within minutes after the first game of the regular season. The future promised more of the same if the slightest excuse could be dragged up. It was an unusual situation.

However, this did not account for a definite air of unease as takeoff time for the flight to Denver and the opening game on September 19 approached. Better reasons were etched clearly in the turf of Minnesota, when the Dolphins played their last of the six preseason games.

From the moment Clint Jones touched the football on the opening kickoff, the Miamians were in deep, deep trouble. Jones boiled back for sixty-nine yards to the Miami twenty-seven and, six plays later, bolted across for a touchdown on a ten-yard run that followed a fourteen-yard scamper by Bob Lee on that ancient but honorable maneuver, the quarterback keep. It is merciful to merely record that the Vikings' final total was 24–0. While Csonka and Kiick maintained their thunderous pace, averaging 5.2 yards each against the "Purple People Eaters" of the Vikings' Front Four, Dolphins' mistakes did what the big Minnesotans couldn't.

Griese had a pass intercepted by Ed Sharockman that stopped the Miami attack at the Vikings' nineteen in the early going, after an eleven-play march that proved that Miami's power was still intact. Later, another drive was drowned out at the Viking twelve. . . . It was that kind of day.

For historical purposes, the other results of the 1971 preseason:

Cincinnati 27, Miami 10—The Bengals didn't have Greg Cook and some other people who would make them even tougher, but all they needed was elbow room in the Orange Bowl. Only in the second period did the Miami offense hum—this was during the limited service of Csonka and Kiick, who had reported the previous Monday—and Cincinnati was much the better. Miami's touchdown came in the third quarter, after Stofa and Mercury Morris got together on a pass that carried to the three. Otherwise, it was all Bengals.

San Francisco 17, Miami 17—The first half was a beaut from Miami's standpoint. The offensive line blew apart San Francisco's usually hard-nosed defense, although the results were tempered by an early field goal by San Francisco's Bruce Gossett. Griese to Warfield scored on the first play of the second quarter. Later Kiick punched over after twenty-seven yards in six plays. . . . Shula admitted in September that this was the best pair of quarters in the preseason games. The '49ers caught up later as Shula tried reservists in the lineup freely.

Green Bay 10, Miami 7—A ragged game, it did little for either team, except that it gave the Packers a chance for Scott Hunter, the Alabama grad, to find his nerves at quarterback. Stofa, third of the Dolphins' QBs, steered a drive that included eleven plays, with Hubert Ginn slipping through for the TD. Injuries to Mercury Morris, Frank Cornish, Dean Brown, and Wayne Moore proved important later; a pattern of foolish penalties for the Dolphins was set in this game and lasted into the regular season.

Miami 28, Detroit 24—A wild game, fiercely fought and well received, it also revealed something not known before about Don Shula—the chief Dolphin was willing to gamble for victory, given square odds, even in a preseason exercise. The gamble, a pass from Griese to Warfield in the end zone, pulled the Dolphins ahead permanently. A field goal from the thirteen would have been surer and brought a tie. Griese scrambled to advantage several times in this affair. Shula was satisfied.

Miami 27, Washington 10—Shula's opponent here, George Allen, is his closest rival in total victories for a currently active pro coach over the past nine years. Prior to 1971 play, each averaged ten victories per season, with Shula having a slight edge between the two of four victories to three, with one tie, before Allen brought his first Washington team to the Orange Bowl. Both teams needed a decision to solidify a wobbly preseason. But, after a Washington lead of 3–0 in the first period, the Dolphins moved out evenly, with a second Yepremian field goal giving Miami a 6–3 halftime lead. Then Mira found the range and two TDs, followed late in the fourth period by an eighty-six-yard run to score by Ginn, countering a Washington TD. The most significant news from this affair was the arm injury of the Redskins' master, Sonny Jurgenson, and the hip-pointer of the popular Stofa.

The shambles made of the Dolphins by Minnesota's lines—coming and going—is recorded above and perhaps is best forgotten. The Vikings afterward gave the Dolphins a heap more credit than did the fans who cowered in front of their TV sets in Miami and watched the purple people flail the visitors without mercy.

It was a proper prelude to the opener with Denver, anyhow.

It should be noted that the rocky results of the preseason games meant little more than mild, personal embarrassment to the Dolphins' owners. The excitement held over from the 1970 season and the obvious prospects for even better luck in 1971 caused an astonishing rise in ticket sales that began before the 1970 playoffs ended and continued into the new season.

The payoff can be determined from the 61,452 average attendance for the four home games of the preseason, each customer representing an average ticket price of $6.50. This figures to a total income of $1,696,752, with 40 percent of that going to the visiting four teams. The Dolphins grossed about $100,000 for each of their two road games. Even the princes of commerce at Miami's First National Bank had to be impressed with these numbers.

But artistically, they still could have some doubts about the football club.

II

1971 Season—the First Half

When the Dolphins' chartered Eastern Airlines jet landed in Denver on the Friday night before the Sunday opener with the Broncos, they mushed into the heart of the earliest major blizzard in the city's history. The white stuff was so thick that the pilot debated the wisdom of diverting to Omaha, Nebraska.

But he shrugged off the idea—the Dolphins' first piece of bad luck on a wretched expedition—and brought the Boeing in safely. Six hours later, there was more than a foot of snow to contend with and temperatures in the thirties.

Norm Evans, thinking about the prospect of fighting Rich Jackson in a blizzard, muttered that this was no weather to take on a grizzly barehanded. But, at the two-o'clock kickoff, the scene had changed completely. The field in Mile High Stadium was free of snow and—despite the baseball infield, where slabs of grass turf had been laid a few days previously—offered good footing, according to Paul Warfield. He should know. Paul used it up freely while giving his usual, excellent performance—a lonely role, as it turned out.

Before the two teams completed the rather wacky business in fiftyish airs, on a pleasant day and literally a mile above sea level, the unseemly odor of burned chicken was noted in the area of the Denver command post. What the Dolphins didn't do to themselves—although, gad, how they tried!—Broncos' Coach Lou Saban didn't do, either.

A record crowd of 51,200 assembled to watch their Broncos seek another moment of rapture like the one of two weeks previous, when they whipped the malevolent Vikings for their only preseason victory. Since the Vikings then went on to lash the Dolphins unmercifully in the last weekend of the exhibition trials, football fans of the high Rockies felt justified in thinking that the Broncs might club down the Dolphins in their first game of the 1971 season.

They didn't only because of the stubborn pride of individual Dolphins. Heaven knows the Miamians committed enough errors —Griese, Warfield, Buoniconti, and Scott turned over the ball to Denver on fumbles, for a starter—and blew chance after chance to win. Twice the Dolphins were penalized for too much time getting off a play—a practically inexcusable error. Better excused but more critical were the three field goals missed by Yepremian, from forty-one, thirty-six, and thirty-five yards. Since the wee Cypriot had led the NFL in hits with 75.5 percent in 1970, including eleven of fifteen from the forty-to-forty-nine-yard sector, his inept performance at Denver put the Dolphins in a spiritual crunch hardly less depressing than the brutal facts on the scoreboard. Fortunately, Denver's Jim Turner was no less erratic. The former "automatic" scorer for the New York Jets missed one kick from the twenty-five and had another blocked by Jim Riley, so it can be said the breakdown of the kicking was about even.

Even so, the only scores of the first half came from this pair, with Yepremian's twenty-two-yarder giving Miami first blood after an excellent punt return of twenty-seven yards by Dick Anderson to the Denver twenty-one. Kiick butted for seven yards in two tries; Griese, trying for a changeup, hurled a long pass over Warfield's head in the end zone, so Yepremian got his kick chance. It was perfect; the other three were wide.

Bobby Anderson, Dick's younger brother and Denver's No. 1 draft in 1970, pitched a halfback pass to Gehrke that carried for forty-eight yards to begin a Denver counterdrive after Garo's field goal. The Broncos moved seventy yards on seven plays in the march that died on the Miami three, so Turner kicked for three points from the ten.

One of the spectacular failures among the several by a Miami star occurred in the second quarter when Buoniconti—his right wrist encased in a cast extending six inches or so from midhand to forearm—intercepted a pass from Denver's Don Horn at midfield and bolted into a nest of frantic Broncos soon after. The ball squirted from under Nick's left elbow, and Floyd Little recovered it for Denver at his twenty-three. . . . It was that kind of day.

When Horn's pass to Dwight Davidson gave Denver a touchdown with a couple of minutes remaining on the clock in the third period, the Dolphins were in peril and knew it. . . . The spectators sensed it, too, and screamed for more than the 10–3 margin. Instead, Denver's Lou Saban was to play it cozy the rest of the way (after a midseason resignation, Lou returned to Buffalo for 1972) and, even after Griese threw Paul Warfield a perfect strike that Paul carried another fifteen yards for Miami's touchdown with 2½ minutes on the clock, Saban kept his counterattack conservative, satisfied to tie.

Jake Scott, a sure-handed and courageous kick-return expert, had no luck at all with a marvelous chance that came to him with something over a minute remaining. He took a weak punt from Denver's Van Heusen at the Broncos' forty-six and slipped through swarming tacklers with no regard for his personal safety—only to fumble in the region of the Denver twenty-three, where Bob Anderson fell on it to frustrate yet another Miami opportunity. It was a final indignity to a bitter coming-out for a team named two days before as the 6–5 favorite to win the AFC East by Las Vegas' resident swami, Jimmy (The Greek) Snyder.

Denver still had time to move the football, but Saban—as he had done in the previous Broncos series—ordered Horn to stay on the ground. After three plays, having worried forward to his thirty-eight, Horn at last was permitted to throw, and he hit Bob Anderson twelve yards upfield, where he was busted hard by his brother, Dick, the Miami safety. Denver was penalized fifteen on the next formation for holding; and on the game's last play, Saban had his chaps running again—while the mountain folk booed and called for his scalp.

"We tried to lose it once and I wasn't about to give it away at the end by trying to throw from deep in our territory, especially when we had to throw out of the muck. . . ." Saban later explained to the press. The "muck" referred to was the recently planted grass noted previously; it was stable enough to sustain Warfield's incisive moves when he caught the tieing pass from Griese and avoided two deep Denver backs. Indeed, Warfield said later that the turf was excellent. Saban's reasoning sounded like a lame excuse.

Shula demonstrated a consuming interest in victory when he had Griese try for a new series twice on fourth down, rather than punt, midway in the last period. On the first occasion, Miami was saved when Denver was guilty of defensive holding. At midfield, with the count fourth down and ten yards to go, Griese to Warfield got eighteen. Shula's point was proved, although these dares were taken with the score 10–3 against Miami.

At its best, the 10–10 tie with Denver damaged Miami's title chances only because it denied a victory—ties are ignored in determining playoff teams. But the fumbling and floundering by the Dolphins was unsettling to the most cheerful of Pollyannas among fans of the teams.

The four fumbles; Yepremian's three misses in four tries; two unnecessary penalties for delay of game—"training camp" errors, according to Shula—and the five times Griese was sacked for losses of sixty yards by the Denver defense led by Rich Jackson were basic breakdowns, the gut kind that normally would cost a team far more than a tie. Despite good performances from its runners— Kiick and Csonka churned for sixty-six yards each—Miami did not score when it penetrated Denver territory seven times in the last three periods.

Shula has never been able to accommodate defeat. But a script could not be written that would cause him more anguish than the story of the tie at Denver; his team had done almost everything in reverse of Shula's method.

The mother of the rival Anderson brothers had said before the game that she hoped it would be a tie. But she was alone in her happiness. Unless Coach Lou Saban felt likewise.

THE SECOND GAME: DOLPHINS 29, BUFFALO 14

Depressed by what they found in movies of the Denver thing, Shula's staffers went at their people with a new toughness. Taking their cues from the top, the assistants normally treat their people well, albeit with strong opinions. But in preparing for Buffalo, statements were shorter, answers louder. Rumors that The Turk was coming wafted into the dressing room at Biscayne College almost every time the door opened. It was an uneasy week.

Shula bluntly described the failures of Yepremian to kick even one of three reasonable field-goal chances as inexcusable. "Garo hasn't offered any reason why he missed, and I don't know of any—[Karl] Noonan held the ball properly, there were good snaps from center [by Bob DeMarco], and the field surface was excellent. . . . Those are three primary conditions the kicker doesn't control for field goals, and there was nothing the matter with them. He just missed." Any one of the three would have meant victory. Garo was miserable, but put on a good front. "The sun does not shine every day," he told Al Levine of the Miami *News*. Shula described Garo's largest problem as a matter of getting back his confidence. He should have known that this was really not so much of a problem. After what happened to him at Detroit, the little tiemaker hardly would lose his confidence in one week of failure. Half a season?

Perhaps. But observers with the team watched him closely for signs that the yips were getting Garo by the goozle.

The offensive line, where several operatives were sore or otherwise not themselves, got an extraordinary amount of attention. Monte Clark, a realist, growled that the only response fit for the occasion was to admit errors that could even be proved by dry statistics— the five sackings of the Miami quarterback, plus numerous other runs for his life—and come up with honest efforts against the Bills. Tackle Doug Crusan got work at guard now, with Jim Langer also at these positions, plus center, as Clark sought to beef up the bench.

Buffalo's opening loss to Dallas was no comfort, either. The Bills scored thirty-seven points against the vaunted "Doomsday Defense" of the Cowboys. That the Buffalo defense surrendered forty-two points to the Dallas offense was another matter. . . . The second year of Dennis Shaw as the Bills' quarterback promised to be even more exciting than the first.

Marlin Briscoe and Haven Moses, two of football's best catchers, complemented Shaw's considerable ability to throw the ball any distance. . . . Briscoe, leading receiver of the conference the year before, was the prime target, but Moses was in his class. The Dolphins were fortunate that J. D. Hill was not available, too; the swift youngster was injured. O. J. Simpson—employed as a receiver by the new coach, Harvey Johnson, who planned to get him the ball by handoff or throw whenever possible—enjoyed the role and was brilliant against Dallas. Considering the unevenness of their own performance against Denver, the Dolphins had to think poorly of their prospects to regain their equilibrium against Buffalo. Which proves how wrong even experts can be about this violent game with the funny ball.

Only a few times in their history have the Dolphins so thoroughly dominated an opponent. Never before had Jim Kiick and Larry Csonka thundered for more than 100 yards each in the same battle (Kiick for 108, Csonka for 103), and they caught passes for another 48 and 34 yards, respectively.

Yepremian got Miami's first twelve points with field goals of fifteen, forty-six, thirteen, and nine yards in the first half. In the fourth period, Garo thumped another through from forty-eight yards away and had a chance to tie his own NFL record of six field goals set in 1966 with Detroit, but the last try was tipped away by Buffalo's Dunaway. How can this be explained, this change from one week to the next? In Buffalo, early-morning rains and a misting rainfall just before the kickoff had the field surface damp and the ball probably less sure than at Denver, but the Dolphins didn't fumble once, where they couldn't hold the ball with a fishnet at Denver. Instead, hard tackles caused two Buffalo drops; Dick Anderson recovered one shaken loose from Simpson.

The Dolphins' power was displayed in the first minutes when they advanced from their own thirty-two to the Bills' eight-yard line, but Buffalo held, and Yepremian's good kick made it 3–0. The Bills were more impressive on their subsequent try, with Simpson running for twenty-two yards on his first crack, but Wayne Patrick was the one who scored for a 7–3 lead.

Yepremian's three field goals in the second period were impressive, but the Dolphins were bogging down too often, deep in enemy country. They didn't appear able to score a touchdown, and Shula's constant pacing betrayed his worry, although Garo's kicking kept the cushion growing.

> *The play I run most is Ride 34, right up the gut and following Csonka. If he wasn't getting the job done, I'd know it before anybody—and I'm still walking around. . . . What's allowed us to go wide where we didn't before is the addition of Marv Fleming's blocking and the work of Warfield and Twilley, the wide receivers, who help tremendously now with crackback blocks.*
>
> *—Kiick*

When the Dolphins accepted the opening kickoff of the third period and Kiick and Csonka picked up where an electrifying return by Mercury Morris ended at the Buffalo forty-four, the nationwide TV audience knew who was boss. The two big backs—blocking for each other savagely when not carrying the ball—cracked Buffalo's line four times apiece. When Csonka drove across from the one, Miami had scored more than just points. As Shula was to remark later: "Our game plan is ball control, no matter the opponent. We finally accomplished it in the third period at Buffalo. . . . That's Miami Dolphin football."

In general terms, the defensive team posed problems for Shaw the youngster couldn't solve, even with his enormously talented receivers. Riley and Bob Heinz bagged Shaw once each, and the Miami Front Four was infinitely more effective in keeping pressure on the quarterback than it had been for two weeks—firm testimony to the blockers of Denver and Minnesota. Harassed as he was, Shaw couldn't hit the creases in Miami's zone defense when his catchers were in sight. It was a good day's work.

However, the individual quality of Simpson shone brilliantly once, in the third quarter, when he bolted into the middle on a trap play, gave a wrinkle that caused Nick Buoniconti's legs to "prop," ran by Doug Swift, and sped forty-six yards to the score. It was a classical demonstration by one of the major masters of the backfield arts. Equally impressive was Warfield's reception of a Griese pass— the same play that tied Denver—and Paul's sprint to a twenty-three-yard touchdown. Griese called that pass at the line of scrimmage. This was the same pattern President Nixon later suggested for Super Bowl VI.

Late in the afternoon there in War Memorial Stadium—surely one of the most depressing monuments in the world—Jake Scott took an awful whack in the head that took his mind off football and sent it spinning off into space, although his body remained mobile and Jake stayed in the fray. Fortunately, Dick Anderson sensed that his colleague was listening to a different drummer and drifted back to take the game's last punt almost out of Scott's arms. Jake spent the night in the hospital but was back in Miami on Tuesday, saying that the bells had stopping ringing.

And Larry Csonka's nose was bent halfway to his ear, but the great bull of a man didn't even slow down until Dr. Herbert Virgin grabbed him and pulled the broken sniffer straight. Csonka remarked later that it felt better than it had after some of the eight previous breaks.

Although few would vow that the Dolphins had valid claim to it, there they were after the Buffalo game, unchallenged leaders of the Eastern Division of the American Football Conference . . . surely one of the quirks of the century, considering their seedy performance at Denver. But all the others—Baltimore, New England, the New York Jets, and Buffalo—had been flattened at least once in their first pair of games. Miami, with one victory and one tie, was the best of a ragged lot.

But the wrong was soon righted . . . and in a game that surely ranks with the most futile in Dolphins' history, a desperate struggle between the forty-yard lines for the most part; when elsewhere, the Dolphins were cracking their tailbones in pratfalls all over the Orange Bowl.

THE THIRD GAME: NEW YORK JETS 14, DOLPHINS 10
Even at this time and distance from that steaming-hot, grease-slick griddle, one is inclined to ignore several logical factors that brought the Dolphins crashing down and, instead, spend his space belaboring the Miami club for the kinds of errors it didn't commit even when manned by culls and retreads. Certain it is that this one pretty well wiped out convictions that the Dolphins were in the heavyweight class of the National Football League.

Because it became such an issue later, we should set the scene in perspective, for the Poly-Turf surface of the Miami stadium was a part of this game even more than most . . . and it was almost all the aftermath, as reporters and even Shula tried to find something to talk about other than the breakdowns that cost Miami what might have been a permanent hold on the top rung of its division.

Twenty-six stadia used by NFL teams during the 1971 season included eleven with artificial surfaces, with Miami's Orange Bowl the first to choose Poly-Turf, a product of American Biltrite Company. Miami's city manager, Melvin Reese, opted for the Poly-Turf rather than the AstroTurf or Tartan surface because of the substantial differences in bids. The natural grass was wrenched up and the ersatz rug was laid at a cost of $205,000 in the late spring of 1970. Poly-Turf was immediately successful. Many players claimed that it gave a better chance for traction than some of the other surfaces, while not so hard when met headfirst in a fall.

Paint employed for the striking emblems that decorated the field for the Super Bowl game in January, and perhaps other elements brought onto the field at other times, was the obvious answer to its sorry state when the Dolphins played preseason games there in 1971. The turf, instead of having a stiffly erect, brushlike effect, laid hard and matted. It hardly was comparable to the elegant and efficient surface of the summer previous. It even had turned a pale blue, the rich green of the previous season nowhere to be found.

Comment from players and reporters brought city maintenance crews out for extraordinary cleaning efforts, but no particular change was noted. Shula and the other Dolphins' coaches ignored the problem, no doubt figuring that their own players would have a built-in advantage if one could be found in the situation. On that October afternoon when the Jets came to town, however—surely this should be called Skid Sunday—the Dolphins floundered or flopped thirty-three times, the Jets a more dignified twenty-six. If the 70,670 spectators hadn't shown up in hopes of seeing football, they could have had a hilarious time, watching the 250-pounders make like Buster Keaton on an ice rink.

Swarms of factory men and local hopefuls appeared within hours and vacuumed and otherwise cleaned and worked with the rug, but the damage was done. Such measures might prove helpful in the future, but on Skid Sunday nothing worked for the Dolphins, least of all their feet.

The Jets already had been beaten 22–0 by Baltimore and 17–0 by St. Louis and, considering their personnel problems, Weeb Ewbank seemed lucky that these scores weren't higher. Joe Namath out for most of the season with another serious knee problem; Matt

Snell, the Jets' strongest runner, was the victim of an Achilles tendon injury; Verlon Biggs, unhappy but powerful defensive lineman, had been shipped to George Allen at Washington and—unlikeliest cut of all—George Sauer, Jr., a magnificent receiver still not at full bloom, retired with mutters that football was animalistic and demeaning and that Ewbank treated his grown men like children. It was pretty well agreed around the NFL that Weeb had some pretty rough tots, at that. Sauer's loss was a critical blow, magnified by the others.

In the first few minutes of the Orange Bowl exercises, it appeared that the Jets would be lucky to escape with their lives. The spectators weren't much better off, either, for the eighty-six-degree temperature at the kickoff had the Poly-Turf cooking at some 125 degrees; reflected upward from the field and with no more than an eight-mile breeze, the heat was enervating.

The proceedings opened with Al Woodall, Namath's substitute, throwing toward Don Maynard, but Miami cornerback Tim Foley intercepted at the Jets' thirty-six and returned to the eighteen. Csonka grunted off two yards, then busted through left tackle for the last sixteen and the TD. In eighty-three seconds, with Yepremian's conversion, the Dolphins led, 7–0. Three minutes later, Garo's forty-three-yard field goal moved it up to 10–0 . . . and it was just as easy as it sounds.

But then the Dolphins moved into that curious state of mind that sometimes characterized their preseason and early championship games—a state of suspended decisions in which nothing fitted with anything else, yet many individual efforts could not be faulted. Griese's statistics (nine hits in twenty-two throws, one intercepted) were not all that bad, but he missed open receivers and had other lapses that were not like him; Warfield caught five but couldn't spring loose; Csonka crunched for seventy-seven yards and Kiick averaged 7.7 yards per carry . . . yet nothing worked. The Dolphins fumbled three times and lost two; the Jets fumbled three and recovered all three. It was that kind of day.

When a Griese pass was stolen by Earlie Thomas at midfield in the first minutes of the fourth period, the Dolphins' errors suddenly turned fatal. Miami's defense, completely in control of its situation until now, became porous. A Woodall pass to Rich Caster for twenty-six yards put the Jets at Miami's sixteen; five plays later, George Nock fell over the goal line.

There was no particular reason to assume that the subsequent 10–7 margin wouldn't hold. But then came an unaccountable lapse by the usually alert Dick Anderson, and the victory was lost.

As usual, Jack Scott was Miami's deep safety and Anderson a few yards short of him when the Jets' Curly O'Neal punted from near his own goal line. Scott lost the ball in the sun—it's straight into a receiver's eyes when he looks west at that hour of a sunny day— and turned to run off the field. Anderson stayed closer to the ball, and it grazed his left shoulder before hitting one of the Jets. Paul Crane fell on it to give New York possession at the Miami thirty- seven. Later, Anderson admitted the call was correct by the officials; Shula had the cryptic observation, "Anderson should have known where the ball was."

The durable Emerson Boozer got going for the Jets in the ensu- ing moments and ripped the right side of Miami's defenses scandalously. Nock scored, and Bobby Howfield's second conver- sion put the game beyond a Miami field goal in the 115 seconds remaining.

Not that the Dolphins got that close, anyhow. Griese opened up with passes from his own thirty-three and—six plays later—was only a yard better than that, for John Elliott erased a good throw to Kiick by decking Griese for a loss of twelve yards. It was a dismal finish to a day of wild gyrations as the team members tried to keep their footing.

More important than all this, however, Shula still hadn't turned the screw that would tune some semblance of consistency into his offense.

After three games that all hands realized should have been in the bag, the Dolphins were 1–1–1 and mumbling.

THE FOURTH GAME: DOLPHINS 23, CINCINNATI 13

Dan and Mary Shula, now respectively seventy-one and sixty-nine, and six other members of the coach's family came down from the Painesville area to Cincinnati to see Don and his team, but also to celebrate the fiftieth wedding anniversary of his parents. The stands at Riverfront Stadium groaned with kinsmen of other Dolphins, including sixty-five head connected by blood or friendship with Bob Griese. The presence of these familiar faces added no pressure, however; seldom have the Dolphins been so steamed up as they were for this one.

Recollections of the opening preseason failure to the Bengals' and Paul Brown's subsequent successes (six preseason victories) were tempered somewhat by injuries to key Cincinnati people, among them quarterback Virgil Carter. The Bengals were only 1–2 when Miami appeared, but Brown's usually efficient, computerized product is one of the most competitive teams in sports. Shula's respect for his old coach isn't based upon fascination at his personal charm.

The efficiency hardly was there for the Bengals when it counted in this game, however, with Brown telling a reporter later that the day "seemed sort of odd." The Bengals pounded the Dolphins' line for 214 yards rushing and—especially middle linebacker Bill Bergey—the defensive group was little less hostile. Before it was over, Dolphins and Bengals were rolling around on the artificial turf like school kids scrapping at recess.

Brown's observation, taken in the context of customary performance by his teams, was right on the nerve of the situation: His Bengals never got back the momentum lost when Curtis Johnson flew in to block Horst Muhlmann's twenty-seven-yard field-goal try early in the first period. Johnson only got it with a fingertip, but that was enough to stop the sure score. Far more surprising was that this early breakdown so shook the Bengals that they couldn't recover.

Starting from their own twenty, the Dolphins banged forward with Kiick and Csonka, of course, but then came a changeup; with the ball at the Bengals' forty-three, third down and two to go and

Jim Mandich joining Marv Fleming in the tight-end offensive set, it was a natural setup for the old Csonka-to-bust-up-people ploy and a first down. Instead, however, Griese faked to Csonka and looped a pass to Warfield at the Bengal fifteen; and the swift receiver went on in for the first score of the game. It was perfect execution and a memorable surprise to the audience, no less than to the Bengals.

Garo Yepremian's nineteen-yard field goal after five minutes of the second period increased the margin to ten points, but this wasn't the most notable happening in that stretch—rather, a kookie play by the Dolphins that looked like it might have been whomped up on the practice field of Shenandoah Junior High or some other lodgment of free-thinking strategists. Certainly it didn't appear to be a product of the NFL, but investigation proved that it had been around quite a while.

In this one, Griese pitched back to Kiick, who ran a few steps to his right and lateraled back to Griese, whereupon the quarterback wheeled and slung the ball toward Paul Warfield along the left sideline. Paul got it all right but was forced out of bounds by the cornerback, Ken Riley, who didn't take himself completely out of the play by following Kiick. The play was good for twenty-seven yards to the Cincinnati eight, but the drive stalled and Yepremian came on for the successful field-goal try.

This play, incidentally, should have scored a touchdown for Shula's Baltimore club against the Jets in the Super Bowl game of 1969. Earl Morrall missed seeing the frantic figure of Jimmy Orr wide open in the end zone; instead, he threw the forward pass toward another Colts' receiver, but it was intercepted by the Jets' Jim Hudson.

Its presence in the Dolphins' repertoire and the earlier pitch to Warfield suggested a new caution by opponents who earlier might have thought only about ways to break up Miami's ball-control game. Griese, especially, was delighted at the success of these calls, for they added a fresh dimension to his bag of weapons.

They also continued the earlier unease of the Bengals, who got on with a field goal just before the half and another in the third period. Sandwiched between, however, was a second Dolphins TD, resulting from another odd happening for Cincinnati. While attempting a punt from his own twenty-nine, Dave Lewis got a high snap from center and was forced to run, getting only four yards. Griese hit Twilley on a third-down pass for eighteen yards, and later, the same combination scored from the two.

Garo hit a field goal for thirty-six yards early in the fourth quarter, but Cincinnati's powerful tight end and receiver, Bob Trumpy, scored on an eleven-yard pass from the young quarterback, Ken Anderson, to keep the Bengals alive. A dashing runback of the ensuing kickoff for thirty-five yards by Hubert Ginn and a fifteen-yard penalty against Cincinnati on the same play, and Miami was at its own forty-six. In four plays, they reached the Cincinnati fourteen, but a penalty and two incompletions fouled up the drive. Yepremian's field goal effectively put the game in the bag for Miami, however, and the record looked infinitely better now, at 2–1–1.

And some assurance for the future could be found in the game. For example, in the way Griese passed . . . not so much the twelve hits in twenty-three throws, for he remained behind the completion rate of the year previous, but the two touchdown tosses and the gut importance of other completions. Altogether, Bob converted six third-down situations into first downs—the most important trait a quarterback can muster.

Another corner was turned by huge Bob Heinz, the Dolphins' useful but largely undistinguished reserve lineman. The six-foot, six-inch, 270-pound third-year veteran of both offensive and defensive line jobs got to the Cincinnati quarterback twice and shared another sacking with Bill Stanfill. The three kills were high for the young season by the Dolphins' Front Four, and the lift could not have come at a better time.

THE FIFTH GAME: DOLPHINS 41, NEW ENGLAND 3

Finally, the explosion.

It was tremendous, but it was satisfying to the 58,822 who braved the Orange Bowl's heat . . . at last Griese's passes and the runs of the three backs—Csonka, Kiick, and Morris—made some music without clinkers. And the Front Four blossomed at last, with *seven* sacks of Jim Plunkett, the Patriot's superb rookie quarterback. Not only was it a record day for the front-line hunters, but it was accomplished without Jim Riley, who rested a pinched nerve in his neck. The extent of New England's embarrassment can be understood best when it is noted that the powerful Jim Nance and the smaller but quicker Carl Garrett were hammered so much they netted only eighteen yards between them.

Mo Scarry's defensive four had the added satisfaction of discovering new depth. With Riley out, Bob Heinz stepped up and was there or thereabouts almost every time Plunkett got his bell rung . . . and then there was the huge Frank Cornish, even bigger than Heinz, and off the field for a month. Frank reported on Thursday, when it was decided Riley wouldn't be ready, and was supposed to be a bench rider against New England. But John Richardson's right ankle was twisted in the first quarter, so here came Frank, weighing considerably more than a quarter-ton and in poor shape after being dropped from the squad on a cutdown just before the opener with Denver. A badly bruised thigh had restricted his practices for two weeks.

Cornish appreciated the opportunity, or maybe he sought to make the coaches look bad for sending The Turk after him; in any case, he got two clean drops on Plunkett to lead the display of ferocity. Afterward, Plunkett said all this was something new for him. . . . "Until today, we've been lucky. Our line has blocked well." Enemy tacklers had nailed the Heisman Trophy winner only twice previously.

In yet another significant and favorable turn, the Dolphins leaped into a twenty-one point lead in the first period and never let up on the pressure. This despite use of the full squad and another day of slipping and sliding on the Poly-Turf. This time the two teams combined for fifty-five pratfalls, a drop of four below the season's high against the Jets, but enough to cause another major furor and sensible moves by the manufacturer to revitalize the matted, discolored surface it so widely advertised as its prize spread of rug.

Twilley scored TDs of twenty-two and fourteen yards on passes from Griese, and sandwiched between these, Warfield scored the first of his two for the day in that first period. Pete Gogolak kicked a fifty-one-yard field goal for the Patriots, but Garo knocked off a pair and Kiick ran for another touchdown—the Dolphins swarmed the visitors from every direction.

The next day, Upton Bell, the Patriots' general manager, made an official protest about the Orange Bowl's turf to Pete Rozelle.

THE SIXTH GAME: DOLPHINS 30, NEW YORK JETS 14
Considering the circumstances of the Jets' physical condition—everybody but Weeb Ewbank seemed to be in traction or trauma on the riddled New York club—only a sadist could gloat over this one. Yet it had the virtue of notable artistic success, resounding revenge for the embarrassment of three weeks previous, and—twenty-four hours later—leadership in the Eastern Division of the American Football Conference.

The Dolphins broke out on top when Baltimore failed to score a touchdown when only ten yards out and a minute to play in the Monday night feature at Minnesota. The Vikings won it, 10–3, in a smashing exhibition of brutal football. Had the Colts tied there they —and the Dolphins—would have been level with records of 4–1–1. Failure in the Twin Cities left the Colts 4–2, or a half-game back. The Denver tie had some merit, at last, for the Dolphins.

In New York, a chilling rain had been falling all morning, and gusts of wind up to twenty-seven miles per hour were blowing into Shea Stadium's open end when Yepremian kicked off to the Jets' Phil Wise at the goal line. Phil got nineteen yards and then, in eleven plays, Emerson Boozer scored on a pop pass from Bob Davis, the new but courageous young quarterback of the Jets. It was an unsettling beginning for the Dolphins, especially since they had opened the week previous so very well. And the way

Davis hit Don Maynard in Miami's deep secondary—he hood-winked Tim Foley for thirty-eight yards—was a rattler.

> *I've gotten a special kind of charge out of coming back to my home town and playing ball and being recognized for it. As I've grown older, I've become more of a moody person; I'm concentrating on football more than before and I don't think it makes me harder to get along with for my family but maybe for strangers, yes. . . . Right before a game I get into a deep concentration bag, where I really bear down on the game it-self. . . . But if I think about it too long, I tend to get tense.*
> —*Little*

More so was the way Griese's two passes in the Dolphins' first series were overthrown. Later, it seemed to be pretty well established that the wind, largely uncertain gusts from behind the huge scoreboard, was the varmint here. The same thing happened to Davis when he got his back to it. Griese did not enjoy a vintage performance, in any case.

But Larry Csonka indicated the way things were to go very soon when he swept to the short side, turned the Jets' left flank, and broke two tackles as he chopped off twelve yards. Griese was successful to Warfield for eleven more, but the final assault was strangled, so Yepremian took a three-pointer from the twenty-five.

The New York defense was brilliant for the first twenty-seven minutes, but a good runback of a punt by Dick Anderson and a crack by Csonka good for seventeen arranged the setting for what was now a specialty of Shula's troupe—an uncomplicated but perfectly executed pass in the middle from Griese to Warfield that Paul carried for his sixth touchdown of the season. It was a piece of cake when the linebacker followed Jim Kiick's move in motion, leaving poor Earlie Thomas alone with Warfield. Larry Seiple, in for Fleming, broke to the outside, Warfield broke in—Zap!— and the same pattern had produced its fourth TD for the Dolphins. This gave them a 10–7 lead at halftime and, for most of the second half the Jets tried to survive.

This is the epitome—this National Football League—and I don't think zone coverages really have a place [in it]. . . . The artistry is not there in a zone coverage; instead of beating a man with moves, I can give all the moves I can dream up and the cornerback won't pay any attention to me—his job is to patrol his zone and not move until the ball is thrown. . . . It takes away the element of combat between the cornerback and the pass receiver. . . .

—*Warfield*

In the first two periods, Csonka had squished for forty-four yards, Kiick for twenty-one. . . . When they finished their day, the giant fullback had amassed 137 yards in twenty carries, while the smaller Kiick cranked out 121 yards in seventeen running tries —career highs for both and a second time both exceeded one hundred yards in a game. Csonka got two of the Dolphins' three TDs that raw day in a masterful exhibition of making like a redwood. The man simply was fantastic as he leaned against and shoved through the New York line and across several other people before tripping or sliding to the ground with the grace of a water buffalo off a shoot-the-chute.

"I was following Larry Little a lot of times, and I'd see the looks on the faces of the cornerbacks he'd be going for, one-on-one," Csonka said on the bus later. "It was kind of pitiful to see the terror in their eyes."

It's probable the cornerbacks might have had some misgivings about Little alone, but with Little's 260 pounds backed up by Csonka's 240—plus maybe the 220 of Kiick at the tail of the power train—it had to be an awesome sight, indeed, for even healthy defenders. The Jets didn't have many of these that day. Jerry Philbin and John Elliott were not there to harass Griese—he only hit five of eighteen, with one sack, even so—and Al Atkinson and Ralph Baker weren't backing up the line; Steve Tannen and Gus Holloman did not play.

Poor Ewbank reported after this defeat that sixteen of his regulars had missed at least one game of the six to date in the season from injuries; and it was announced the next day that Joe Namath wouldn't return after a preseason knee injury until "some date in the future, not next week as we had hoped." Part of that hope was trampled by the bull's rushes of Csonka and Kiick, for victory over the Miami club would have left the Jets 3–3 and involved, if ever so slightly, in the Eastern Division race. At 2–4 they were dead and knew it—so why risk Namath?

More pertinent to the Dolphins was a painful neck injury for Bill Stanfill, a match for the one that plagued Jim Riley two weeks previous; and, with the Rams in Los Angeles coming up, this was a grave footnote to the excellent second half of the victory in New York.

THE SEVENTH GAME: DOLPHINS 20, RAMS 14

Three hours before the Dolphins' jet took off for this vital match with the West Coast power, Don Shula spent a quiet thirty minutes in his office at Biscayne College. As he flipped through books and pamphlets, he made careful notes. Later, he used these as his text as he talked to his squad in one of the several sessions in which he psyched up his people.

The notes were simple facts on past performances of the Rams over the years.

Shula did his own research and his own evaluation of what the numbers meant. In a word, they came out: quality. This was his point and his preaching as the Miami club wound itself tight for a tremendous effort . . . quality on a defense led by Deacon Jones and one of football's most formidable front lines, quality on an offense led by the gangling figure of Roman Gabriel who, when at his best, has no peer as a quarterback. In the 1971 season, Gabe wasn't enjoying memorable success until the Sunday before the Dolphins appeared in the Coliseum, when he slung three whistlers for touchdowns against Green Bay and the Rams won, 30–13.

While Shula's Baltimore teams had defeated Los Angeles nine times, against four losses and a tie, and they had prospered even against the great defensive Rams' clubs when George Allen was their coach (4–3–1), the bitter taste of 1967 was unforgettable. The

Colts and Rams crashed into each other at season's end and
Baltimore lost for the first time in that campaign. Although their
records were identical (11–1–2), Los Angeles went to the NFL
playoff because it scored more points in their matches than did
the Colts. No wonder Shula was careful in his approach as he
brought the Dolphins west for their first game against the old pros
under the new coach, Tommy Prothro.

Prothro's remarkable successes at UCLA were in the class of
Shula's in the NFL. After a wobbly start (a 24–20 loss to New
Orleans, then a 20–20 tie with Atlanta), the Rams had rumbled
forward over the Bears, San Francisco, Atlanta, and Green Bay.
Leaders of the Western Division of the National Football Conference, their record was even with and comparable to the Dolphins' 4–1–1 and leadership in the Eastern Division of the AFC.

Curiously, the Los Angeles press wasn't impressed by Miami's
weapons or its standing. Reports in area newspapers before the
game indicated that only 60,000 fans would attend, suggesting
Miami still was a maturing squad and couldn't be expected to pull
like Green Bay the week before. When the Dolphins kicked off in
the Coliseum, 72,903 spectators were in the stands; the most
exciting team in football had found its mark among Los Angeles
fans via television.

> *I wish to be known as Armenian, rather than Cypriot. I
> follow Ben Agaganian, who was a field goal kicker with the
> Giants. . . . We are a great Armenian tradition!*
>
> *—Garo*

Shula stressed the gut importance of ball control even more than
usual as that kickoff approached. Csonka's right knee had a lump
the size of a small cantaloupe above it from the Jets' game, but the
giant fullback was ready; as always, the game scheme called for
throws to Warfield when possible but control of the ball with runs
by Kiick and Csonka. If this could be accomplished, Shula felt he
could win; if not, he believed defeat was inevitable, for the Rams'

defense had all the elements needed to do a job on a team going for the big strike—or so it seemed.

Defensively, the Dolphins hoped to hector Gabriel by concealing their linebackers and safeties whenever possible . . . faking blitzes to keep the towering quarterback jumpy for a half-count, anyhow. Since Miami had blitzed very well against Boston and New York in its last two games and Gabe doubtless had seen the movies, this fakery proved effective, especially in the first half. But control the ball Miami didn't, nor did the Rams behave as advertised in the last, critical moments when they had a substantial chance to score the tieing touchdown, with a subsequent kick giving them the victory.

The first play from scrimmage established the Rams' mood for the day. After the kickoff to the end zone produced a touchback, the Rams opened from their twenty with a double reverse by wide receiver Lance Rentzel that snapped up eleven yards before Mike Kolen nailed him. Later, this success would snare the Rams, as we shall see in a moment.

A screen pass to Willie Ellison and a reverse by Bob Klein for thirteen were the best moves as the Rams moved on to the Dolphins' forty-one, but Gabe was smacked by Manny Fernandez in the first of four sacks by Miami, and Los Angeles punted.

As might be predicted, Griese tried to worry forward from the Miami nineteen with first Kiick and then Csonka carrying. They got seven yards between them. On third down, Deacon Jones, the great defensive end, was pulled offside by the irregular, staccato beat of Griese's snap cadence, and a flag was thrown. Griese, under pressure from the Deacon and others, swung around behind a knot of struggling giants and, running full throttle and almost to the line of scrimmage, pitched truly and hard to Paul Warfield, who had three steps on both his convoying defenders. Warfield took the ball at the Miami forty-five and sped for a touchdown, seventy-four yards from the scrimmage line.

It was a version of the same pattern that had scored for him so often before, but it still caught the Rams' defense flat. The flag thrown when Jones jumped offside probably caused a couple of defenders to relax. The same thing had happened to the Dolphins the week before, in New York. But the seven points on the board called for no excuses.

Larry Seiple's kicking figures were the least impressive in the AFC at this point in the season, but the durable utility man—no doubt smarting from a blocked kick that resulted from his own carelessness against the Jets—boomed them in Los Angeles. He kicked five times and averaged 43.2 yards, a substantial improvement and important as the struggle moved into the second period.

Early on, the passes of Gabriel—including one to Jack Snow for twenty-four yards—cut into the Dolphins, moving the Rams to the Miami twenty-six. But a five-yard penalty and a sack by Jim Riley for eight broke the rhythm, and David Ray's field goal went awry from forty-six yards away. Again the Dolphins started upfield, from their own twenty, with Csonka pounding away twice and Kiick picking off fifteen on the third of his eight pass receptions for a first down at the Miami forty-two. Now Griese went to Warfield again, for eighteen more, and then scrambled off a first down at the Rams' twenty-two. Csonka, turning his own right end behind the grunting, straining form of the powerful Little, thundered away for another eleven.

On first down, Griese pitched toward Howard Twilley in the yonder corner of the end zone—this pattern by Twilley had become no less effective than the reliable post pattern of Warfield—and Howard, his feet stuttering their contacts with the field inside the corner lines, had another six points.

The big Coliseum crowd responded with more enthusiasm than one might have expected. The eighty-yard assault was a classic, really, and the fans appreciated its quality, perhaps, for it had all that one could ask from a drive against a determined opponent. The eleven formations included only one dud—a penalty of five yards for too much time between plays—but this one was not a matter of carelessness; Griese had to correct a lineup mistake by one of his people at the line of scrimmage, and the clock caught them.

Now, with fourteen points on the board and having proved that the Rams could be attacked from all directions and could be repelled when they countered, Miami had the initiative.

The Dolphins' Front Four never was more impressive than at the end of the subsequent drive by the Rams.

Gabe got his troops up from the Rams' twenty-three to the Dolphins' eight just before halftime, but Bob Matheson decked Rentzel for a six-yard loss on the reverse mentioned earlier. The towering Bob Heinz crunched Gabriel for a ten-yard loss, and Fernandez embarrassed him again for another ten on the next play. Ray's attempted forty-two-yard field-goal try flopped.

At the halftime horn, Yepremian also tried a fifty-one-yarder. It was partially blocked . . . but the Dolphins had those fourteen fat ones on the scoreboard.

In those first two quarters, Miami's offensive line kept the ferocious Rams off Griese, except for one seven-yard drop. The Dolphins cracked Gabriel four times, with thirty-two yards lost, but more important than the yards was the field position each time—and now Gabe knew Miami's alley fighters not only could get to him but knew how to tackle him when they got there.

Shula, insisting that no one rusher can bring Gabriel to gaff with a normal tackle around the thighs or lower, had emphasized all week that Gabe must be bear-hugged. "He's too strong and tall to deal with any other way," is Shula's tribute to the big fellow. "Tackle him low and he'll just stand there until he gets off his pass, and that's the one that'll hit some receiver sixty yards away. . . ."

The Los Angeles club is a remarkable assembly of strong people, with the quarterback only one of many. Larry Little reported an occasion during that fateful afternoon in which Merlin Olsen held off Little's bullrush block with one arm and brought Larry Csonka down with the other. Such an accomplishment should be immortalized in bronze, at least.

Having accommodated to the situation in which they couldn't establish the power game they preferred, the Dolphins had shown resiliency. Now they would be hit with everything the Rams could muster. It was considerable.

They jammed the Dolphins against the goal line after the third-period kickoff, and it took a fifty-three-yard punt by Seiple to break out at all. A pass from Gabriel to Larry Smith got thirteen, and Williams sliced through Miami's left side for seventeen yards that brought Los Angeles to the Miami thirty-six.

But Williams, racked by Buoniconti when he came up on a center trap, fumbled, and Fernandez recovered at the Miami thirty-five . . . and Griese had room to operate. He hit Kiick for twenty-seven yards—Jim had been seen to limp earlier, but not now—and Marv Fleming for eleven and Kiick twice more, for fourteen yards, in a sweep to the Rams' six.

Again he went to Twilley, and Howard took it on a perfect reception in that corner of his—but Bob Kuechenberg was flagged for tripping, and the play was called back. Another pass to Kiick was good for a few, but Yepremian had to be called for a twenty-yarder, and he rolled the count to 17–0.

The Dolphins and millions watching on TV waited for the hammer blows they knew were coming. And they came.

Youngblood almost broke out of the Dolphins, who sought his head on the kickoff, but he was dropped at the Rams' thirty-nine. Gabe went to Ellison twice with quick tosses and to wideout Jack Snow for eleven yards to the Dolphins' thirty. A fourth-down pitchout to Ellison got the three yards for a new Los Angeles series at the twenty, and Smith sped for eleven on a pass. The Dolphins gave way as Ellison ripped the middle for eight and then Larry Smith, the old Florida Gator, finally scored off tackle.

This was on the first play of the last quarter and the 17–7 margin did not look at all impossible for the Rams, especially when Seiple was rushed and got off his poorest kick of the day, for thirty-six yards. Haymond made a fair catch at the Los Angeles thirty-four.

Ellison got thirteen on a screen pass and Gabe missed a pair before connecting again to Ellison, for eight.

Then Gabriel faked the double reverse to Rentzel that had gained once and lost once . . . but Jack Snow was all alone to Gabe's left front near the sideline when the quarterback looked for him. It was a cheap touchdown but perfectly executed; the Miami defenders flowed to their left with Rentzel—and Ray's second conversion closed the gap to 17–14, with eleven minutes, thirty seconds on the clock.

No team enjoys playing catch-up, and most don't have enough weapons to make it work. The Rams had the weapons, and they still had the time, and all the season could be wrapped up for both teams in those minutes. They were gut-grinders.

The Dolphins used up more than four minutes after the kickoff, with Warfield and Kiick the main instruments for Griese. And the quarterback saved what appeared to be complete disaster when, after a thunderous tackle by the Rams' Robertson on a blind-side sack, Griese fumbled but then turned back and recovered as two huge Rams leaped for the ball. It was a very near thing.

Seiple's high, lazy punt from midfield forbade a return, so the Rams opened up from their seventeen, with seven minutes remaining.

Two wide tries and one at the middle got them nine yards—Scott hammered Ellison back on that third one—and Ellison, on fourth and one yard, cut toward left tackle, but John Richardson hit him so hard that he lost the ball. Dick Anderson's recovery gave Miami possession at the Rams' thirty-two, with five minutes to go.

It didn't go quickly. Two efforts by Kiick got three yards, and Griese lost four when he fled after finding his receivers covered . . . so the Dolphins settled for another Yepremian field goal, a forty-yard beauty, that made it impossible for the Rams to tie with a field goal.

Three minutes and as many seconds were left to the Rams' great effort for a touchdown. . . .

Two passes brought Gabriel up to the Rams' thirty as the Dolphins frantically patrolled their zones, forbidding the long winner but sacrificing ground to the short throws . . . it was a race between real estate and the clock now.

Two minutes were still up there when Gabe's throw to Rentzel beat Anderson for a first down at the Rams' forty-seven. Gabriel changed targets and went to Les Josephson twice with good results, and the Rams were at the Miami thirty-four, with 1:36 to play.

Across the continent, Miamians at their TV sets turned green when Rentzel caught a hummer from Gabriel along the left sideline and was not brought down until he reached the Miami seven. But the tall receiver shoved Anderson a moment before the catch, and the penalty pushed the Rams back to the Miami forty-nine.

After passes to Ellison and Rentzel, Gabriel had them back on the Dolphins' thirty-two, with the fourth-down situation finding the Rams three yards short of a new series but with plenty of time—a minute, five seconds—to break through.

One must wonder what factor finally determined the Los Angeles strategy here. . . . Was it that everyone in the stadium thought Gabe would pass, and that a changeup would fool the Dolphins? Did Gabriel think he could solve his problem by playing on the inexperience of Bob Heinz at defensive right end for the Dolphins? Any number of factors may have entered into the fateful next move.

In the simplest kind of play pattern, Gabriel handed off to Ellison, who had only one blocker ahead of him as he tried to sweep outside Heinz. It was a shattering mistake. Heinz battered into Cowan, the tackle before him, and got enough of Ellison to brace him upright, where Jesse Powell piled into him and Anderson and Buoniconti nailed the trap shut.

Thus did the great battle finish, although thirty-five seconds still were left. Griese went into his worm act on two snaps, and it was over.

The way it ended, with the lunge by Ellison that failed, will be a subject for discussion among the Dolphins for years to come, for they expected almost anything else from Gabriel and his solid cast.

"I didn't dream they'd try any such thing," admits Nick Buoniconti, the man who called Miami's defense on that play. "We were in a 'four-three pass' front. . . . The linemen had absolutely no responsibility against a run.

"But I'm glad they didn't haggle about who should make the tackle. . . ."

There was an air of concern among team insiders as they took the long flight home from Los Angeles. Jim Kiick had remained to the end of the battle with the Rams, but he couldn't bend his left leg on the plane—it hurt too much. The knee was bruised badly and needed careful handling. This would deny Jim a chance to fatten his statistics against Buffalo and Pittsburgh after he and Csonka completed the first half of the season with more than 500 yards each on the ground, Csonka's 529 yards leading the AFC and Kiick—Oakland's Marv Hubbard and Baltimore's Norm Bulaich were sandwiched between—fourth to his pal, at 502.

The gleaning prize in the Coliseum resulted from many efforts, but none was better than Griese's. Bob hit for thirteen of nineteen passes and two TDs, with a third called back.

The kid had upstaged Gabriel on Gabe's home grounds.

Meanwhile, according to Csonka, "Butch Cassidy" was trying to be reasonable and rational in the face of adversity. Csonka says he came upon his pal Kiick twisted out of shape after a fierce encounter with numerous Rams.

"Kid, find out who these guys are," moaned Kiick. "We ain't coming back here no more." . . . a line straight out of the movie from which this splendid pair has come to be famous.

12

1971 Season—the Second Half

With the towering threat of Los Angeles eliminated and the season's midpoint reached, the Miami club had reason to believe it could lick any football team in America on a given day. . . . Even the brooding presence of Baltimore down the line wasn't too frightening, for the Dolphins had dealt the Colts stunning defeats in two of their three meetings in 1970, and now Miami was stronger than ever.

The unease and unevenness that characterized their first three games were gone, a swelling reservoir of first-class replacement parts were available—no better example can be found than Bob Heinz' enormous contributions, especially in the Rams' game while occupying Stanfill's end position—and those areas where Shula had demanded improvement were improved. These were the Front Four, the linebackers, cornerbacks, and the general work of the offensive line.

No permanent damage to Kiick was expected, although Jim hobbled after the Los Angeles trip. His bum knee was stiff and sore, but the puffiness one might expect did not develop. Csonka's massive gam had responded to treatment, and Stanfill was sprung from the hospital after the weekend. His ten-day stay had taken ten pounds off the big fellow and his legs were shaky for a couple of days, but he would play against Buffalo for a time and report that the nerve in his neck no longer bothered him.

Statistics are always tricky but sometimes significant. For example, the Front Four at this stage had accounted for twenty-two drops of quarterback, or "sacks," as these have come to be known. In the whole of 1970, they only reached the passer eighteen times.

Bob Griese wasn't throwing so often as he once did, because he had great runner support, but his 51 percent hits, with eleven touchdowns, made him the best in the AFC at this point. Csonka's 529 yards led the division, with Kiick at 502 and fourth. Warfield had no peer as a receiver, and every team had to double up on covering him, often to no avail.

Ahead lay Buffalo, Pittsburgh, Baltimore, Chicago, New England (there), Baltimore (there), and Green Bay.

It was a formidable prospect but hardly terrifying.

THE EIGHTH GAME: DOLPHINS 34, BUFFALO 0

It's quite possible that the 61,016 witnesses to this one knew more about the measures taken to make the Poly-Turf right than they did about the hapless Bills, who had played—at least sporadically—sound football, but not the winning kind. They had not won in seven games. The Dolphins were favored by more than two touchdowns.

The desperate cast of officers and technicians from American Biltrite Company who came down to study the miserable field conditions found in the games against New York's Jets and the New England Patriots (114 skids or falls in the two) had muttered publicly about "too much ozone" and "nitrogen, plus a contami-

nant the nature of which we're still investigating." . . . Those
Miamians with a residue of memory of their ninth-grade science
classes were intrigued.

Mostly, or so it seemed, the manufacturers of the ersatz grass
just steam-cleaned the massive rug, again and again. In any case,
it passed the exam given it by the Dolphins and Bills, both of whom
worked out on it before their game. Instead of the pale blue surface
of weeks before, the Poly-Turf was restored to a recognizable
greenish hue, and one could stand up on it without fear of doing a
belly-flop.

Mercury Morris opened with Csonka in Kiick's place at running
back, while Kiick strolled the sideline with his sore knee and cussed
some. Heinz took Stanfill's place at defensive right end in the early
going, but Bill also got in some licks as Buffalo desperately tried to
cope with the Dolphins while doing things to themselves that
seemed unbelievable.

For openers, take the first Buffalo series. Wayne Patrick cut
from the Bills' twenty-one for five, then shot through the Dolphins'
overshift for forty-one yards, when Doug Swift and Dick Anderson
fetched him up. On the next play, Jim Braxton fumbled the ball
when belted, and Jim Riley recovered for Miami on the Dolphins'
thirty-three.

In seven plays—an artful mixture, including Griese passing to
Warfield and a fruitful scramble by the quarterback—Csonka
scored, bursting through the Bills' line and blowing aside safeties
John Pitts and Jackie Allen as if they were children. It was a
twelve-yard effort and, as it did other times, it seemed like the big
man was running his own interference. The absence of Kiick, a
sound blocker, was noticeable only to the expert; however, Mercury
Morris was all over the field and, for the day, ran for a total of
116 yards.

In the second period, Griese flashed a hit to Warfield in the
end zone—Paul's eighth TD catch of the season—and the Bills
reeled under the pressure as the AFC's top quarterback (Griese)
joined its top receiver (Warfield) to make even tougher its top
rusher (Csonka), who was backed up by the flashing form of

Morris, leading kickoff return expert in the league; when needed, the NFL's top scorer of that week, Garo Yepremian, trotted on to do his kicking thing. Garo hit field goals at thirty-eight and twenty-four yards.

Meanwhile, O. J. Simpson had lost another Buffalo fumble to the omnipresent Riley, at the Miami forty-five, and, in the second quarter, a second Braxton drop was covered by Curtis Johnson when poor Braxton was trying to score from the Miami one-yard line.

We shall spare the details of this game, since Buffalo did almost as much to defeat itself as Miami was able to bring about through its own efforts. True, the Bills' seven fumbles were caused by hard licks, but three fell where Dolphins could flop on them, and the luck was with the winners, who made no critical errors, although allowing the Bills a total of 364 yards.

This was the first time in Dolphins' history that they were not scored upon in a regular-season game. Buffalo could have gotten a three-pointer easily enough in the last moments but tried for a TD instead and failed, by two yards, to get a new series on fourth down at the Miami twelve.

Morris enjoyed a brilliant success in his first starting role of the season, including a forty-five-yard run for a touchdown after turning his own right end and teetering along the sideline until the flow of Bills was established, when the flying Mercury turned upstream—to his left—and wasn't touched.

Apparently the measures taken to restore the Poly-Turf did the job. There was no slipping, no sliding whatever. The City of Miami administration was no less relieved than were the high swamis of the American Biltrite Company, who probably watched the game's early play from behind laced fingers.

As the work week opened after this game for the Dolphins, they spent Monday evening watching the Rams fritter away one opportunity after another in their blood-letting at Baltimore. When the Colts won 24–17, without much help from their graybeard quarterbacks, it was testimony to their great defense.

The old workhorse, Tom Matte, and the new one, Norm Bulaich, were tough and able runners. Had they been anything else, even the weird pattern of play calls by Roman Gabriel would have been successful.

The Colts' victory left Miami ahead in the AFC's East by one-half game.

The next morning, the Dolphins settled down to cases in preparation for Pittsburgh, where Chuck Noll had his Steelers actually believing they could win at least a division title. Even this honor had escaped the Steelers since they were formed in 1933. Their smashing defeat of Cleveland, 26–9, on Sunday had left them tied with the Browns for the Central Division's lead—heady wine, indeed.

Both these teams were 4–4. The Dolphins were 6–1–1 when they went to work in a nerve-bender that gave the Miami club a new insight into itself and the National Football League a startlingly clear view of its most exciting strike force.

THE NINTH GAME: DOLPHINS 24, PITTSBURGH 21

A few minutes after eleven o'clock on Saturday morning, some twenty-six hours before the kickoff, Bob Griese was seen to stumble away from a group of teammates in the Orange Bowl and throw up near a sideline . . . the first public indication of a major crisis for the team.

Griese had awakened at his home early that morning with a queasiness that rapidly turned into something more dramatic. By the midday practice at the Orange Bowl, the quarterback had spent restless hours with chills, nausea, and a moderate fever.

Early that evening, Dr. Herbert Virgin sent Griese to Mercy Hospital for tests. He was in there some hours before the media learned that Griese very likely would not play against Pittsburgh and that George Mira would start in his place in any case. The backup quarterback had a hard night with his books and tense sessions with Shula, Howard Schnellenberger, and the other coaches.

A Miami loss would drop the Dolphins into a tie with Baltimore, and they would meet the Colts next in the Orange Bowl, eyeball-to-eyeball. Mira's play could be decisive in the season, although a wan and drawn Bob Griese was sprung from the hospital during that Sunday morning, his troubles with food poisoning moderated but still present. Later, he was to say that he had no idea what potions were shot into his veins, but they were numerous.

Weather conditions were excellent, some 66,435 spectators were present, and an uneasy doubt was heard among these fans when Yepremian kicked off to the Steelers. This quickly dissipated when, on third down at his own twenty-three, Pittsburgh's strong young quarterback, Terry Bradshaw, hurled a pass toward Pearson. Nick Buoniconti deflected it into the arms of Jake Scott, who was dropped on the Steeler's forty-five—a bright opportunity, indeed.

The runners, Csonka and Morris, got a first down but, from the twenty-eight, Mira's pass to Warfield was dropped, an unheard-of error by the great receiver . . . proof, if any were needed, that Mira's passes have characteristics unlike those of Griese's throws. The same usually is true of any two passers, which makes the desperation employment of alternating quarterbacks—as Dallas used them for a game or so in 1971—a completely unsatisfactory compromise.

Ben McGee sacked Mira for eight, so Yepremian came on and got a field goal, running his point total to eighty. Moments later, Bradshaw started twenty minutes of terror for the Dolphins, and it didn't end until the big blond had led his club to a 21–3 lead.

The first came after Bradshaw popped five quick passes short of the Dolphins' zone coverage—with Miami's linebackers dropping back to cover zones, the underside was wide open—and the Steelers moved to the Dolphins' thirty. Here, on a third-and-two situation, Bradshaw flashed another to Dave Smith fifteen yards down his left sideline, and the wideout went the other fifteen for a touchdown.

On Miami's first formation after this, Mercury Morris fumbled, and Pittsburgh's L. C. Greenwood covered it at the Miami thirty-two. On second down, Bradshaw completed a throw to Ron Shanklin at the five, and he carried it across for another score. Slightly deflected by Dick Anderson, the pass almost was intercepted—a lost chance.

These dramatic turns in that first ten minutes found Miami trailing, 14–3, and the Steelers stronger than ever on a defense led by "Mean Joe" Green, a malevolent tackle playing knocks in the line with Larry Little. It was a fair match but, eventually, Little seemed to get the best of it.

Not for a time, however . . . many a bell had to be rung first.

After another pass by Mira was short of his intended receiver and a punt was forced, Shula was seen talking with Griese on the Miami sideline. A few moments later, the sick quarterback began his warmup throws and, when Miami began another attack at the Pittsburgh forty-six—Jake Scott's good return brought a punt fourteen yards to place it there—Griese went into the huddle, amid cheers. But not for long.

On the first snap, Griese fumbled and Andy Russell recovered at the Steelers' forty-nine. The crowd was stunned into silence and, five plays later, Pittsburgh had a third touchdown, on a pass from Bradshaw to Smith for the last sixteen yards. It was 21–3 a moment after this, on Roy Gerela's third conversion.

In the second period, no pro team with recognizable offensive power is deeply concerned if trailing by a touchdown; if behind by two, it's a worry; if behind by three touchdowns, it's time for even the best to begin work on a better plan for next week's game. Pittsburgh, a very physical team and going for the jugular as the brilliant Bradshaw enjoyed one of his good days, appeared quite capable of restraining the Dolphins, while adding another score or two in the forty-three minutes remaining.

Gerela's kickoff boomed through the end zone, and the Dolphins started up again from their own twenty.

> *I didn't feel there was any way I could play . . . I'd had a needle in my arm all night and hadn't eaten anything all day Saturday; they let me out of the hospital around ten o'clock Sunday. I hadn't even looked at the game plan for a day and a half, although I had it in the hospital with me. . . . Judi and I finally decided I'd go to the game and just watch, so I tried and finally got a hamburger down about eleven o'clock.*

. . . I've always had a weak stomach and don't play well unless I've got food in me. This goes back to the days when I was an altar boy and I really got weak, serving those summer pontifical high masses. . . . When Shula asked me if I could go, I told him I didn't think so. He said he'd just as soon I'd suit up and be the second-string quarterback that day, even if it meant just handing the ball off. . . .

After three or four series and all we had was three points and were behind 14–3, Coach Shula came over and asked me: "Can you go?"—he had kind of a helpless look on his face, the look that means he doesn't want to hear anything but "yes"—so I said yes. The next series, I went in and after that I'd come to the bench after each series and Dr. Virgin gave me a lot of juice to drink and kept looking after me.

—Griese

Csonka cracked for nine and Morris for three. Griese rolled slightly to his right and hit Twilley with a pass along the right hashmark, and the little Texan darted and twisted for forty-one yards. Morris and Csonka advanced to the Steelers' twelve where —on second down—Griese passed to Warfield for Paul's ninth TD of the season, despite the wildly waving arms of two defenders.

This was closing the gap the way the Miami crowd enjoys it most.

After an interception of a Terry Hanratty pass by Miami's Tim Foley and a subsequent exchange of punts, Scott returned a Pittsburgh boot to the Miami fourteen.

On first down here, Griese set Csonka and Morris to his right rear, believing the Steelers would rotate their zone defense in that direction. This happened. But Csonka was covered when the quarterback picked him up and Griese rolled and turned, escaping a couple of flying bodies in Pittsburgh suits.

Suddenly he saw what he was looking for, the speeding form of Warfield. Paul turned and came back a couple of steps, then whirled and sped off again, with Mel Blount desperately trying to catch him. He never did, for Mel had come forward on the move, rather than rotate for a deep receiver—and Warfield quickly was even deeper. It was an eighty-five-yard scoring pass—off a play fouled up when Csonka was covered.

It looked like good execution on a practice field, for nobody in a Pittsburgh shirt was within shouting distance of Warfield when he turned and hit high gear . . . beautiful.

Now, with ninety-two seconds remaining in the half, the gap closed to 21–17 and Miami was near a score again—down on the Pittsburgh thirty-five—when a Griese pass to Warfield was intercepted by Chuck Allen at the sixteen.

This was the first interception for Griese in eighty-eight throws and he was to have another later, the only blemishes on an otherwise perfect day for a man with a sour stomach.

Pittsburgh reacted as might be expected: Violently.

But Miami controlled the ball early in the third period. On the second Steeler interception (by John Rowser) at Miami's forty-one, Bradshaw had another opportunity and homed in on it. But two critical, fifteen-yard penalties against the Steelers broke the back of the drive, and Jake Scott strangled it at the twenty when he intercepted and returned to midfield.

On the last play of the third period, Csonka crashed for a yard; then Griese sighted the swift Warfield again, forty-five yards beyond the scrimmage line. His strike hit Paul at the fifteen and he scored again from there, with the inevitable conversion by Yepremian completing the significant pattern of the day's scoring, with the final 24–21, Miami.

After that, it was rip and tear and groan . . . a crashing battle as the Steelers tried to regain initiatives Miami wouldn't surrender. Bradshaw was able to generate what could have been a dangerous drive from his twenty-six that reached the Miami thirty, after Curtis Johnson was nabbed for pass interference against Pittsburgh's Dave Smith.

A Steeler was found holding a couple of formations later, and this slowed the tempo. When Smith dropped a Bradshaw whistler at the twenty, a punt to the seven by Walden was downed there by Hughes.

A subsequent Miami punt produced the break that ensured a

victory for the Dolphins: Seiple's punt was off line a trifle, and Jon Staggers' feet went out from under him when he tried to reach it on the fly: the ball caromed off Staggers' leg, to be covered by Charlie Leigh, the quick running back who doubles on the special teams. Jim Riley fell on his face and kissed the Poly-Turf where Staggers had crashed down.

This was the clincher, as it turned out, although Seiple's poor punt in the last few seconds found the Steelers at midfield. Bradshaw passed to Fuqua for eight and this brought Gerela into field-goal range.

He missed a fifty-two-yarder that would have tied the game— then got another chance when a Miami player was found offside. This time, Curtis Johnson swept in and blocked it as the gun went off amid bedlam.

Shula called this one "a high point in the life of this team—to get behind, 21–3, and come back to win while holding a tough, well-coached club that had plenty of scoring weapons. . . . It showed the Dolphins have a lot of character, not to mention confidence in their ability to do a job, no matter the circumstances. . . ."

Asked to name the turning point, Bill Arnsparger grunted: "When Johnson blocked that field goal. . . ."

For the pale Griese and his superb partner, Warfield, it was a day to remember for all time.

Griese was named the NFL's offensive player of the week for the three TD throws to Warfield and his 9–14 passing performance after a night in the hospital.

Warfield's receptions for touchdowns now reached eleven, equaling the most scored by any Dolphin in a season. Karl Noonan ran up eleven in 1968, but now Warfield had a chance to leave that far behind.

The eighty-six-yard catch also was a Dolphin record—exceeding one made on an eighty yard pass from George Wilson, Jr. to Bo Roberson against Houston in 1966—and this had to be satisfying.

But such marks were of little moment now, for Baltimore was coming into the Orange Bowl in seven days—after slipping, 14–13, by the amazingly resilient Jets—and the Dolphins were in wretched physical shape to meet them.

Jim Kiick, absent with his bum knee since the Rams' game, except for two plays against Pittsburgh, still was sore and stiff; Csonka's lower right thigh was one big bruise (from Poly-Turf coming up to meet it, Larry growled), and Nick Buoniconti's left knee was extremely sore, while he still wore a cast on the hand with the freak fracture of a small bone months previously . . . the list was longer, but this gives the drift of the casualty roster. It was distinguished.

As usual, Shula mentioned injuries only when asked for comment. "We're now in a position to win from Baltimore—something we have known for a long time we have to do. We can't depend on somebody else doing it for us. . . . We've got the chance, and it's got to be done."

The last three thousand tickets were sold a couple of hours after Charlie Gesino opened up for trade on Monday morning.

And now the tension set in.

THE TENTH GAME: DOLPHINS 17, COLTS 14

The task for both Don Shula and Don McCafferty was complicated by total knowledge of each other.

If this sounds ridiculous, let's reduce it to a less complex situation than this rivalry between two groups of fifty intensely competitive males dedicated to reducing each other to jelly, either physically on the field or psychologically through the national media.

Shula was McCafferty's boss at Baltimore and looks upon him as a good friend. Their close association in those years of many great victories and occasional moments of bitter disappointment gave both the chance to study the other and get a pattern of behavior that, instinctively, was stored away in memory. Perhaps McCafferty's position was even better than Shula's in this respect, for it was Shula who made the final moves when they were associated and the assistant could evaluate his chief with some objectivity. He got to know Shula's predictable reactions.

At least one famous football coach—the late General Bob Neyland, of Tennessee—was embarrassed early by former assistants and afterward refused to schedule games with their teams. "They know better than I do what I'll do in a given situation," the general told the author. "You let me have time to study a man's style when he's under pressure and I'll have him by the throat if he comes at me."

If such thoughts occurred to Shula or McCafferty before their teams collided in the 1970 season, neither mentioned it. Nor was the subject brought up before the climactic battles of 1971 . . . but it was in the background of this meeting of two excellent football clubs.

Each confident of his ability to anticipate the other's moves, the coaches stood the chance of losing their cool when the anticipations turned out wrong. It sounds like a trifling thing, but no game is so intimately influenced by the decisions made on the sidelines—by men too old and out of shape to participate as players. Take away the value of their experience, and you've got a couple of over-weight bum guessers. Shula and McCafferty were to remain true to their normal reaction patterns in this game, however; at least there was no great surprise evident.

The Colts and Dolphins mirrored each other, almost down to the fine details.

The Dolphins were younger but, over-all, not by much. (24.30 years to 26.15). At quarterback, however, they had Griese (26) just reaching the fullness of his years while John Unitas and Earl Morrall were respectively 38 and 37, even on the program. Baltimore had no receiver to match Warfield. If the Colts had any marked advantage on defense, it was not evident despite their record as the best defensive club (mathematically) in the AFC. Perhaps in linebackers, with Mike Curtis, Ted Hendricks, and Ray May, were they a trifle tougher to handle than Buoniconti, Swift, and Powell, but they had no more depth at these positions.

During this Baltimore game, watchers of the NBC telecast across the nation saw the first results of a radio man's promotional brain-storm that created a Dolphins' trademark that doubtless will re-main for years—a sea of white handkerchiefs when the Dolphins score or otherwise please their home fans. Rick Weaver, of WIOD, called for fans in the stadium to wave handkerchiefs when he asked them on the air to do so. . . . The idea quickly caught on and today is a fixture at every Dolphins' appearance.

Baltimore's best runner, Norm Bulaich, was no better off physically than were Miami's Kiick and Csonka. As he teamed with the wise and completely dedicated Tom Matte, Bulaich lacked the power of Csonka in a ramming situation, but his foot movements get him places most big backs can't match. Norm's left ankle was a bother for some weeks before the Miami game and he was seen to shuffle off in obvious pain, although he didn't seem any slower than usual when carrying the ball in the Orange Bowl.

For the first time in 1971, McCafferty announced he would open with Johnny Unitas at quarterback.

It was Unitas who rallied the Colts in the squeaker over the Jets the Sunday prior to the Miami invasion, and even with the good work of this grandest of all pro quarterbacks it took a block of a conversion try by Ted Hendricks and a field goal try blocked by Jerry Logan to keep the Colts ahead of the scrappy New York club that seemed to defy nature. No matter how many first-stringers he lost through injury, Weeb Ewbank seemed to come up with others equally adequate.

The Colts staggered home against New York, the Dolphins started late but collared and outstripped Pittsburgh with what it took to win. . . . This was the immediate background of that matchup on November 21 in the Orange Bowl. Miami was favored by three or four points, with the home field advantage the only rational explanation. The weather was perfect, six miles of wind in seventy-five degrees, when Baltimore's Jim O'Brien sent a high tumbler toward Hubert Ginn at the Miami five-yard line.

Hubie evaded the first two white shirts to take a shot at him and was on the verge of splitting the first wave entirely when Ken Mendenhall nearly snapped his head off with a shoulder tackle at the twenty-eight . . . it was the kind of boyish enthusiasm shown by hitters on both sides for the next sixty minutes.

Shula indicated after the first play that Kiick would not be used

in his customary iron-man act. When he had carried on that
opening formation for six yards, Jim was replaced by Morris.
Mercury took a pass in the flat from Griese that Jerry Logan
almost reached. It got only a pair. Baltimore braced for Csonka.
Larry hit like a ton, but was short of the first down. Rick Volk
caught Seiple's kick fair at the Colts' twenty-three and, with a
roar of affection from Miami fans beating upon him, No. 19
trotted out to the Baltimore huddle. Johnny Unitas was in his
office and open for business and, for the next eight minutes and
fifty seconds, he was the artful master of his prime years, before
age, a sore arm, and a ruptured Achilles tendon combined to
reduce his effectiveness.

Doug Swift and Dick Anderson had the opportunity to study
Bulaich up close when Unitas sent him on a nine-yard rip on the
first play. Matte lost a couple when Jesse Powell combined with
Anderson to bat him back—so Unitas passed to Tom Mitchell for
eleven good ones. In the remaining part of that seventy-seven-yard
drive, Unitas was to get first-down yardage in three critical situations (third and eight, two, and five yards). Two were by passes,
one by a Matte buck; the wise old quarterback still was the master
mixologist, as they call a Miami Beach bartender if he is discovered
to have a touch of class.

On the last of those third-down successes, Bill Stanfill and
Manny Fernandez pressured Unitas, who broke out of the pocket
to his left, peering downfield. His right arm cocked, John waved
instructions to Bulaich, who was running just inside the left sideline. Norm cut to his right and Unitas hit him with a pass
for twenty yards. Two plays later, Don Nottingham busted left
tackle for the touchdown.

Later in the period, O'Brien missed a forty-five-yard field goal,
but the 7–0 lead was strong stuff, as the crowded watchers wondered when the Dolphins would escape the box Baltimore's flinty
defenses had stuffed them into. Almost twenty minutes of the
game were gone before Griese passed to Csonka on third down for
a new series at the Baltimore forty-seven and the Dolphins broke
the pattern. The quarterback next threw to Fleming for sixteen,

and the Colts obviously were shaken when Mercury Morris flashed around Miami's left side for a touchdown as Csonka cut down two of Baltimore's finest.

An official called Csonka for clipping, however, and the ball was returned to the thirty-four; the Dolphins had gained confidence in what they were trying to do, and—largely through a couple of passes to Kiick—Griese had them back down at the Baltimore seven in a few moments.

This drive was strangled and Griese was almost decapitated, however, when Jim Bailey was ignored by Miami's blockers and blind-sided the quarterback for Baltimore's lone sack of the day. It could have been a fatal mistake for Miami, for Newsome recovered for the Colts at their sixteen and they had the initiative for the rest of the half, except for one instance when Tim Foley made an exceptional interception of a Unitas pass. This resulted in a Yepremian field goal try from fifty-four yards out.

It was short. There were some watchers who felt that the Dolphins would be, too, for the Colts were much better for the whole first half, if we discount the lone Dolphins' big move, the one blasted by Bailey.

Superb defensive work by the Dolphins in the Colts' first series after the intermission changed the beat, however.

The Colts contributed toward a slowdown even before that, when Charlie Pittman's runback of the kickoff produced a clipping penalty against Mendenhall that—brought back to the point of the foul and marched off—rolled Baltimore back from its own forty-two to the eleven.

Unitas flipped a screen pass to Matte that Buoniconti anticipated and drilled old Tom for a loss of two, and then Nick captured him again for a loss of one, as Matte hit his helmet with his open palm in frustration. When Bulaich failed to grab the next pass, David Lee punted for the Colts to midfield.

The ensuing response by Miami ended with a touchdown. Equally important, it left the Colts raging at both Miami's deception and the officials' calls. Remarks by Mike Curtis about the first and Ted Hendricks about the latter were to draw derisive responses from the South Florida press in the next days.

Griese started the torment of the defending champions by escaping from a noose of Colts linemen and racing safely out of bounds nine yards downfield, at the Baltimore thirty-seven. Kiick chopped off two and then nineteen more as the Dolphins' Norm Evans, Bob DeMarco, and Larry Little took turns on the inside front of the giant Bubba Smith. . . . Bubba was up and down like a Yo-Yo in this second half as the Dolphins dealt him particular misery.

With a first down at the sixteen, Csonka popped through on a quick trap for nine, with Kiick inching over for the first down. A five-yard penalty for Little's premature pullout moved the ball back to the Colts' ten where, on second down, Griese passed toward Warfield as Paul raced from left to right behind the goal post with the able Jerry Logan in lockstep with him. Logan's hand touched Warfield twice, and it was ruled interference; there is some doubt that Paul could have reached the pass, but, as Warfield patiently explained afterward, that became academic when he was denied the *chance* to reach the ball.

From the one after the penalty, Jim Kiick nosed into a heaving pile of bodies and, eventually, wormed across for the score. Yepremian jammed the count at 7–7, but it stayed that way only a couple of minutes.

Deep in his own country after the kickoff, Unitas tried to break out with passes. The first was hastily thrown as Stanfill stormed in for Unitas' throat. The second was headed toward John Mackey —having his best day to this point in the season, by the way—but John didn't have a chance for it. Instead, Doug Swift, pride of Amherst and the "potted Ivy League," hardly had to lift his hands to take it in, and Doug gave the runback a good go for twelve yards until he was dragged down by the bitterly disappointed Unitas. Surely that couple of moments when he intercepted a pass from a boyhood idol and then was tackled by Unitas had to be the highlight of Swift's young career as an NFL linebacker. His bulk also bruised the idol. Unitas left the field hurting.

On the first down at the Baltimore ten, Griese sent Warfield

to the left corner, with Twilley and Kiick toward the right—and
passed for the touchdown across the middle to Marv Fleming,
who had been jammed but only momentarily by Mike Curtis and
slipped between Mike and Ted Hendricks to catch the ball with
no Colts within eight yards or more. It was Marv's first touchdown
in his two years since coming to Miami from Green Bay. When
the magnificently built tight end held his long arms high and the
football in his hand, the Dolphins not only had the go-ahead
touchdown, they had a weapon all their enemies for the rest of
the season would have to conjure with seriously . . . Warfield,
Twilley, Kiick, Mandich, Csonka, and now Fleming, plus some
others—an impressive fleet of proved catchers, indeed.

With Garo's conversion, the Dolphins led, 14–7, but more than
twenty minutes remained on the clock . . . plenty of time for the
Colts to strike hard.

The strike was not long coming.

Charlie Pittman almost broke the kickoff return but was cut
down at the Colts' twenty-four by Captain Crunch—Mike Kolen—
who hung on despite a 360-degree whirl by the fleet carrier.

Unitas passed to Richardson for nine and Matte got a first
down at the thirty-five, where Unitas sent Ray Perkins around the
left side on a double reverse—the same play Warfield employs so
often with good results for Miami—but both the quarterback and
the wide receiver were cracked by Dolphins. Unitas, blocking Fernandez, was shaken up. Perkins purred along for eleven yards and
was in position to get out of bounds but chose to contest the sideline
with Jake Scott. It was a mistake. Scott's head proved the harder
in a crash heard in the press box. Perkins laid motionless for five
minutes before he was taken away on a stretcher; he had a severe
concussion. Scott went back to his free safety position, for there
was more fire in the Colts.

Earl Morrall relieved the wounded Unitas and started a drive
from his own forty-six that ended with Bulaich punching through
right tackle for the touchdown from four yards away. This was an
even more impressive attack than the one Baltimore pulled for
openers. Morrall hit Mackey for eighteen and Ed Hinton for sixteen

on the way, and the malevolent Matte—attacking with the fury of a shark after a wounded snapper—ripped for five and later twelve, and it was a terrible thing to see for the Dolphins' rooters when Bulaich scored, with O'Brien's kick jamming the count once more.

One play later, the third period ended . . . fifteen minutes remained.

Baltimore's defense forced a punt and Seiple—unimpressive against both Pittsburgh and the Colts up to this kick—was helped by Mike Kolen, who touched the ball down at the Baltimore three. On second down, Morrall slung a beaut to Mackey on the left sideline for twenty-eight yards, and the Colts had kicked the stopper out of the bottle. But a holding penalty against John Williams snapped the rhythm and—despite an excellent scramble by Morrall for sixteen yards—the Colts' counterattack died on their own thirty-seven, when David Lee punted.

Scott caught the high, arching spiral fair on his twenty-seven and the Colts' defense crushed the Miami forward troops to get at Kiick and smash him for a four-yard loss . . . and now Griese sensed an opportunity. With the Colts so aggressive and in what amounted to an eight-man line, he sent Csonka on a quick trap through the middle that Larry almost took for the distance, but he finally was tripped on the fifty-yard line by Logan—with Fred Miller charging up and onto Csonka and drawing a fifteen-yard roughness penalty that just about sent poor Fred off his rocker. He argued bitterly, to no avail.

Griese passed to Karl Noonan for fourteen and then drew Baltimore offside with his erratic snap count—Garo was warming up by now on the south side of the Orange Bowl—and this was the end of the line. The Colts, angry and afraid, fought with a tiger's desperation to stay alive. Logan and then Curtis cracked Csonka at the line of scrimmage and Morris came on but he, too, was held for no gain at right end as Stukes and Logan met him headlong.

Yepremian trotted out, the picture of concentration, his head down all the way from the bench. The snap from Kolen was faultless, Noonan touched the ball down with no hesitation, and Garo knocked it true through the wishbone goal post . . . and it seemed that the whole season was riding with it as the count rose to 17–14.

Again, Pittman gave a good runback, but it ended with a crash when Bob Matheson hit with full power at the Baltimore twenty-nine. Two passes to Bulaich were good from Morrall, but they only got four yards; not so Earl's next pitch. He pumped one out to Hinton on the sideline for thirty-three—Kolen was there, but the pass and catch were perfectly executed—and Matte reached the Miami thirty-five, well within field-goal range. Morrall overthrew Richardson on a short pattern, bringing up a third-and-eleven situation at the Dolphins' thirty-five.

This time he threw a strike, for his man Mitchell was deep in the end zone and the pass came straight down at him. It was caught, however, by Dick Anderson, while Doug Swift—he had moved downfield with Mitchell, step for step—screened the big, talented tight end.

It was a touchback. Miami out to the twenty and with the ball, with three minutes, twenty-eight seconds remaining. Plenty of time for the Colts to force a punt and get possession in marvelous field position for one more mighty try. But this was not to be.

Miami's offense just plain whipped the Colts' defense in those remaining moments of a great football game.

Kiick opened this winning move with a seven-yard crack at right tackle; Csonka took a pitchout to the short side for no gain, but Griese used a counter on the next play, throwing to Warfield for his only reception of the day . . . and it made all the difference, for the thirteen yards gave Miami a first down at the forty. Csonka popped through one one of his trap specialties again, this time for twelve, and eighty-six seconds remained after Kiick chopped off five more. Csonka's ten-yard lunge put the last rope on the Colts.

Against the defense generally considered the toughest in football in 1971, the Dolphins had hacked out fifty-seven yards and three first downs to kill the clock and win this gut test—certainly a champion's way, and it took this kind of effort to stun Baltimore.

In his seven years with the Colts, Shula's seventy-one victories to twenty-three losses gave him the best percentage (75.7) of any active coach in pro ball. After this sweet victory over the Colts, his Dolphins in two seasons had won eighteen while losing five, for 78.2 percent.

Old-timers will recall it was said by some that Shula's great success at Baltimore was simple enough to explain—he had inherited a deep squad of proved and winning veterans from Weeb Ewbank, and the presence of Johnny Unitas ensured victory for the young coach.

If that be true, then those partisan to Don can point to the first two seasons in Miami as a happy accident—for he had no deep squad of proved and winning veterans. He did have a talented quarterback, but not even the most frantic of Griese rooters would claim for him just yet the majestic competence of Johnny U., circa mid-1960s.

Perhaps certain observers are hard put to explain away that rather impressive comparison of victory percentages with two squads so different and circumstances so unrelated.

THE ELEVENTH GAME: DOLPHINS 34, BEARS 3

It was antiseptic and without flaw, a laboratory example of how to disassemble and destroy an enemy football team with a minimum of interference from people—say a Dick Butkus—who would have it otherwise.

The menacing Chicago linebacker, the epitome of malevolence and violence in professional football, was a tabby cat this time. He admitted later that the Dolphins "came at me from all directions, I didn't know where they'd be coming from next."

Nor, it seems, did Don Shula.

Shula had seen Howard Twilley sail into one of the big Baltimore linemen the week before, and Howard's bell rang for hours afterward. "I didn't figure to see the little guy go for anybody of size any more," the coach reported, "but then we saw the movies of this Chicago game. . . ."

The play was away from the stumpy wideout's side of the field, but Howard angled behind Chicago's defensive linemen and linebackers—the defender watching to see that Twilley caught no pass trailing along with him—and then he chose Butkus. "Butkus never knew what hit him," Shula says in delight. "Old Howard knocked him flat on his face!"

It was that kind of effort by all who had a hand in the Miami victory—the most letter-perfect yet.

The Bears came to the bowl with legitimate hopes that Minnesota and Detroit could fall on evil times and that they might still (with a 7–4 record if they could beat Miami) sneak to the top of the NFL's Central Division, the justly named the "black and blue" division. Chicago Coach Jim Dooley finally had achieved a measure of balance, despite the loss of Gale Sayers and other stars from injury.

The Dolphins' week began with the shipping out of John Stofa to Denver for a medium pick in the coming winter's draft. John had recovered from the bothersome hip-pointer of early fall that forced him out at the height of a battle with George Mira for the job as Bob Griese's support quarterback. Now he had a chance to play regularly, for Denver was in foul shape at the position.

Practices at the Biscayne College grounds went well after the first glow of self-esteem receded and the players accustomed themselves to the idea that they had dispatched Baltimore and now had to defend their position at the top of the hill. The Bears were unlucky victims of the new mood.

A second sellout crowd in the Orange Bowl witnessed an amazing first half.

Starting from their own twenty after Mac Percival's kickoff went through the end zone, Griese passed to Warfield for twenty-four yards on second down, after which Csonka and Kiick got two more first downs to reach the Bears' forty-three. When a pass toward Warfield was short on third down, Yepremian came in and kicked a forty-three-yard field goal, the sixteenth game in a row for a score by the irrepressible Garo.

Chicago couldn't move in its first try with the ball and punted, so the Dolphins started slugging forward this time from their own twenty-four. On the tenth play, including a penalty for illegal motion, Csonka lunged into the end zone.

The customers were hardly seated before Bill Stanfill fielded a fumble by the Bears' quarterback. Bobby Douglass, and the Dolphins were back at the Chicago forty. On the sixth play from that point, Griese popped a rollout pass to Fleming at the goal line and Marv lurched over, with a Bears' defender helplessly trying to stop his legs. And the Bears' wretched misfortunes continued, as Bobby Joe Green got a high pass from center trying to punt and threw a forward pass instead. It failed, and Miami took over control on the Chicago forty-seven.

Two penalties throttled a budding Miami drive from that point, but Yepremian got another pound of Bear meat with a thirty-five-yard boot that gave the Dolphins a 20–0 lead at the half. To this point, the Bears had gained 76 yards to 259 yards by Miami—certainly one of the most impressive halftime comparisons the Dolphins ever enjoyed.

With the beginning of the third period, Douglass took up where he had left off—this time hurling a bomb on the first play—but Jake Scott interrupted it short of the intended receiver, and Miami was in trade once more, at its own forty-three.

In five plays—including a twenty-three-yard fling from Griese to Twilley and a naked rumble by Csonka for nineteen yards around the short side of the formation—the Dolphins were at the Bears' ten. Griese tossed a screen to Csonka, who went another eight yards for the score.

Later in the period, after an agonizing march from their own twenty-nine to the Miami eight in eleven plays, Percival kicked a field goal for the Bears that kept them from being skunked in a game that meant so much. But Mira—in relief of Griese, who got a sore left shoulder from a blitzer early in the fourth period—moved the Dolphins seventy yards in thirteen plays for yet another touchdown, this one on a pass to Otto Stowe, a first for both players in a regular-season Dolphin game.

When Dick Anderson intercepted Douglass on the last play of the game, it somehow seemed appropriate.

The Dolphins now had the best record in the whole National Football League, with a 9–1–1 season to date. Baltimore kept the pace, however, by pummeling Oakland on the day before Miami's Monday night triumph over the Bears.

This gave the Colts an 8–3 record. The Dolphins needed to win over New England to establish themselves as a certain playoff participant. . . . The wild-card assignment would be theirs for the second season in a row if they dumped the Patriots.

But this was not to be.

THE TWELFTH GAME: PATRIOTS 34, DOLPHINS 13

The Futile Fight at Foxboro opened in the most auspicious circumstances of weather and psychological one-upmanship.

The Dolphins, having belabored the Patriots earlier, 41–3, had every reason to presume they would flail them whenever and how they pleased. And nothing in the first sixteen seconds of the fray led any among the record turnout of 61,457 spectators in the new stadium to presume otherwise.

Mercury Morris took the opening kickoff from Charlie Gogolak and sliced the middle of New England's first wave, gave a couple of wrinkles to two Patriots, got two good blocks, and sped all the way to the touchdown. The ninety-four-yard beauty was a classic of its kind and stunned the mob. But then something curious, even strange, occurred:

New England didn't give up.

The Patriots exploited the weapon they used to garrote the Dolphins all day—the passes of Jim Plunkett—to move fifty-two yards on eight straight passes after the ensuing kickoff, and that left six to go for a touchdown. Jim Nance got it with the first running play for New England, and Gogolak's conversion tied it, 7–7.

This drive was dead, for all intents and purposes, at the Pats' forty-four when, on third and eight, Plunkett's pass toward Crabtree fell uncaught. But Tim Foley was convicted of interference, and New England got new life that led to a TD.

This was Plunkett's twenty-fourth birthday, and surely one so young couldn't continue to perplex the wise men of the Dolphins' secondary. But there was an ingredient missing for the Dolphins that they had plenty of when they denied the 1970 Heisman

Trophy winner earlier in Miami. This was the sack. Frank Cornish got to Jim twice in the first game, with Stanfill, Fernandez, and Buoniconti also flailing him. At Foxboro, nobody got to Plunkett. New England's laboring front troops made certain of this, and the Dolphins' Front Four seemed to accept it without a real argument. But less subtle developments also would contribute to the breakdown of the Dolphins in the thirty-degree chill.

This was demonstrated when the Dolphins accepted Gogolak's second kickoff and Hubert Ginn came whirring upfield, making like a Mercury Morris . . . except that Ginn was struck heavily by Atessis and another Patriot, and the one who busted into Hubie's right shoulder dislodged the ball he was carrying. A Patriot who used to be a Dolphin, Randy Edmunds, flopped on it under a pile of people.

That was at the Miami twenty-six and a satisfactory spot for Plunkett to go into his act. He just flipped a pass to his former Stanford University receiver, the diminutive Randy Vataha, beyond Foley's straining figure and Vataha got the first of his two touchdowns for the day.

So the Patriots kicked off a third time.

And for the second time in a row, Ginn received it and came speeding back up the track. This time, he bumped into Charlie Leigh, a teammate who was the only one 'twixt Hubie and a touchdown, and the two fell to the Poly-Turf. The ball squirted out of Ginn's clutch, and Bob Gladieux had it for New England at the Miami thirty-seven.

Although Miami's defense was not so permissive this time, the Pats got a field goal out of this giveaway and New England had a 17-7 lead . . . and Miami's offensive team had not touched the ball yet.

Finally, Leigh brought back a New England kickoff without fire or backfire. Charlie was downed on the Dolphins' twenty-nine with a good return of twenty-two yards. Csonka, on Miami's first scrimmage play, broke through the middle and tacklers peeled off him as the big man ran for twenty-one yards. Strangely, he was to carry only ten times this day for sixty-one yards and his spare chances are hard to explain, for Larry always has enjoyed notable success against the Pats, even with an upset in the making.

> *Young quarterbacks can have a hot day against us but a guy like Jim Plunkett is taking potluck. The old tigers—Unitas and Morrall—they knew what they were doing. . . . They used gimmicks to hit us in the tender parts of certain defenses —stuff like a delayed pass to the tight end or to a trailing back or swing patterns to the backs or they take advantage of a linebacker's drops, little stuff like that.*
>
> —Scott

The Dolphins' most impressive assault of the day came soon after this, with the advance carrying from their own forty-two after a poor Pats' kick, to the enemy eighteen. There, a pass from Griese to Seiple hit the goal post, so Yepremian kicked a field goal from the twenty-six.

Another good opportunity went to smash after Warfield's twenty-nine-yard reception carried to the Patriots' twenty-seven. But now Kiick—he had handled the ball on runs and passes 164 times in fourteen games without error—dropped and dribbled Miami's third fumble picked off by the Pats; Webb jumped on it at the New England twenty-one. In nine plays—most of these "nibbler" passes by Plunkett—the Pats had another field goal by Gogolak from the thirty-five and led at the half, 20–10.

We shall not agonize the details for the remainder of this sad affair for the Dolphins; one piece of business by the steady and alert Larry Seiple deserves attention, however.

Still very much in the game, the Dolphins stalled at their own forty-seven early in the third period, and with fourth down and two to go, Seiple came on to punt. Instead, he noticed that New England's wide rusher on his right dropped off the line to make a block. Larry put the ball under his arm and ripped for fourteen yards while breaking two tackles and kept the drive alive. Not really large enough (215) to play tight end constantly, the onetime wideout and running back is to the Dolphins' ball-handling troupe what Bob Heinz is to the front folk—a dependable utility man who meets all challenges. Shula nearly fainted when Larry pulled this run-on-punt trick against Washington in the preseason game in 1970, but has not questioned his judgment on it to this day—a rare compliment from a coach who believes that only constant attention to every detail will bring success in the modern game.

Eventually, this move carried to the Pats' fourteen, but Griese—his left shoulder painfully sore—tried to hand off to Kiick and just didn't get the ball to Jim. Bob fumbled but recovered, forcing another field goal by Garo.

With the 20–13 score at this point, Miami's chances looked good, but the Plunkett-Vataha combination quickly changed all that.

From his own twenty-four, Big Jim hit his former schoolmate at the thirty-eight, and the little scooter got down to the Miami twenty-five before Swift caged him. On the next play—a broken defensive one helping considerably—Vataha was wide open for his second touchdown reception.

Two minutes later, Griese tried to float a pass to Twilley between two defenders along the right sideline, but the near one (Larry Carwell) intercepted and raced back fifty-one yards for the score, and the Pats had moved out to an astonishing 34–13 lead. Worse than this for the Dolphins, Griese was shaken up on the play for the second time in the afternoon and Mira came on in relief.

Jake Scott gave Miami a fat chance for a more competitive final count when he brought a punt twenty-seven yards to the Pats' nineteen. Mira threw two passes incomplete and had the third intercepted by Outlaw.

And that was the old ball game . . . with the Baltimore Colts rallying after a scoreless first half to plaster Buffalo, 24–0, and close the gap. The Dolphins still led by one-half game in the Eastern Division of the AFC, but they had dropped a chance to make certain of a berth in the playoffs as the wild-card team.

But, when they arrived at the Miami airport at nine thirty that night—after a slow bus ride from the stadium to the Boston airport when the driver lost his way—some four hundred fans were there with signs and loud cries of loyalty and respect. It got to Shula and his players, who knew quite well how thoroughly they had botched all sorts of chances in the New England game.

Their fate was complicated a mite further when Kansas City defeated San Francisco in the Monday night game following their own defeat. Had the Forty-Niners won, Miami automatically would have qualified for the playoffs. They still could lose their last two against Baltimore and Green Bay and make the playoffs, if Kansas City beat Oakland the following Sunday.

But the overwhelming thought now was the invasion of Baltimore on Saturday night.

THE THIRTEENTH GAME: COLTS 14, DOLPHINS 3
At the start of the week, Don Shula received a letter from a Baltimore lawyer he had known in which the supplicant requested Shula's aid in nailing down four tickets for the coming battle— but the sometimes lethargic fans of Oysterburg long since had cleaned out the supply.

Shula had a few left, so he shipped off the four tickets with a warm note saying he hoped the fan and his party enjoyed the game. Back came the reply:

"Thank you so much for the tickets. . . . I'll feel a little bad, sitting in those seats while rooting for the Colts!"—and no check was enclosed.

It was still the high point of the week for Shula.

After eight straight victories, his club had been mightily embarrassed by the events at Foxboro. Worse, Griese's shoulder was sore as a bad tooth, and the quarterback was unhappy . . . the pressure and pain were thinning his customary calm as Bob wore his left arm strapped in a sling for most of the week. The Miami area teems with legitimate reporters whom Griese normally deals with generously; he kept faith with them during the days and hours approaching Friday evening's departure for Baltimore, but it was hard going for him.

Larry Little had fierce headaches Monday and Tuesday, until medication relieved a sinus condition; Larry Csonka's right knee

224   THE MIAMI DOLPHINS

had companion pains in his left ankle. Paul Warfield's thigh
continued sore but gradually was improving, while Manny Fernandez favored a shoulder bruised in the Futile Fight at Foxboro.
Every squad late in the season has such wounds and the Dolphins
were no exception; however, theirs seemed to center among the
core of outstanding talents on the club. Shula was frank to admit
on the day of departure that Griese's shoulder was a worry, and a
final decision on him would be delayed until the warmup at
Memorial Stadium in Baltimore. All week, George Mira was kept
abreast of all plans and alternate schemes for the battle, for it was
suspected that he would have to carry the major part of the
load.

As the game approached, another quarrel deflected the attention
of Miami fans feverish for at least a televised view of the key game
of the late season.

On Tuesday night before the Saturday affair in Baltimore,
serious reports of a move by the NFL to authorize a closed-circuit
telecast of the game's live action into Greater Miami were heard
through sources in the National Broadcasting Company, which
held rights to the game. These were discounted, since the NFL
and NBC had backed off earlier in the face of federal prohibitions
against telecasting of a professional game into an area in which a
college or high school game might be financially hurt by such a
program. Florida A&M's annual Orange Blossom Classic was to
be played in the Orange Bowl on the coming Saturday night (the
reason for the original switch of home dates for the two games
involving the Colts and Dolphins) and, since the telecast of the pro
game would start at four in the afternoon, the legalistics of the
situation were such that both sides of the argument could take a fair
hold on the opposition.

The squabble became real on Wednesday afternoon, when the
NFL and NBC announced that the closed-circuit telecast had been
arranged and that auditoriums in Miami Beach and the main-
land would carry the live action. The customers would be charged
six dollars each, with all proceeds above expenses to go to the
Belafonte-Tacolcy Youth Center, a struggling private institution in

the Liberty City section of Miami. The resulting furor and a last-ditch effort to eliminate the public telecast consumed acres of newsprint and hours of air time in Miami, plus the efforts of judges in three federal courts and one circuit court.

At roughly the same moment that the Dolphins landed at chilly Friendship Airport at Baltimore, the last of the lawsuits was decided . . . the closed-circuit telecast was allowed. Bitterness developing over the complicated circumstances involved in this argument promised to linger. Knowledgeable observers agreed that the principal ingredient in all this was the gut rivalry between the National Football League and the National Collegiate Athletic Association—pros versus the colleges—and that Florida A&M was the unhappy centerpiece of their battlefield.

The absolute sellout crowd of 60,238 in Memorial Stadium and the nationwide television audience couldn't have cared less about such matters as the two giants of the AFC Eastern Division came to grips for a second time in perfect weather. It was clear and sixty-two degrees when the Colts' Charlie Pittman took Yepremian's end-zone boomer and brought it out to the Baltimore twenty.

What followed must stand for all time as a masterpiece of the quarterback arts, for it was Johnny Unitas at his purest and best, offering insoluble problems to the Miami defenders and yet dangling before their eyes the most glittering opportunities. . . .

The opening march of eighty yards consumed eight seconds less than ten minutes, with the great quarterback passing three times for new life on third-down situations and sending Tom Matte afoot for another. The crafty oldster was successful on seven passes in this relentless advance—but not one was for more than eight yards. He did it by cutting the Dolphins in the short ribs—under their zones and in the flat. For nine years, Johnny U. had been throwing—in practice or for real—against the faceless zones of Don Shula, and the wise man missed no tricks in this attack. Its classical simplicity lent it a special luster to studious observers.

Yet there was a breathless instant when the Dolphins were an inch or so from breaking up the parade. This came on Big John's pitch under heavy pressure to Ed Hinton on the left sideline. Mike Kolen took a chance and lunged in front of Hinton and missed breaking it up at least by no more than a fingernail; but Hinton got it at the forty and reached the forty-six and a first down.

At the end of the stormy passage, Matte broke through center for the last seven yards and the Colts were away to a notable victory in a great game.

Shula's strategy was evident in the first series after the kickoff, and it depended upon a healthy quarterback. Fortunately, Griese seemed to be his old self, at least in the first fifty minutes or so, despite his lack of hard work during the week. On his first choice, he sent Csonka into the line, then popped a quickie pass to Twilley that gained five yards to the Miami thirty-five. With four yards needed for a first down, Shula sent Karl Noonan to join the starting wideouts, Warfield and Twilley, withdrawing Csonka from the lineup.

Griese passed perfectly to Noonan for much more than the needed four yards, but Doug Crusan was convicted of holding, and Miami was pushed back to its own twenty. A draw with Kiick carrying bringing only five yards, Seiple punted long—his twister carried fifty-three yards—and the Dolphins at least got out of the pocket.

At the end of the first period, the Dolphins seemed to have something stirring with two good plunges by Csonka that got them to the Colts' forty-nine but then—on third and one—the Colts' Rick Volk and Rex Kern sensed what was happening and felled the big man for a two-yard loss on a wide pitchout.

Now came a second display by Unitas, and it was equal to the first in its deadly effectiveness and exceeded the first in total yardage, for it began on the Baltimore thirteen after Seiple kicked fair to Volk.

In moving the eighty-seven yards to Baltimore's second touchdown, Unitas had to make the third-down conversion only once, and he made it clean, with a Bulaich plunge. The quick and powerful running back opened the drive with two runs good for twelve yards and contributed a couple more of his line-busting

(17) Howard Twilley—Everyman's Walter Mitty—eases up after
another touchdown. Smaller, slower, and more susceptible to
bone breakage than his contemporaries among NFL wide receivers,
the tough little genius only beats them into the end zone.

(18) TOP When Baltimore's Norm Bulaich (36) carries, Nick Buoniconti (85) calls for a mass rally of Dolphins. In this case, only Curtis Johnson (45) and Bob Matheson (53) showed up to help the middle linebacker man the ramparts.

(19) TOP RIGHT The kind of thing that permits a quarterback to see his loved ones for another week: Norm Evans (73) and Larry Csonka (39) keep Deacon Jones (75) at bay long enough for Bob Griese to get off a fling in the Los Angeles game in 1971.

(20) RIGHT Attorney Nick Buoniconti appears to be practicing his speech to a jury between plays. . . . No. 85 seldom is more than inches away from enemy ball carriers, and he closes the gap with enthusiasm.

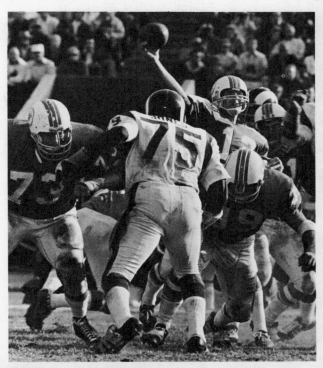

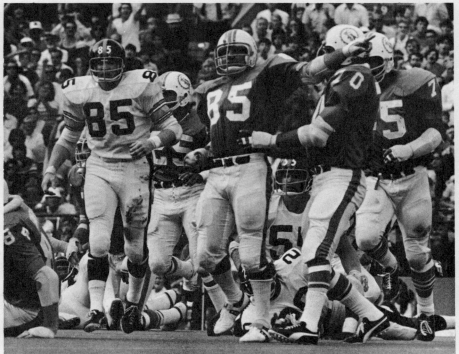

(21) ... And he held onto it when he lit. Jim Kiick is best known as a runner, but the 220-pounder consistently winds up in the AFC's top ten in pass receiving, too. Knee problems kept him out of two games in 1971—the first time he didn't play since junior high.

(22) LEFT This leap of a ballet master is worthy of the Bolshoi. . . . The comparable grace of Paul Warfield on a football field is no less impressive than what he does with a football after he gets it. The former Ohio State long jumper once leaped two inches over twenty-six feet . . . and his NFL opponents—including San Francisco's secondary people—could be made to believe Paul did it straight up.

(23) TOP Sometimes, things don't work out so well . . . and Jim Kiick is lucky his head isn't in that helmet he's losing as four Chicago Bears put him through the meat grinder.

(24) This twenty-yard field goal by Garo Yepremian was the difference in the first 1971 meeting between the Dolphins and Baltimore. Karl Noonan (89) held for the soccer-style, left-footed expert. The final score: Dolphins 17, Colts 14.

(25) The Rams' last gasp . . . and it belongs to Willie Ellison (33) as he is decked short of a new series deep in Dolphin country on a fourth-and-three situation. Bob Heinz had slowed him; now Jesse Powell (56), Jake Scott (13), and Nick Buoniconti (85) finish the job.

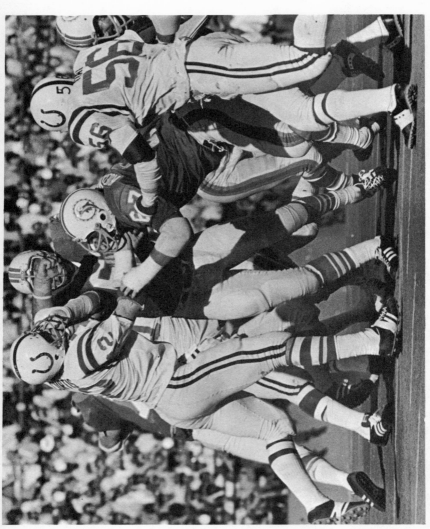

(26) One would have to believe that Baltimore's Mike Curtis (32) doesn't get on with some of his Dolphin acquaintances, among them Bob Kuechenberg (67) and Jim Langer (62). The Colts' Ray May (56) appears to be choosing a helmet to rap.

rushes as Unitas wove a bewildering pattern that included a personal sneak for three yards at the Dolphins' twelve. But it was Matte who bumped the last yard for the score.

Mercury Morris made a spirited run of the kickoff return and the Dolphins ground forward from their own twenty-four to what appeared to be a fat chance. . . .

Fleming took Griese's pass in traffic twelve yards to the forty for a gain of sixteen to begin it, and Kiick reached the forty-six on the next play, a swing pass. Noonan caught the next one, too, but it was out of bounds . . . and a clipping penalty against Bob Kuechenberg broke the rhythm of the drive.

Still, the Dolphins didn't run out of gas until they reached the enemy's twenty-four, where Garo came on for a field-goal try.

It was blocked by Ted Hendricks, the six-foot, seven-inch native of Hialeah, a Miami suburb, and three-time All-American defensive end at the University of Miami. Now one of the best of NFL linebackers, Hendricks was a pain to the Dolphins throughout this furious fight, but never more so than at the moment he leaped —his fingers close to ten feet in the air—to tip Yepremian's kick off course.

Instead of reassuring themselves with a score, the Dolphins were trailing by fourteen points when they went inside for the halftime rest.

The lights had been on since before the four-o'clock kickoff, and now it was dark in Baltimore. But no more so than the Dolphins' luck in the first two quarters; at the intermission they could point to only seventeen offensive formations, while the Colts had the ball for thirty-nine. Baltimore's advantage in first downs was fifteen to three, and Unitas had missed only one pass in thirteen.

Griese was eight for eleven—a sparkling effort, indeed—but everybody knew who was boss man at that point.

Miami very quickly established that it wasn't dead when the third quarter opened with an assault that carried from the Dolphins' thirty-three where Bob Matheson received the short kick and struggled back to the thirty-nine.

Ten plays later, Miami was at the Baltimore five-yard line with a second-down chance to score, but Griese's feet went out from under him as the quarterback retreated to set up for a throw, and he hit the bare dirt of Memorial Stadium's dreary battleground with a crash heard loudest in Miami, a thousand miles away. On third down, a pass toward Noonan went haywire and, on the last down, Yepremian finally kicked a field goal midway through the quarter.

In the subsequent Baltimore series, Norm Bulaich was carried off the field with one of his recurrent leg or muscle problems, and even the most ardent Miami rooter was sympathetic as this brilliant youngster was seen to fall flat on his face while walking later near the Colts' bench.

Another promising Dolphins' move was killed at midfield, but Seiple's punt denied Unitas decent field position. Yet the aging genius maneuvered his people over and around the defenders to the Miami forty-five, and then came another of the game's significant breaks . . . David Lee's punt was allowed to fall to the ground by Jake Scott at the Miami goal line but, instead of a normal forward bounce from there, the silly thing bounced laterally, and Tom Curtis touched it down at the Miami one. It was a dreadful break for the Dolphins, for the last period was half gone and desperate measures were called for, even if they had the benefit of good field position.

Still, they came out of there against the best defense in the National Football League, with Griese hitting Kiick twice and on third down getting a fresh chance. However, a third attempt for a new series at midfield resulted in the interception of a pass toward Noonan by the omnipresent Hendricks—effectively shutting off all chance for a Miami victory, although the Dolphins were to get the ball once more. Griese says his low throw apparently was caused by the ball slipping off his hand.

The Dolphins improved their statistical comparison with the Colts a trifle on that last occasion, slogging forward from their own twenty-six to the Colts' thirty, but Ray May intercepted Griese once more to bring the drama to its effective close. When the gun sounded a minute later, Baltimore had the ball at mid-field.

But nobody really cared. What Johnny Unitas did with it fifty-five minutes earlier had decided the issue. . . . The Colts now had overtaken the Dolphins and passed them for a half-game lead in the American Football Conference East and the Dolphins were even in danger of losing a spot in the playoffs, although they had been football's winningest team no more than six days before.

They were saved from any such ignominy by the skull-busting game between the Chiefs and Oakland the next afternoon in Kansas City.

Although George Blanda had performed numerous miracles and seemed to have the Chiefs by the goozle in their decisive match, they slipped away in the last ninety-five seconds and beat him and the Raiders, 16–14, on Jan Stenerud's field goal. It also assured Miami of a playoff position as the "wild-card" team for a second year under Shula in the AFC.

The Dolphins still had a chance to win the Eastern Division title, but only if they defeated Green Bay while Baltimore lost to New England the next weekend.

A thin reed, that last, for Johnny U. was his own, great self and enjoying his Indian summer, and even the sparkling youth of a Jim Plunkett was dimmed by comparison.

The statement completing the above paragraph stands, despite the shattering events of the next weekend, last of the regular season and the one that scrambled football minds from Biscayne Bay to the far reaches of the wide Missouri.

Before this mad afternoon was completed, the whole superstructure of the AFC's Eastern Division was turned about, with Miami struggling for the first thirty-five minutes before tromping the Packers, while weird things were said over the loudspeaker in the Orange Bowl. . . . These things made little sense: The Patriots, who hadn't won a road game all season, were thumping the Colts in Baltimore.

It could be said of this game that Jim Plunkett did to the Colts' great defense what he did to that of Miami, while Unitas did very little that was reminiscent of his electrifying work against the Dolphins. Yet the memory of Unitas in his two marches against the tough Miami defense remains the quality performance of the season, in the author's eyes.

The actions of Plunkett and his small pal, Randy Vataha, were decisive in the final arrangement of the Eastern Division championship—Miami winning over Baltimore by one-half game—and the Patriots wound up third after a splendid season that had to be enormously satisfying to Bill Sullivan and the other owners, the players, and their coaches.

For the Dolphins, the final accounting was a mixed bag. They won their first championship of any division, but they turned up playing Kansas City instead of Cleveland in the first round of the eliminations toward the Super Bowl.

THE FOURTEENTH GAME: DOLPHINS 27, PACKERS 6

The margin sounds comfortable and it was . . . once it began to accumulate. There was a time or two in the first half—when Griese's passes were sailing over the heads of receivers or when the passes were being dropped like so many hot irons by the catchers— when the ten-point favorites seemed so many schoolboys.

Ten full quarters—four each against New England and Baltimore, plus another pair against the Pack—had elapsed before Shula's attack group scored a touchdown.

Meanwhile, a twenty-six-yard field goal by Yepremian in the first period brought the Dolphins even with Green Bay's eager young troops—it also marked the nineteenth straight game in which the kicking artist had produced such a goal—and then Garo added a twenty-seven-yarder before the intermission. And Larry Csonka was presented the ball with which he crashed over the one-thousand-yard rushing mark for the season.

Tim Webster equaled Yepremian's six points in the third period, and it appeared that the rotation might continue. Bart Starr, starting his first game of the season for the Pack, was having problems with Jim Riley, who sacked him three times during the game while Stanfill got Starr once. But the Dolphins had shown little flash in attack.

However, this changed quite abruptly the first time they got the ball in the third period. For no perceptible reason, but quite definitely, the Dolphins came out of their fog.

In ten plays, Miami moved eighty-four yards to a touchdown, with Csonka ripping nine through tackle for openers. Griese converted the assault's only third-down requirement with a sharp eleven-yard pass to Otto Stowe, who showed real quality with a sideline move that jooked one Packer out of his shoes and got five yards more than seemed possible. Kiick, whose knee showed no sign of the malaise that slowed him for most of the late season, bucked over from the one. And it was about this time that the loudspeaker boomed that the Patriots were still breaking through the Colts at Baltimore. After this, the Miami team settled down and rapped the Packers proper.

Green Bay's Donny Anderson fumbled when Riley belted him, and Bob Matheson fell on the ball at the Packers' twenty-four. Warfield swept around on his copyrighted reverse for seventeen yards, and Ray Nitschke—the Packers' aging middle line-backer who had just come onstage a few moments before—was tagged with a roughness penalty when he lit on Paul. From the three, Kiick and then Csonka cracked the line, and Larry scored shortly before the quarter ended.

Starr maneuvered the Pack into Dolphin territory as the fifth straight sellout crowd—a record 76,812 to see a regularly scheduled game—tried to learn more about what was transpiring at Baltimore. The proceedings on the Poly-Turf were interrupted, however, when Tim Webster's field goal attempt from the Green Bay forty-six was blocked by quick little Lloyd Mumphord, and Curtis Johnson fielded it perfectly and ran it in for a Miami touchdown from forty-seven yards out.

Starr was till firing away at midfield when the gun sounded, although the Packers were too far gone to have much punch left. But the Dolphins still didn't know how they were doing in the battle for the division title, for news from Baltimore was fragmentary.

The Miamians went into their dressing room and most had

showered before they learned the final news, that New England had won. Shula endured and finished numerous interviews, only to backtrack with reporters who had waited. Don was hugely pleased, although the upset of the Colts meant that his team would now play the Western Division winners, the Chiefs, in Kansas City. . . . Baltimore, finishing with the best record of any non-winner (the basis on which Miami reached the playoffs of 1970), would now go to Cleveland. The Browns had trimmed the Colts, 14–13, earlier but were considered substantially less formidable than the Kansas City team of Hank Stram.

The final standings of the Eastern Division of the American Conference for 1971:

	W.	L.	T.	Pts. For	Opp. Pts.
Miami	10	3	1	315	174
Baltimore	10	4	0	313	140
New England	6	8	0	238	325
N. Y. Jets	6	8	0	212	299
Buffalo	1	13	0	184	394

(See the Appendix for the final standings of all NFL teams.)

Numerous bruises resulted from the Green Bay game: Warfield's ribs were pounded severely; Howard Twilley had a bruised knee, Anderson a bruised hip, Little a bruised toe, etc.; but Tuesday's work day at Biscayne College found the training room people optimistic about all hands, although Jesse Powell had a kidney bruise that needed close surveillance. He would not play against the Chiefs.

In the afterglow of the weekend's events and the Dolphins' first division title, it was noteworthy that this team that had won three games two seasons previously now had gone into the playoffs one-half game in front of the Baltimore Colts by whipping the Green Bay Packers—nothing at all like the old days. Strictly dream stuff.

And the unpleasant tie at Denver in the season's first game finally meant something. It could mean everything.

It was by this tie alone (see the standings) that Miami edged Baltimore for the Eastern Division championship; if the Dolphins had lost to Denver, rather than tied the Broncos, the title issue would have hinged on the two meetings with Baltimore (even), and the points scored in them (in which case, Baltimore would have been the victor). It was a satisfying compromise to what had been a nagging embarrassment.

In any review of the Dolphins' season, it had to be counted enormously successful despite the uncertainties of the first three games. Shula frankly admitted at season's end that those bothered him, they made him feel that he probably had not read his people right . . . disturbing to a man of Shula's temperament for several reasons not found on a scoreboard. In the long run, however, his players responded as he thought they could, given enough hard work and realization of the opportunities winning could bring.

Suddenly, thousands of South Floridians announced that they had known all along that the Dolphins would win the division title . . . but the same savants usually admitted it was too bad that the Miami club must now play powerful Kansas City.

Their memories of the Chiefs' superiority still were green, although the teams had not met in two seasons.

13

The Playoffs

It is well at this point in our narrative that we review what happened in the weeks immediately prior to the meetings of giants that led to Super Bowl VI.

In the American Football Conference, Miami reached the round-of-four by winning the Eastern Division championship with victories over Buffalo (twice), New York Jets, Cincinnati, New England, Los Angeles, Pittsburgh, Baltimore, Chicago, and Green Bay. They lost to the Jets, Baltimore, and New England and were tied by Denver.

Kansas City won the Western Division in a most exciting fashion, coming from behind with seconds to play with a Jan Stenerud field goal that frustrated Oakland, 16–14. A postscript to this is interesting: the field goal was made possible—or at least made infinitely easier—when Jimmy Warren, one of the original Dolphins who wound up as Oakland's right cornerback, was called for tripping Otis Taylor on the Kansas City twelve-yard line; Stenerud's kick from there was almost automatic.

The Chiefs, in their regular season, had a record equal to Miami's, at 10–3–1. They had victories over Houston, Denver (twice), San Diego, Pittsburgh, Washington, Cleveland, San Francisco, Oakland, and Buffalo. They lost to San Diego, the New York Jets, and Detroit and were tied (20–20) in a midseason battle with tough Oakland.

Cleveland generally was thought to be the weakest of the playoff participants. The Browns were 9–5, with victories over Houston (twice), Baltimore (by 14–13), Pittsburgh, Cincinnati (twice), New England, New Orleans, and Washington. The Browns lost, sometimes by a ton, to Oakland, Denver, Atlanta, Pittsburgh, and Kansas City . . . not a very imposing rundown, but nonetheless effective under the National Football League's system.

The fourth playoff team, the "wild card," was Baltimore when the dust settled on the last day of the season and New England had done its dirty deed to the Colts. By virtue of their 10–4 season, the Colts were best among the nonchampions of the AFC's three divisions.

Baltimore's victims were New York's Jets (twice), New England, Buffalo (twice), the New York Giants, Pittsburgh, Los Angeles, Oakland, and Miami. The Colts lost to Cleveland, Minnesota, Miami, and New England.

Without a laborious breakdown of their fortunes during the regular season (it can be found in the Appendix, however), National Football Conference teams reaching the playoffs were Dallas (11–3), Eastern Division, vs. Minnesota (11–3), Central Division; San Francisco (9–5), Western Division, vs. Washington (9–4–1), wild-card qualifier.

In the AFC's two games, Miami and Kansas City were matched in the latter's stadium on Saturday, Christmas Day, with Baltimore at Cleveland the day after. In the NFC, Dallas at Minnesota were paired for the Christmas game, with Washington at San Francisco on Sunday.

To digest the results: Miami defeated Kansas City, 27–24, in the longest professional football game ever played; Baltimore crushed Cleveland, 20–3; San Francisco defeated Washington, 24–20, while Dallas bested Minnesota, 20–12.

Then, in the second round, where the conference championships were determined, the Dolphins broke down the Colts' tenacious defense with three long strikes for a 21–0 victory, while—in a dull and strangely unappetizing counterpiece—Dallas overcame San Francisco, 14–3.

Thus Miami reached Super Bowl VI in New Orleans' Tulane Stadium on January 16, 1972, there to oppose the Dallas Cowboys, who had lost Super Bowl V to the Colts in the Orange Bowl, 16–13, on Jim O'Brien's field goal with five seconds remaining.

The digest is not enough for understanding, however, for the victories over Kansas City and Baltimore will remain vivid in the memories of all who saw them, no matter whom they cheered during these furious games. The manner in which Miami won these two suddenly brought attention to the Dolphins that even their significant progress under Shula in 1970 did not approach.

It is one thing to win in the National Football League's regular-season play. It is quite another situation in the playoffs, where each game is for all the marbles on the day it is played. The losers get less gold, but this is incidental. To the first-line troops who participate, victory is everything . . . the ultimate answer, but also the only answer.

Cynics with fewer wits than most brayed their doubts of such dedication by the Colts, defending champions of football. These whining incompetents—some in print—suggested that the Colts dumped their game to New England on the season's last day so they could play Cleveland, rather than Kansas City, in the first-round playoffs, and that the Pats' 21–17 win thus was contrived rather than earned.

As the playoffs advanced, this canard was revealed for what it was . . . Baltimore defeated Cleveland easily enough but then was flailed by its most bitter enemy, Miami, on the Dolphins' home grounds. Don Klosterman, the Colts' general manager, further destroyed this shameless lie by revealing that Baltimore's coaches and several players lost contract performance money when they failed on the last day of the season to nail the title with a victory over the Pats.

The Colts had played six preseason and thirteen league championship games when they blew the finale to New England. To suggest that they would negate all that labor for so dubious an advantage is to reveal a monumental ignorance of what makes football players suit up in the big league.

THE FIRST ROUND: DOLPHINS 27, CHIEFS 24

Once or twice in a lifetime there is an experience so sweet that nothing else before or after quite compares with it. . . . Only a game of this unique quality could stand alone for the Dolphins in a season where astonishment and satisfaction became everyday emotions.

Even for the most jaded observer, the 201 minutes between the opening kickoff by Kansas City's Jan Stenerud and the flawless field goal by Garo Yepremian that won for the Dolphins will remain one of the exciting memories of football history.

In official playing time, the battle in perfect conditions of weather and other factors consumed 82 minutes and 40 seconds. . . . deep into a sixth, or second overtime, period. It became a struggle for breath and the will to run for the players, no less than for points. The moment the regular game time ended, every one of the 50,374 fans in the packed stadium and millions along the TV cables—including all the hundreds of thousand yelling at their sets in South Florida—knew only a miracle could keep the issue from being settled by Stenerud or Yepremian, a Norwegian or an Armenian born on Cyprus, neither of whom ever played football as a schoolboy.

This was especially in focus at that time, since Stenerud had just been named to the Pro Bowl American Football Conference team by coaches who ignored Garo's supremacy in the AFC and, indeed, in the NFL, as pro football's top scorer.

But let us retell the tale. . . .

The Dolphins couldn't break out of their back country after Stenerud's kickoff went for a touchback, and Seiple punted for the first of six times in the gusty, sixty-degree breeze. In nine plays, the artful Len Dawson cut into the Miami defense with a screen and two other short passes that featured a move from the Chiefs' forty-three to the Miami seventeen. Nick Buoniconti leaped to deflect another throw toward Ed Podolak—the Chiefs' running back who had a great day in a losing effort—that killed the drive, but Stenerud got first blood with a field goal from the twenty-four.

Bob Griese found Paul Warfield loose shortly thereafter and hit Paul with a twenty-three-yard pass that got the Dolphins out to their own forty-three. However, Bob pitched one of his two interceptions (this one by Willie Lanier) among twenty hits in thirty-five tosses for the day, and the Chiefs were in charge once more with excellent field position.

When Larry Little decked Lanier, Kansas City was at Miami's thirty-five and the knots of Dolphins' fans at their TV screens back home set up a universal moan . . . recalling the seven previous times the teams had played since 1966 (including one preseason) and the seven Kansas City victories.

Dawson sent Elgin Hayes on a nine-yard rip through guard to the twenty-six, then for another seven on precisely the same play. Miami stiffened but soon was penalized for offside by Curtis Johnson, and this gave the Chiefs a third down, one yard to go, at the ten. . . . Dawson flipped a quick pop to Podolak, and that inspired citizen hauled it on in for the touchdown.

With more than two minutes remaining in the first period, the Chiefs had a ten-point lead and Miami's offense had hardly turned a wheel, while the defense staggered, uncertain in the face of a bewildering array of Kansas City formations and offensive people who can run faster and hit harder than any other group in football.

However, as the quarter ended, progress was being made. Griese stubbornly stayed with his power-back attack, and it bit into the ground defended by Hank Stram's awesome array of Buck Buchanan, Curly Culp, and associates.

Jim Kiick and Larry Csonka busted on up to the Miami thirty-nine from the twenty, and Griese faked a handoff to Kiick before passing to Warfield, who broke out of trouble at the sideline to race to the KC twenty-one before Jim Lynch and Lanier finally fetched him up short.

A sweep by Csonka failed, but Griese evaded a battalion of heaving monsters before passing successfully to Marv Fleming, who was almost unhinged when hit by the fierce Bobby Bell at the Kansas City four. Kiick tried guard but got only a yard, so Griese went toward Fleming again, for Warfield was smothered off to his left. . . . Marv didn't get it, but the Chiefs' Kearney felt the wrath of the fuzz; the interference penalty edged the ball to the KC one, and Csonka crashed through for the score.

This drive probably was the key to the whole monumental struggle, for it proved that the Dolphins could rally. They could stab and club their way through the maze of tall, powerful men whom Don Shula found to be a much better football team than he presumed before this first personal experience with the Chiefs. "They run, hit, throw, and catch with anybody," the weary coach of the Dolphins admitted when it was over . . . but such reflections were for later.

Having gained their offensive equilibrium, the Dolphins might have expected relative peace for a time, but this was not to be . . . here came Dawson and friends, with one of his amazingly quick flips to Podolak on a short screen breaking through the Miamians for twenty-nine yards. When Curtis Johnson knocked Ed out of bounds at the Miami thirty-nine, the Chiefs had their momentum once more and Dawson struck for the kill, throwing long for his best receiver, Otis Taylor, an All-Pro who had found himself in a morass of Dolphins' zones and personal escorts that he could never unravel. For the day, he was held to three catches worth twelve yards, and this was surely one of his least effective performances; this time, the omnipresent Johnson slipped in at the last fraction of a second to intercept and, though Taylor belted him down immediately, Miami had broken the flow.

Griese's big backs hardly budged the ball as the Chiefs saw through their moves and Seiple punted out while standing on his own eight; Homan caught it fair at Kansas City's thirty-nine—a superb job by Seiple when one was needed.

Podolak swung around his left end for thirty-two yards, however, so the Chiefs were holding Miami by the short hair again . . . and even a fifteen-yard penalty didn't strangle their threat. After Elmo Wright got back ten of the fifteen on an end-around, Dawson again proved his appreciation of old things that wear well when he sent Elmo back around on the next play. Jake Scott, who had joined Bob Matheson to bat Wright down the first time, did it alone now, but the five-yard gain carried to Miami's twenty-two —two yards short of a new series.

In came Stenerud for the fourth-down field-goal try—and he failed under a savage rush from the Dolphins, the ball sailing off to his right. This obviously shook the blond kicker and no doubt contributed to later events of larger magnitude.

Another solid punt from midfield by Seiple a couple of minutes later drove the Chiefs back to their eight. Podolak was slashing away at the twelve when three Dolphins popped him on the next play and Anderson leaped on the ball at the Kansas City twelve.

Griese worked one pass to Warfield for five but overthrew Twilley once and had another to Twilley broken up by Jim Marsalis before Garo came on to bring the Dolphins even, thirteen seconds before the halftime break. It was a chance compromised, if not entirely wasted, but at least the Dolphins had proved their spunk, and the 10–10 jam on the scoreboard in the old ball park indicated that they were far from out of it.

Kansas City's power when the new period opened was typical of the veteran linemen who have figured in so many victories for Hank Stram.

Heartened by the young Podolak's twenty-four-yard runback of the kickoff, the old boys joined him in a savage assault from the

Chiefs' twenty-five. An early key to this was the fifteen-yard throw from Dawson to Wright, and a six-yarder to Taylor got fresh life at the Miami forty-eight. . . . Seconds later, Taylor caught another short job, and his lateral to Podolak was correct, but Frazier was clipping, and the beat slowed—only to be picked up again by Jim Otis, who made the remainder of the unstoppable advance his personal triumph. Included in this was a jarring passage from Miami's thirteen to the one, after a pile of assorted body parts blocked a path Jim expected at guard. Then he shot through right guard for the touchdown, and Miami—for the second time —was behind. The Chiefs had gulped down ten minutes worth of clock in that one long drive. The count now stood: Kansas City 17, Miami 10.

A great deal of football remained to be played in this epic battle, the clock notwithstanding. . . .

Mercury Morris broke one tackle and almost busted loose but was dropped at the Dolphins' twenty-nine on his runout of Stenerud's deep kickoff and, for the second time, Miami's offense got the job done.

On the first of eight formations, Griese passed to Twilley, and Howard worried his way twenty-three yards through the Chiefs' defense to reach the forty-eight. A couple of plays later, Griese went to him again and it was worth another five, with Csonka and Kiick pushing on down to the KC thirty. Now, after a beautiful fake on a play-action move, Griese threw to Warfield, and the great receiver was sorely used by Lanier and Reardon when they hit him at the seven. Another pass, this to Kiick, was a yard short of the touchdown, but Jim got it on a second try from that point; again Garo came on and, for the second time, the Dolphins had pulled even.

Buoniconti—who may have had his greatest day as a Dolphin— was one of a bunch who smashed Hayes at midfield early in the fourth period, and Nick recovered his victim's fumble. But the fat chance escaped the Dolphins a few plays later, when Griese's pass toward Kiick was caught instead by Jim Lynch on the Kansas City nine.

The school solution suggested that the Dolphins contain the Chiefs there or thereabouts, awaiting a punt or a break and keeping relentless pressure on the big men in flaming red war gear. But it didn't work out that way.

Instead, the Kansas City offensive group gained ground in huge chunks, with Hayes tearing off fifteen yards in two carries, Len Dawson throwing to Frazier for fourteen and Elmo Wright for another thirty-one . . . and Podolak carried over for another touchdown in less time than it takes for the telling. With Stenerud's conversion, the Chiefs now had their twenty-four and Miami was looking like a frazzled loser, seven points behind with seven minutes to play.

Again Morris got the Dolphins out of the ditch, however, with a crackling good runout from behind the goal line, all the way to the Miami twenty-nine.

If he felt either despair or the pressure of time, Bob Griese didn't show it as he kept the usual cadence of huddle-and-break-and-play, continuing to use the staccato, uneven count that is his mark. The Chiefs were equally disciplined and refused the bait.

Griese hit Fleming behind the Kansas City right linebacker for fourteen yards; Bob DeMarco saved the situation when he flopped on a fumble of Warfield's when the fleet catcher was caught on his usually productive reverse. Griese passed to Warfield then to make another seventeen on a third-down conversion that was a classic. Two plays later, on a third-and-four situation, Bob went to Paul again, although everybody in sight knew this was his inclination, and it worked for twenty-six more, down to the KC twelve, and only two minutes were left on the clock now.

After a throw to Twilley got five more yards, Griese hit Fleming deep in the middle end zone, and the State of Florida breathed again. Garo's kick pulled the Dolphins even for the third time, 24–24, and ninety-six seconds were left.

It was considerably more time than Kansas City actually needed to nail down the victory—but time wasn't the only factor now, despite the magnificent runback of Yepremian's kickoff by the courageous Podolak, as he continued one of the NFL's most glittering performances in this memorable season.

Accepting the kick on the goal line, Podolak came straight upfield for perhaps thirty yards, angled off to his left when little Garo made like a kamikaze pilot, and Ed was home free for a winning touchdown except for the desperate lunge of Curtis Johnson. The big, fast Miami cornerback didn't drop his man, but he nudged Podolak just enough for him to career out of bounds by a foot or so, and that stopped his flight. But he was then at the Miami twenty-one—cinch distance for any field-goal kicker in the NFL, you say, and the minute, twenty-five seconds remaining was no great problem.

Twice, Podolak was held to inches on third down—Miami was taking time out between each of these plays, trying to put off the inevitable—and Tim Foley blitzed to nail him for a three-yard loss. But this was of no real consequence in the drama, for Stenerud had been swinging his leg on the sideline and now he came on to join Dawson, who holds for him, and every fan in the old stadium was on his feet.

There was a roar and groans as the linemen attacked each other and Lloyd Mumphord sprinted in from the left side of Stenerud. Lloyd didn't quite get there, but his near-miss and that of two other Dolphins threw Stenerud's mind or timing off. In any event—miracle of miracles!—the man voted the AFC's best field-goal kicker by its coaches three days previous missed, the ball flying to the right of the goal!

The Dolphins' bench went balmy and the players on the field couldn't believe it, but there it was, rescue in the teeth of doom. . . . No man in his right mind would have predicted this course of events, but it was there to be seen—or its track was to be seen—in the unblinking lights, 24–24, on the scoreboard.

The Dolphins tried line plays for a gain of only six, after which Seiple punted and the game died a tie.

As was his usual fate, Buoniconti lost the coin toss that determined which team would kick off to open the fifth period, when sudden death—or "sudden victory," according to the oversweet explanation of the network telecaster—would determine the winner. Kansas City naturally elected to receive. Anything else, especially with a return artist of Podolak's capability at hand, would be madness.

Yepremian's kick went to the far edge of the end zone, where Podolak grounded it for a touchback, but one of the Dolphins was tagged for illegal procedure, and the boot had to be made again.

> *It's ironic. . . . I sincerely felt, as the game went on, there was no way in the world we could lose it. . . . When Miami tied it and Eddie Podolak came back with a 78-yard kickoff return—our longest of the year—we felt it was poetic justice. . . . I was more concerned with the protection of Stenerud than I was the actual kicking of the field goat attempt. I still think Jan kicked the ball well but it . . . was a little bit off line. In a big game like this, you've got to take advantage of the shots you get or you're dead.*
>
> *—Hank Stram*

This time Garo squibbed it, and the giant Buck Buchanan caught it and lateraled to Podolak—quick thinking—and Ed twisted and sprinted to the KC forty-six, where swift Lloyd Mumphord collared him to save the day for Miami.

A screen pass and a butt by Hayes got a fresh series at the Dolphins' forty-two, and Jim Riley slammed into Podolak to cost him a yard. Miami refused an offside penalty now; Podolak almost escaped, but was held to a gain of six at his right end . . . so Dawson came back with the same play, but this time Podolak fumbled and Ed Budde recovered for the Chiefs at the Miami thirty-five—setting up a Stenerud kick from the forty-two or so.

The tension at this point was a living thing. Stenerud, rattled by his two previous failures and understandably nervous in the present situation, came on to win the game and give the 1970 victors over Minnesota a giant step toward a third appearance in the Super Bowl . . . but again, it didn't work out just that way.

With every Dolphin on the line and straining every muscle in his body, the diminutive but dedicated Mumphord whirred in from Miami's right flank on the snap of the ball, as Johnson leaped to his immediate left, taking the minds and attention of the blockers off Mumphord. Buoniconti and the other linebackers blitzed as best they could through the heaving hills of linemen and Nick and Mumphord got to the ball simultaneously, a split second after it came off Stenerud's toe. . . . Instead of defeat, Miami had the initiative at its own twenty-three!

The counterattack by Miami did not produce points, either. The Dolphins managed one third-down conversion after Kiick picked up eleven yards on a sweep, but this one—a fourteen-yard pass to Twilley—reached only the Chiefs' forty-eight and, three downs later, the Chiefs were still holding there.

Seiple punted and Podolak caught it fair at his seventeen—and the Chiefs were no more able to advance than were their tormentors. Scott brought back Wilson's kick eighteen yards to the Miami thirty-nine. Griese, careful and conservative now, went for Twilley for a new first down at the Chiefs' forty-six, but Earlie Thomas broke up a subsequent third-down pass to Warfield, and Yepremian's attempted field goal of fifty-two yards fell far short.

As the first extra period ended, Jake Scott pulled in a Dawson pass toward Wright and raced it back thirteen yards to the Miami forty-six.

The Dolphins now seemed to be the stronger team for the first time in the game. They had gotten "second wind" from their repeated frustrations of Kansas City, perhaps no less than they did from the exhaustive hard work Shula subjected them to from July forward.

Yet the Miami offense couldn't get untracked, and one line try by Csonka was followed by two unsuccessful passes, forcing Seiple's sixth punt. This time, Curtis Johnson lit on Podolak as he caught the ball and wrestled him down at the Kansas City fifteen.

Hayes snapped off four hard ones at his left tackle, but—in a display of the energy mentioned above—Fernandez and Riley caught the elusive Podolak on a sweep to his right and cracked him for an eight-yard loss. The good deed seemed in vain, however, when Podolak caught another screen from Dawson in an inviting situation; appearances were deceiving, however, for Riley and Buoniconti accumulated from somewhere and stopped the hardy fellow after nine yards, five short of a new series.

Jerrel Wilson's tall, hanging punt arrived with tacklers deep in Miami territory, and Scott called for a fair catch at the twenty. And then came the break that had been eluding the Dolphins for so long.

After Kiick wrenched off five yards, Csonka finally broke out of the cage of giants created for him by Kansas City linemen. It was a trap play off his own left guard, and Larry raged forward for twenty-nine yards—he netted eighty-six for the oversized game —and only a savage tackle by Kearney dropped him at all. As usual, however, Csonka fell forward.

Two more line tries gained six yards to the KC thirty, where Jim Lynch and Aaron Brown met Kiick at the line for no gain.

From the sideline, where he had been praying and swinging his left leg in sweeping motions, came tiny Garo Yepremian and tall Karl Noonan. The bigger man took the snap from center with relaxed hands and set the ball just so on the torn turf even as Garo's foot sped toward it, and the thump of their collision was the most momentous sound in the Dolphins' short history.

Arrow true, the ball sailed over the mass of struggling, tired men and through the goal's uprights, thirty-seven yards away, and Miami—for the first time—had the lead.

The Dolphins also had the victory—the "sudden victory" about which the voice on the television talked so much—and they had become the most intriguing team in American sport, into the center ring at last.

The usually inscrutable Shula surged forward with the leaping and laughing two dozen Dolphins from the sideline and looked for Hank Stram, his worthy adversary in a game significant for countless reasons beyond the benchmark in the history of long games.

The bitterly disappointed Kansas City fans, who had seen the Dolphins collar their people three times and finally surpass them in a manner almost copyrighted by the Chiefs, didn't take out their pain on the visitors. Instead, they suffered in silence, and some even cheered the Dolphins, for what they had witnessed was a kind of moving experience that happens in sport only once in a decade or so.

When the Dolphins arrived at Eastern Airlines' Gate 77 late that night at Miami International Airport, at least fifteen thousand screaming fans teetered on the edge of hysteria. . . . Women with babies in their arms shrieked their praises, and the bone-weary players staggered and pushed among the fans and traffic to reach their cars in the parking lot.

When Don Shula finally reached his big, freebie Chrysler— Don hasn't paid for a personal car since becoming a head coach at Baltimore in 1962—the battery was dead. The head coach of professional football's new glamor team asked a fan for a lift home, and this bedazzled citizen was invited into the coach's house when they reached it.

Meanwhile, Garo was a prisoner of his own popularity. While the other stars of the great battle in Kansas City finally reached their cars and went away with their happy families, the winning kicker wiped his moist brow in the airport police headquarters. Security officers, fearful that the little tiemaker would be crushed by his admirers, literally trampled into the concrete, held him for more than an hour, until the parking lot cleared enough for a police escort to get him out with no broken bones. The ecstatic fans who did get near him that exciting night usually came away with that they considered the greatest of rewards—a rub of Garo's stone-bald head.

Yepremian, his dignity unruffled but his response to the acclaim that of a happy child, told a reporter in a masterpiece of understatement: ". . . I was determined to prove that I am competent in my profession. . . ."—oblique reference to his disappointment about the all-star selection of Stenerud.

It hardly is possible to imagine a more meaningful victory

for a young football team than this first Miami victory over the only member of the former AFL that it had not bested at one time or another. Seven times previously, Kansas City had batted back the Dolphins; now, in the most significant game of the eight, the younger team had won in a bloodletting that exceeded in time even the one between the Houston Oilers and Dallas Texans— now the Chiefs—in 1962. That one lasted seventy-seven minutes, fifty-four seconds. Hank Stram was the winning coach in the first, loser in the second.

Reflecting upon the wreckage in Kansas City, Joe McGuff, of the Kansas City *Star*, wrote: ". . . It was such an eventful game that just when you seem to have it in proper perspective another element comes to mind and changes the picture.

"There's one obviously simple explanation for the defeat. Jan Stenerud missed a thirty-one-yard field-goal attempt seconds before the end of regulation play, while Garo Yepremian kicked a thirty-seven-yarder after twenty-two minutes and forty seconds of sudden death. . . ."

That's about it.

The Armenian whipped the Norwegian in their private showdown, and his team happened to be carried to its greatest victory as a consequence.

Since the Colts dispatched Cleveland, as expected, the next day, Miami now would entertain Baltimore in the Orange Bowl Stadium on January 2.

A few hours before the Dolphins came home from Kansas City on Christmas night, Bob Devaney landed in Miami with his undefeated national collegiate champions, the Nebraska Cornhuskers, to get ready for their Orange Bowl Classic meeting with Alabama's undefeated Crimson Tide on the approaching Saturday night. Alabama would arrive on December 26.

Thus began the wildest, craziest week of emotionally charged football rivalries any city ever offered. With Nebraska ranked No. 1 all season and Alabama ranked No. 2 after its smashing defeat of Auburn on November 27, the collegiate national title was at stake less than eighteen hours prior to Miami's first AFC title game . . . all in the same stadium and with the largest number of reporters ever seen in town, save for a Super Bowl game or two.

To begin the week, on Monday night, the Mahi Shrine's North-South College All-Star game began at nine o'clock, mostly for a national television audience. . . . The next night and on Thursday night, the National Intercollegiate Soccer Championships were held in the stadium in the first such event sponsored by the Orange Bowl Committee. Howard University would win the soccer title, with dramatic victories over Harvard and St. Louis Universities.

These games by college athletes are mentioned here for a reason pertinent to our story of the Dolphins. Their presence made it almost impossible for Colts' fans or Dolphins' fans who needed hotel accommodations or drive-yourself cars, etc., to get them. Followers of Nebraska and Alabama long since had wiped out the supply. Another factor that soon added to the tension was the refusal of NFL Commissioner Pete Rozelle to lift the television blackout of the pro game on January 2, forcing those South Floridians with fierce devotion to the Dolphins but with no game tickets to travel to Naples or further for a view of the television presentation.

Which brings us to the most volatile of all the pressures in that unbelievable week: the struggle by Dolphins' season-ticket holders to purchase tickets for the Colts-Dolphins game.

Space forbids an accounting of all that happened or of even a sample of the comments by those who kept the faith and got the tickets. Joe Robbie later admitted that his plan for distribution was faulty; however, it must be said for Robbie and the Dolphins that they tried mightily to give the season-ticket holders (some thirteen thousand individuals purchased forty-seven thousand tickets for the season) a break on the available ducats for the title battle.

Briefly, the plan was for each season-ticket holder to have access to as many tickets as he had purchased for the season, plus

50 percent extra if he wished. Thus, a citizen purchasing four season books could buy six title-game tickets . . . or he didn't have to buy any, but no such animal was found.

Expecting a steady flow of purchasers, the Dolphins sent out a letter to each season book holder, inviting him to come to a designated window at the stadium on Monday, Tuesday, or Wednesday and buy his usual seats, plus the extras noted on the letter.

Instead of a steady flow, however, it seemed that every one of the eligible season book holders was in line long before the first window was opened on Monday morning, December 27. It was an unbelievable mass of people, soon engaged in a press and tangle that erupted into fights and bitter outcries against the Dolphins' management—although it is quite possible that the same management's determination to make available extra tickets to those in line caused most of the aggravating delays for purchasers.

On Tuesday, when six windows at the stadium were available rather than Monday's three, the lines were even thicker and tempers shorter—some had been in line for most of thirty-six hours—and it was not until the Wednesday sales, with eight windows working out of a central room, that the end finally was in sight. On Thursday, the last of the sufferers was heeded and the last tickets disposed of, but the wounds in egos were raw and bleeding. In retrospect, psychologists might deduce that at least some of the sturdy thousands who sweated and swore in the lines got a spiritual charge out of their suffering . . . it gave them some identity with the hardy football players they were trying to see perform with the tickets they sought with so much determination and fortitude.

However, it did the club's relations with its patrons little good.

With Baltimore's crushing 20–3 victory over Cleveland on the day after Miami's monumental decision over Kansas City, the sixth meeting in two years between the bitter rivals was automatic. Miami, winner of three of the five previous clashes, would be the host—certainly no small advantage.

To avoid what was termed the "lack of acclimatization" when they were bested in Miami earlier, 17–14, the Colts moved into Tampa early in the week. This lent weight to reports already flying thickly that the club would move to Tampa from Baltimore permanently, unless spectacular progress were made in the seeming stalemate between Carroll Rosenbloom and city fathers who had dragged their feet in prior commitments on stadium facilities in Baltimore. (In early January, Commissioner Rozelle said the franchise would not move.)

But all such conjecture was just that. The Colts had no part in the gossip, for they had a big worry: the unsatisfactory physical condition of their splendid running back, Norm Bulaich, who now had a severely pulled hamstring to go with the bad wheel that had bothered him all fall. Before Sunday's game, Norm was taken off the Colts' roster and even the tough old warhorse, Tom Matte, was slowed by his wounds. The Baltimore attack was not itself, although the stubby Don Nottingham had done very well, indeed, against Cleveland and had the confidence of his colleagues.

Bubba Smith had one of his great days against the Browns and led the Colts' defense as it smashed quarterback Bill Nelsen four times and intercepted three passes, in addition to blocking two field-goal tries—a brutal display.

Miamians discovered that Jake Scott had played the whole first-round game—after the first two Kansas City formations—with a broken hand. But Jake didn't make much of it and gave no thought to laying out of the big one. Griese's shoulder had permitted him to have one of his great performances against the Chiefs—twenty completions in thirty-five passes for 263 yards, one TD, and two interceptions.

Better even than his mechanical performance was his hold on the tactical situation. Bob's play calls were consistently impressive, despite the physical problem of getting around or through or over football's fastest defensive heavyweights. His call on Csonka for the twenty-nine-yard, roll-trap play that set up Yepremian's field goal was the ultimate move for the quarterback, but there were others in the great battle. Now, for Baltimore, he knew the Colts and they knew him, and he was playing with a different set of building blocks.

Suddenly, attention reached the Dolphins that they never had known before.

While his constituents thirsted for his blood outside the Orange Bowl Stadium—the scheduled events noted previously made it impossible for the championship game tickets to be distributed as the Dolphins wished—Joe Robbie was acclaimed "Man of the Year" by *Football Weekly*. It's the kind of honor Robbie responds to and enjoys. But he had to accept the testimonial in the quiet of his office. Had he done so at the big game on Sunday, the poor man would have been strung up on a light tower.

Attention to individual players poured in from everywhere, with seven Dolphins—Warfield, Griese, Little, Csonka, Stanfill, Scott, and Morris (for kick returning)—already named to the AFC's Pro Bowl team. After the Baltimore game, Griese would be given the most coveted of all honors in pro football: the Jim Thorpe Award, with the voting done exclusively by league player representatives and team captains, recognizing him as the NFL's top player—a supreme victory for Bob.

Yepremian's leadership of the NFL in scoring with 117 points, and his consistent effectiveness—he scored at least one field goal in all fourteen Dolphins games—brought him the "Golden Toe Award," proffered by an opportunist shoe manufacturer . . . and so it went.

As the swirl of activity reached its peak with the weekend football games, Nebraska dealt Bear Bryant and his Alabama team a devastating 38–6 drubbing on Saturday night to retain the national collegiate championship. The jammed house for the Orange Bowl Classic was amazed at the ease with which Nebraska's superb battalions destroyed a team Bryant had admitted might be the best he ever produced at Tuscaloosa. Certainly Nebraska proved to be one of the best of modern college teams, anywhere.

Within minutes after that surprising development, stadium manager Al Rubio had double work crews cleaning up the debris, which included raincoats and other gear designed to fight the elements. Heavy rain that night in the early hours gave way to a light spray before the pros took the field for a four-thirty kickoff in the afternoon. This late beginning was set by Commissioner Rozelle so that the NFC championship game—Dallas vs. San Francisco—could be on and off the CBS Television Network before the AFC's show came from the Orange Bowl on NBC. The previous winter, the AFC game had been played first.

Long one of the nation's football centers, Miami has never known such excitement as was felt by its veterans of the Ticket Rebellion when their heroes took the field against the detested Colts.

THE SECOND ROUND . . .

THE AFC CHAMPIONSHIP GAME: DOLPHINS 21, COLTS 0

In their first two games, the Colts had scored two touchdowns in each and, in the second, strangled the Dolphins' offense except for Yepremian's field goal. Another boot by Garo had given the Miami club the victory in the first match, 17–14. In each of their six encounters since Shula appeared in Miami, kicking—the over-all kicking game—was a prominent feature.

In the championship game, it was vital to Miami's defense, which kept Johnny Unitas and friends out of the end zone and Jim O'Brien out of the goal posts for the first time since 1965, when the Chicago Bears skunked them, 13–0, with Shula the Baltimore coach. That was ninety-seven games in the past when the Colts—purple from frustration at every hand—trudged into their dressing room in the Orange Bowl while tornadoes of sound hailed the Dolphins as conference champions for the first time. It was a bitter moment for Unitas, the aged warrior who must see in young Griese flashes of himself in a former time.

For a while, however, there was no hint that the attacks of the Colts would be slowed, much less stopped, for long.

The Dolphins moved out to their thirty-eight after the initial kickoff, halted, and Seiple lofted the first of his six kicks; it was in his customary pattern—high and slow, perfect for his people to get down and nail the return specialist. In this case, Rick Volk got it back on what amounted to a long runback, six yards, before Langer popped him. Volk had a total of twenty yards on the five punts he handled that climactic day, and Seiple had a right to be satisfied.

Don McCauley, a good rookie running back, got five, and then caught a Unitas pass for sixteen down the middle, and it looked like Unitas might be building up for another precision display comparable to the beauties he offered in Baltimore but—on his second try for a third-down conversion, for two yards at the Miami forty-seven—John sent Nottingham over guard and he was batted back.

Baltimore's punt resulted in a touchback, and Kiick notched five yards on the first down.

On the second, Griese faked handoffs to Csonka and Kiick on a play-action rollout and Rex Kern suckered on their moves; Volk started away from the sideline on the zone rotation when suddenly he and Kern realized simultaneously that they had been had—Paul Warfield was flying between and then beyond them at a dead run, after slanting out in front of the play-action maneuvers of Miami's backs . . . Paul caught Griese's perfect pass without breaking stride and continued into the end zone, completing a seventy-five-yard touchdown strike that could not have been executed more perfectly on the practice field at Biscayne College.

The perfection of the execution left the press box occupants stunned. Most of these citizens see a lot of football through the course of a pro season and assume postures of bored indulgence when a perennial champion, in the Baltimore mold, is working over a victim in championship competition. Griese's call and throw, supplemented by Warfield's superb reception, caught them in mid-grumble. From that moment forward, they silently absorbed the strange things that were happening out there on the grubby rug of the Orange Bowl. . . .

The first quarter died with O'Brien missing a forty-eight-yard field goal when it was five yards short. Late in the second period, the fellow who had edged Dallas, 16–14, to win the Super Bowl game on the same grounds the winter before was to fail once more—this time because the catlike Lloyd Mumphord swept in from Miami's right side and blocked the thirty-five-yard attempt.

One more time in this game, the Colts were within easy field-goal range, but Coach Don McCafferty chose instead to try to keep a march going. This was early in the second period, the one time Unitas got a substantial drive going and advanced from his own twenty to the Miami nine-yard line, making four first downs along the way, two of them on third-down conversions.

Doug Swift pounded Nottingham down at the nine on a draw play, two yards short of a new series, and the human fireplug got the call to try once more. This time, Buoniconti and Bob Heinz didn't give him a chance, and Miami took over . . . a play call of debatable merit, of course, since Baltimore trailed by only one touchdown at the moment, and the three points would have been as certain as any field goal can be before it's tried.

However . . .

The Dolphins took their seven points into the half and, after a snap of the ball in the third period, got seven more in a manner even more spectacular than Warfield's great pass reception.

Unitas was throwing deep, straight downfield from his own nineteen and toward Ed Hinton, when the ball was tipped by Curtis Johnson a fraction of a second before Ed could catch it. . . . Bounding upward and to one side, the ball came down in the arms of Dick Anderson, and the onetime Colorado All-American halfback knew what to do with it.

Wheeling around toward his left, Anderson had the benefit of a ferocious block by Jake Scott on Tom Mitchell as he headed for the right sideline and—behind blocks you wouldn't believe— suddenly veered left and careened along the south sideline. On his final switchback, Unitas was wiped out, setting Dick free at about the ten-yard line of Baltimore, and he galloped on in for the touchdown from there. A moment later, the joyous Scott leaped upon his colleagues as the stadium was a bedlam of sound.

At least six total blocks were laid by Dolphins on that runback by men supposed to be defensive specialists!

Mike Kolen, Swift, Heinz, Tim Foley—and all the others save Buoniconti—had some part of the action. Nick admitted later that he was toddling around behind Nottingham, trying to get bore-sighted on the fireplug man when one of Anderson's cuts

sent Nottingham flying in a new direction, so the veteran linebacker gave up and just watched the fun.

For Miamians, it was hilarious. For Baltimore's people, it was
devastating: A noticeable shift in emphasis followed Anderson's
coup, and Baltimore never was in it after that, with a Colts' move
from their own twenty to Miami's forty-three the only offense. And
even this was garroted by Scott, who intercepted another Unitas
pitch toward Hinton as the third period died.

The Colts only had the ball twice in the fourth period and
did little with it then, while another perfect pass from Griese to
Warfield—the second of Paul's two catches for the day—put
Miami at the Baltimore five.

On the first down here, Csonka blew through right guard and
on over for the touchdown, and there was no more spark in the
Colts.

Analyzing this final triumph that brought their first conference
championship, the Dolphins had to give their defensive line
enormous credit. Unlike the game in Baltimore, the pit crew dev-
iled Unitas all day and Heinz decked the old boy twice, while
Miami's line gave Griese time, although Bubba sacked him once.

The astounding finish of their American Football Conference
play—the almost interminable uphill fight that won in Kansas
City, the 21–0 squelch of Baltimore—stunned the Dolphins' fans
even more than it did the players . . . a pair of conquests of
comparable magnitude had never been experienced before by players or rooters, and the Dallas Cowboys, in contrast, seemed far
away.

Besides, there were two weeks for building up to that.

They would be used by the Shula staff to break apart statistics,
films, and all the other sources that might give a hint how the
Doomsday Defense might be cracked or circumvented. President
Nixon called Shula to suggest that Griese throw to Warfield on a
deep slant pattern! While Dallas had finally settled on a quarterback—Roger Staubach was named by Coach Tom Landry after
the first seven games, in which Staubach alternated with Craig
Morton for a 4–3 record to that point—continued troubles with

the moody Duane Thomas indicated that the offensive Cowboys might have problems. The Dolphins believed they could overcome the perennial No. 2s of the NFC (Dallas had lost the wretchedly played Super Bowl V to Baltimore in the last five seconds in early 1971) if the Miami attack group could control the ball at least a simple majority of the time. Doing so against the veteran Dallas defenders seemed the key to the game in New Orleans, as, indeed, it proved to be when the time came to test the theory.

The participating teams were allowed ten thousand tickets each by the NFL commissioner's office, and—in what seemed a natural sequence to their earlier embarrassments—the Dolphins got a lot more static from fans over the way these were dispensed. After an overnight stay in the Orange Bowl parking lot for many who came to Gates 8 or 14, available tickets were gone in a couple of hours. The howls were loud and sometimes ugly; an impromptu group of protesters went to the Dolphins' downtown office and bellowed some, but the tickets were gone. It was a perhaps predictable last spasm of devoted fans who simply couldn't believe they were to be denied. . . . But the tickets were sold and not stored, for there was not a vacant seat in Tulane Stadium (the Sugar Bowl) when a record mob of 81,035 sat through a near-freezing wind to watch the game.

Airlines added at least fifty extra sections to accommodate Miamians going to New Orleans, and others went by car or private aircraft—a procession of the faithful that, in another time, could have been spurred only by religious zeal. Now it was part and parcel of the Dolphins' story, one of sport's loudest chapters.

Shula was determined to reduce distractions that might interfere with his players' rest and concentration on the enormous job at hand. But the commissioner's office ordered both teams to appear in New Orleans on the Sunday preceding the game of January 16. The Dolphins arrived early that evening (January 9) and were housed in the Fontainebleau Motel, a downtown New Orleans establishment ideal for the purposes of the team and the reporters who seethed in every corridor. Organized by Harold Rosenthal, public relations chief of the AFC working under Don

Weiss, PR boss of the NFL, two press conferences—one by Shula, another by five different players—were held each morning. Otherwise, the "picture day" held on Monday was supposed to suffice. However, the players cooperated with reporters who weren't too demanding as the week wore on.

As a direct result of the Baltimore experience in Super Bowl III, wives and families of the players were not allowed to join their husbands in New Orleans until a quiet dinner for the whole group on the night before the game, held at a suburban restaurant, Masson's. After that the players went back to their bachelor quarters and the families to another hotel. They wouldn't see each other until the Cowboys had done their foul deed. . . .

At Fort Lauderdale, getting ready for their Super Bowl loss (16–7) to the Jets on January 12, 1969, Shula allowed Colts' families to accompany the players, and the scene was a madhouse of reporters collaring everyone in sight to comment upon the brazen remarks of Joe Namath. Constant inquiries by reporters compounded Namath's boyish enthusiasm into the gospel from some sort of oracle, with results far more important than one might expect.

It was Shula's intention to bring his club into the New Orleans game in a relaxed—not to say happy—mood. He and Tom Landry allowed the players of both squads to have the Sunday and Monday nights prior to their game without bedcheck. The Dolphins meandered around the French Quarter and had a few beers, but there was no report of excessive relaxation. As always, the specter of Shula's displeasure perhaps had its influence, but this assembly of players also possesses a tremendous loyalty to a common goal of excellence. This was no moment for a stupid mistake in behavior.

However, an event that occurred a thousand miles away—in Miami—broke at least some of the concentration Shula was trying to maintain . . . including his own.

In an interview, George Wilson, Shula's predecessor and onetime boss (with Detroit) let his bitterness overrun his good judgment and he told Charlie Nobles of the Miami *News:* "I've been silent too long. . . . Joe Robbie fired me just when the team was ready to go. . . . As far as I'm concerned he [Shula] took over a ready-made team. Joe Doakes could have coached that team. . . . You go over the roster and you'll see most of the guys who are doing the playing were committed to the Dolphins before Shula ever got here."

Wilson also said—as he earlier had told the author—that he was instrumental in Shula getting the Baltimore head job and "I practically wrote his contract for him. . . . Carroll Rosenbloom wanted me to take the job and I had twelve meetings with him about it. But I got him to take Shula. . . ."

There was more in this vein, but the damaging part was in the unfortunate reference to the now extinct cartoon character, Joe Doakes, who might have done as well with the Dolphins as has Shula. Any fairly competent observer of football for a time knows better than this, much better. Shula not only reformed the character of the squad through changing individuals—only nineteen of the forty-man Dolphins' 1969 squad reached Super Bowl VI— but added a sense of sacrifice and organization not always apparent when Wilson ran things.

The crack angered Shula. His relations with Wilson prior to the succession were warm, but the night Wilson was told by Joe Robbie that Shula would succeed him made the difference. We shall not labor the point now—it is noted elsewhere in this report—but the incident on Tuesday before the playing of Super Bowl VI on Sunday was a disturbing factor.

There can be no doubt that the unfortunate timing of the blast by Wilson injured his own image in the esteem of Dolphins' fans more than it injured their opinion of Shula. The team's record of 20–7–1 in regular-season play and 2–2 against the toughest of competition in postseason playoffs for Shula's two years in Miami speaks for itself—and for Shula.

As the week progressed in New Orleans, however, the attention of that city turned toward its visitors and the traffic building up. It was said that eight hundred private aircraft landed before the kickoff, there wasn't a drive-yourself automobile available for three hundred miles, and all who went to New Orleans for the occasion can attest to the logjam of hopefuls at every restaurant entrance in the French Quarter.

On Saturday, a weather front brought in cold winds of more than twenty-five miles per hour and, that night, the temperature sank to the twenties. Fortunately, the day of the game was sparklingly clear and the wind dropped; although still a factor, it was only nine miles per hour and out of the north at the kickoff.

The 39-degree temperature had Dolphins' fans and Dallas followers bundled and blanketed as they crowded into the huge saucer; thoughtful ones had arrived by bus, for there are few parking places at the old stadium and these were taken hours before football's most remarkable team took on the tough old boys who had been to the well so often and never had won the National Football League championship.

The day before the game, Florida Governor Reubin Askew quoted from the Third Book of Daniel, verse thirteen, as he spoke at the West Palm Beach prayer breakfast: "You Dolphins and all water creatures, bless the Lord and exalt him above all, forever."

"Nowhere," said the governor, "do I find mention of Cowboys. . . ."

When the Miami club took the field from the south-end dressing room of the Sugar Bowl, acres of white handerchiefs waved and swayed in the bright sun, and they knew they were not alone.

14

The Super Bowl Game:
Cowboys 24, Dolphins 3

When Nick Buoniconti went against form and won the toss, the Dolphins were at their high point of the day. After that, Dallas had all the options.

> *We're the kind of club that attacks the other team. . . . We didn't have it in New Orleans, we just weren't aggressive. . . . We were as well prepared for that game as you can be for football. . . . It's a different kind of week . . . unreal. . . . It was almost like a comedy, with people bothering you for tickets and hotel rooms and the press asking the same questions, over and over and over. . . . It's not the players' week—it's the commissioner's week but the players are the ones bothered.*
> *—Buoniconti*

Mercury Morris—who was to finish his afternoon with a bitter rundown for reporters of his frustrations as the "third back" in the three-back concept Shula seeks—brought Mike Clark's kickoff twenty yards to the Miami twenty-six to open proceedings.

Shula always calls the plays in the first Miami series of downs, and his first one wasn't in character: Griese pitched toward Howard Twilley in the short middle, where Lee Roy Jordan's leap enabled him to bat it aside. Twilley was open enough, but Jordan must have jumped six feet straight up.

Kiick swept left end for seven, but Dave Edwards cracked him for no gain on the other side and Seiple punted forty-five yards—his forty-yard average in five tries wasn't too impressive, but Larry never has been more accurate or effective than he was that day—and Mumphord dropped Bob Hayes for a loss of one on the return . . . an auspicious beginning for the special troops.

Roger Staubach opened with a pass—to Bob Hayes, a short one in the flat off to the right—for five yards. And the uncommunicative Duane Thomas made his intentions loud and clear when he tore off eight yards at his own left tackle before Mike Kolen drilled him. Staubach, the former Navy officer, now tried to throw deep on a changeup maneuver, but Fernandez chased and decked him for the first of two Miami sacks for the day. This one cost Dallas six yards. And Staubach was in trouble immediately when the next play started; his receivers covered, the renowned scrambler tried to do his thing, but Jim Riley hacked him down after only a yard; when Staubach did get time to throw, he slung it over Lance Alworth's head, and Dallas had to kick.

Ron Widby's effort was a real clinker, only twenty-nine yards' worth, and a teammate, Cliff Harris, saved it a worse fate when he downed it at the Miami forty-two. Though only five minutes had been used on the clock, the Dolphins were in their most promising posture of the whole bitter afternoon at this moment. It passed quickly.

Larry Csonka, working on his short-side specialty, careened twelve yards behind Larry Little around the right flank, and it looked like the Cowboys might be had by the customary Dolphin moves. Then Csonka tried to take a handoff from Griese while looking up to see what was happening to Lee Roy Jordan and Chuck Howley, two Cowboys with vicious tackling habits, and missed the transfer. The ball, low on his left thigh, was joggled out of Csonka's hand by his own knee and fell to the Poly-Turf, where Howley leaped upon it. Dallas had possession at its own forty-eight.

Instead of an assault from midfield, the Dolphins had to regroup for defense, and they never regained the momentum that seemed theirs before the disastrous fumble. This cannot be counted the "turning point" reporters like to refer to, but it certainly was a grievous mistake that must be laid to both Griese and Csonka. They collaborated perfectly on every handoff of the great season until that miserable instant.

Dallas, considerably heartened by Howley's fetch of the ball, fought now to keep the Dolphins' Front Four from beating a tattoo on Staubach's rib cage.

This storybook character, on a third-down scramble and trying for three yards, was pursued hotly from the rear but was stopped only when Bob Heinz got a shoulder into him four yards downfield. This golden opportunity was lost and cost the Dolphins a chunk, for it signaled the pattern of things to come . . . not that Staubach became a running threat, but it seemed that everybody else from central Texas did.

Walt Garrison's powerful pair of dashes now cost Miami another eighteen yards, and the Cowboys were at the Dolphins' twenty-three. Staubach slid back to pass deep but Riley pursued and bulldogged him down, a thirteen-yard loss that seemed vastly important at the time. But it wasn't. Staubach whipped a pass to Hayes down the middle for eighteen yards and then another to Thomas that carried to the seven and a first down. Only at the two was Miami really contentious—the Dolphins' Anderson racked Thomas for no gain on a third-down screen, but Clark got a field goal to give Dallas first blood.

The Miamians were fortunate to get out of that headlong attack with only three points against them. But the observer got an impression of Cowboy confidence no matter what the Dolphins might do to shake up the situation. It was a completely justified emotion, as events proved time and again in the remaining forty-six minutes.

Witness what happened after Hubert Ginn hauled the kickoff back to the Miami thirty-seven, where Mel Renfro brought him down.

Cornell Green dropped Kiick after one yard, and Renfro got an arm between Warfield and a Griese pass down the middle—this was the one President Nixon told Don Shula he figured would work against the Cowboys; and then came the most depressing play since Ingrid Bergman ran off to an island with that fat Italian director so long ago.

It started with Miami at its own thirty-eight and Griese looking downfield for Warfield or Twilley. It finished with the 260 pounds of Bob Lilly grinding the 190 pounds of Griese into the ersatz grass, twenty-nine yards back downfield, almost under the goal posts. The great tackle—an All-Pro long before Griese finished Purdue—didn't give the NFL's highest-rated individual player time to even raise his arm to shed the ball. With Larry Cole, Lilly piled through the Dolphins' line and then beat Cole to the victim. It was a magnificent demonstration of a superb veteran at his best, but the artistry of it was lost on the Dolphins, who were deep in a hole now as the first quarter ended.

In the first fifteen minutes, Miami had the ball two minutes, twenty-five seconds, and did nothing with it whatever.

Early in the second period, however, they got two whole first downs in sequence and had something going. Kiick gained eleven yards in two formations for the first one, and a Griese throw to Twilley got another twenty but, after a line try failed, Warfield was overthrown and a toss to Kiick got only four yards when seven were needed—a typical Dolphin ploy that chilly afternoon.

Yepremian found the forty-nine yards too long for his newly gilded No. 7, and a couple of punts were swapped before anything much happened.

When something did, it happened for Dallas.

The inscrutable Thomas opened with a five-yard shot at right guard and the first Cowboys' drive was on, moving from their own twenty-four to a touchdown on eleven formations, with all three of the Texas running backs contributing heavily as the Miami line cracked. But Staubach got his big move and then the touchdown with passes to Lance Alworth, the famous "Bambi" of earlier times in San Diego and a fellow who never had a bum day against the Dolphins. He took a seven-yard pass for the touchdown, deep in the end zone.

That seventy-six-yard drive produced a 10–0 count, and only a minute, twenty seconds were left on the clock.

The game's first penalty (there were only three) gave Dallas a five-yard setback and another kickoff, after which Griese opened from his thirty-two with passes to Warfield and Kiick that reached the forty-eight. After a pass to Mandich failed, Warfield caught another to reach the Dallas twenty-four.

With fourteen seconds left, Griese went to Warfield again, but the omnipresent Herb Adderley got a fingernail on it and the ball was deflected just enough to throw off Warfield's timing. The ball hit Paul in the face mask and fell to the ground, and there wasn't enough clock left to take further chances. So Garo came on and kicked a field goal.

It was the only scratch the Dolphins could manage on the steely Dallas defense in the first half, although they were considerably encouraged by the success of that late rally.

"We only had the ball twenty times to thirty-five for Dallas in the first two quarters," Shula mused later, "but we felt the issue would be decided in the third period. If we could hold them their first time with the football then, we had a chance to get their heads down and keep them there. . . ."

The wish was not father to the deed, however.

The Cowboys came out and blew the Dolphins in all directions, while shielding off Buoniconti or fouling up his usually instantaneous recovery when Nick committed himself quickly to a Dallas running play. Tom Landry had said before the game that the Cowboys could beat the Dolphins' defense if they could neutralize Buoniconti and his mercurial quickness. They did their job so well that Nick was sent into worlds far beyond the Sugar Bowl. After a particularly savage rap from Blaine Nye late in the third quarter, Nick was on his feet but not his rocker. Leaving the field later, he asked if the score was still 10–3 . . . he was fourteen points behind. Bob Matheson finished the day in Nick's place.

It took the Cowboys only eight plays to move from their twenty-nine to their second touchdown after receiving the kickoff that opened the third period. And this, in the later evaluation by Shula, was the climactic event of the total disaster—the clincher or, as advertised, the turning point.

It looked so very easy, too, with Staubach turning a third-and-three problem into a twelve-yard gain with a pass to Calvin Hill, whose bad knee seemed sound enough. In two efforts, Thomas tore off for another thirty yards and Bob Hayes reversed for sixteen. No other team had so whipsawed Shula's ground defense since he came to Miami.

Thomas took a pitchout for the last three yards and the touchdown that made the score 17–3 as tall men with big belt buckles bellowed and waved their bright blue cowboy hats in the stands. White was for funerals only, it seemed. Dallas controlled the ball for twenty plays in that quarter, Miami for ten.

As the fourth period opened, however, Griese passed to Warfield for a first down at the Miami forty-three. And something may have come of this but, on third down, Chuck Howley threw himself at Twilley, yet had time to leap up and intercept a throw toward Kiick from Griese. It was an extraordinary piece of work for the 225-pounder, topped off with a pell-mell run down the sideline for forty-one yards, to the Miami nine.

On third down, Staubach hit Mike Ditka with a touchdown pass in the far right end zone, and the final count of 24–3 was established with Mike Clark's conversion.

However, there was one more piece of business that left a poor impression on the Dolphins and their followers.

This occurred during a Dallas drive with slightly more than two minutes remaining.

Dan Reeves, holding for what appeared to be another field-goal try by Clark at the Miami twenty-seven, picked up the ball and ran for a first down at the thirteen—a petty maneuver, in Dolphins' eyes, especially when Coach Landry explained later that he "never can be sure of a game until the last whistle." But if he wasn't sure of it, he was alone in the crowded stadium.

Incidentally, that attack ended when Calvin Hill leaped over his own left guard—perhaps to test his bum knee—and dropped the ball. Fernandez fell on it, ninety-six yards away from a Miami touchdown.

It might as well have been ninety-six miles.

SUPER BOWL GAME

TEAM STATISTICS

	DALLAS	MIAMI
Total First Downs	23	10
First downs rushing	15	3
First downs passing	8	7
Total Offensive Yardage	352	185
Total No. Offensive Plays (inc. times thrown passing)	69	54
Average gain per offensive play	5.1	4.2
Net Rushing Yardage	252	80
Total rushing plays	48	20
Average gain per rushing play	5.3	4.0
Net Passing Yardage	100	105
Gross yards gained passing	119	134
Times thrown and yards lost attempting to pass	2–19	1–29
Passes attempted—completed— had intercepted	19–12–0	23–12–1
Average gain per pass play (inc. times thrown passing)	4.8	4.4
Punts—Number and Average	5–37.2	5–40.0
Had blocked	0	0
Fumbles—Number and Lost	1–1	2–2
Penalties—Number and Yards	3–15	0–0
Total Return Yardage	76	143
No. and yards, punts returns	1–1	1–21
No. and yards, kickoff returns	2–34	5–122
No. and yards, interception returns	1–41	0–0

INDIVIDUAL STATISTICS

DOLPHINS
Rushing

	ATT.	YDS.	AVG.	LONG
Kiick	10	40	4.0	9
Csonka	9	40	4.4	12
Griese	1	0	0.0	0

Passing

	ATT.	COMP.	YDS.	TD	INTC.
Griese	23	12	134	0	1

Receiving

	NO.	YDS.	TD	LONG
Warfield	4	39	0	23
Twilley	1	20	0	20
Fleming	1	27	0	27
Kiick	3	21	0	11
Mandich	1	9	0	9
Csonka	2	18	0	16

Punting

	NO.	YDS.	AVG.	LONG
Seiple	5	200	40.0	45

Punt Returns

	NO.	YDS.
Scott	1	21

Kickoff Returns

	NO.	YDS.	LONG
Morris	4	90	37
Ginn	1	32	32

COWBOYS

Rushing

	ATT.	YDS.	AVG.	LONG
Thomas	19	95	5.0	23
Hill	7	25	3.6	13
Garrison	14	74	5.3	17
Staubach	5	18	3.6	5
Hayes	1	16	16.0	16
Reeves	1	7	7.0	7
Ditka	1	17	17.0	17

Passing

	ATT.	COMP.	YDS.	TD	INTC.
Staubach	19	12	119	2	0

Receiving

	NO.	YDS.	TD	LONG
Hayes	2	23	0	18
Alworth	2	28	1	21
Ditka	2	28	1	21
Thomas	3	17	0	11
Garrison	2	11	0	7
Hill	1	12	0	12

Punting

	NO.	YDS.	AVG.	LONG
Widby	5	186	37.2	47

Punt Returns

	NO.	YDS.
Hayes	1	—1

Kickoff Returns

	NO.	YDS.	LONG
Waters	1	11	11
Thomas	1	23	23

Interceptions

	NO.	YDS.	LONG
Howley	1	41	41

SUPER BOWL RECORDS BROKEN BY DALLAS AND MIAMI

INDIVIDUAL RECORD SET

Most Super Bowl appearances: Herb Adderley, 4 (Green Bay, 2; Dallas, 2)

TEAM RECORDS SET

Most first downs, one team: Dallas, 23
Most first downs rushing, one team: Dallas, 15
Most first downs rushing, both teams: 18 (Dallas, 15; Miami, 3)
Fewest touchdowns, one team: Miami, 0
Fewest total yards gained, one team: Miami, 185
Most rushing attempts, one team: Dallas, 48
Most rushing attempts, both teams: 68 (Dallas, 48; Miami, 20)
Most yards rushing, one team: Dallas, 252
Most yards rushing, both teams: 332 (Dallas, 252; Miami, 80)
Fewest touchdowns rushing, one team: Miami, 0
Fewest passes attempted, both teams: 42 (Dallas, 19; Miami, 23)
Fewest net yards passing, one team: Dallas, 100
Fewest net yards passing, both teams: 205 (Dallas, 100; Miami, 105)
Fewest punt returns, both teams: 2 (Dallas, 1; Miami, 1)
Fewest punt return yards, one team: Dallas, —1

INDIVIDUAL RECORDS TIED

Most kickoff returns: Mercury Morris, Miami: 4.
Most kickoff-return yards: Mercury Morris, Miami: 90
Highest kickoff-return average: Mercury Morris, Miami: 22.5

TEAM RECORDS TIED

Fewest touchdowns rushing: 1 (Dallas, 1; Miami, 0)
Most touchdowns passing, one team: Dallas, 2
Fewest punt returns, one team: 1 (Dallas and Miami)

15

After the Crash

The bitter taste still lingers. It is even stronger in the mouths of the Dolphins' top players now than it was on that cold night in New Orleans when they stumbled from the dressing room in the archaic old pile that is the Sugar Bowl and headed downtown.

Most seemed to snap out of it pretty well then. Howard Twilley was an exception. His square face was a mask of frustration as the party for the players at the Royal Orleans, with the club as host, swelled far beyond the list of those actually invited. Among these invited, Twilley's parents were there—most of the players' families were represented in one way or another—and they took the disappointment far better than the players. Shula moved around in the company and Joe Robbie, his attention constantly called from one minor emergency to another, still showed the shock of the scalding defeat.

What ate into Shula's insides was the way Dallas controlled the ball in the third period and, entirely on the ground, ripped the Dolphins apart. He knew his preparation was sound—otherwise, the first half would have been poor—and Dallas pulled no tactical surprises. But the Cowboys had converted the deadly efficiency of Nick Buoniconti—at least to some extent—to their own advantage.

Nick moves quickly when he senses the point of attack. "That characteristic gets me hit a lot, but it gives me an advantage many times," says the undersized linebacker. At New Orleans, the Cowboys—noticeably in the third period—started wide as if going off tackle or on a sweep and then the carrier, usually Duane Thomas, cut sharply back against the flow and usually got huge chunks of yardage.

Shula was to find upon examination of the movies that the Dallas center or a guard—immediately when Nick made his move—moved to screen him off from the runner . . . and Nick was at least somewhat off balance as a result. "The defensive end or tackle wasn't pursuing the way we wanted him to in almost every case and, when the cutback came, if one man was out of position (for us) there would be a gap. . . . This happened several times," according to Shula. It was a consistently sound move for Dallas, which executed almost without flaw from the first period to just before the game's end, when Hill fumbled. The combination of excellent planning and brilliant execution finally allowed Dallas to win an NFL championship, after six previous chances.

The Dolphins fell short in their only chance, and it was no less painful than the experiences of the Cowboys in years past.

Countless excuses were made for them, but Shula—and most of the players—refused to whimper or play the crybaby. They and their followers knew they had not played their best game in the defeat, but they had played better than their best against Kansas City and earlier, against Pittsburgh, when eighteen points behind . . . and the 21–0 victory over Baltimore, made with three big plays, couldn't be sweeter. . . and the eighty-five hundred dollars for winning over the Colts and the seventy-five hundred dollars for losing to the Cowboys was proof enough that what they had done earlier was worthwhile. For the Kansas City game, each Dolphin received one-fourteenth (one day's pay from the regular season) of his yearly salary.

There were some sour notes, of course. When Mercury Morris sat for many minutes in the dressing room, unloading to reporters how he felt about being kept on the sideline "when we planned to run wide on them but weren't doing it." Shula was irritated. He told newsmen he felt players "should come to me if they have a complaint about the way they are handled. After that, and we can't come to an agreement, then the player can say whatever he wants, to whomever he wants—I have no objection to what a ballplayer says. I wouldn't want a ballplayer who was happy on the bench.

"I respect Merc for wanting to play and, hopefully, we can work him into our offense a little more this next year and continue to progress and move along. We do need his outside speed," Shula admits. "Hubert Ginn is another possibility. We'll find out what Ginn can do, early in the preseason. . . ."

Meanwhile, there was the college draft to consider.

The Dolphins only had three rookies on their 1971 roster—linebacker Dale Farley, wideout Otto Stowe, and defensive end Vern Den Herder—and yet one of the youngest squads in the NFL. Newcomers would have to be what Shula wanted—big, strong, and devoted to tearing people.

Shula's views are uncomplicated by sentiment when it comes to selecting his first ranks.

"Stowe is a prospect and we started him early in the season but went back to Twilley, who gives you that good day-in, day-out performance. I think Otto is good enough to be a No. 1," the coach tips his thoughts of the future. "Hopefully, Stowe will challenge for that this year (1972).

"Farley is going to be on the spot in training camp. He'll be given the opportunity to prove himself. If he does, fine—we'll have a young, strong football player. If he doesn't, we'll look for somebody else. In Den Herder, we have a young prospect we think will make a defensive lineman. . . . He's going to be a lot bigger and a lot stronger and he's a hard worker and very intelligent. . . . He could be a pretty good defensive lineman in the years to come.

"But you have to bring a lot of young people into your organization. We did that in 1970 and, in 1971, we worked with those people to get them to play better than they did the year before. They did, too, and we did a lot of things better. For one, the thing we said we would improve first—the pass rush—was far better than in the season before. There's still room for work there and we'll do it. . . ."

In that direction, a significant move was made in the first choice of the Dolphins and in the draft of college players held February 1–2, 1972. Bluntly saying beforehand that he wanted to get a strong interior lineman, Shula felt he was lucky when Joe Thomas picked off Mike Kadish, a huge fellow of five inches over six feet and 270 pounds, with solid experience at Notre Dame. Mike recognized himself that he perhaps was weak on the techniques of rushing the passer, for Notre Dame's style is for the line to deny the enemy a running opportunity first, then get the passer if possible. "It's different in the pros and I'll have to bear down on getting to that passer and nailing him if I'm going to make it with the Dolphins." Kadish put it very well.

In Gary Kosins, a big running back from Dayton, the Dolphins got a fellow who—if he bangs the line and has some capability to the outside—could blend well into the "big back" offense now employed with Kiick and Csonka. There was no hint that Mercury Morris might be replaced, although reporters speculated that Shula would deal him away after the incident in the dressing room at the Super Bowl.

Calmer observers felt that Shula's irritation was momentary. His tendency is to handle player relations privately, when possible, and sort out his people to win football games, not sit around feeling heads or fretting about a player's psyche, once communication is established. Morris is naturally a cheerful person and has no trouble expressing himself, as does his former teammate—a blocking back then at West Texas State—Duane Thomas. The addition of young Kosins (six-one, 212) no doubt made Mercury thoughtful when he learned about it, however.

In Craig Curry, the Dolphins got a second quarterback (Mira being the first) who established an early reputation in the Miami area. The Minnesota star played his high school ball at Coral Gables, and Shula figured he might use him as a flanker or defensive back if Curry couldn't nudge aside Mira or at least Jim Del Gaizo, of the taxi squad.

Altogether, Thomas drafted seventeen new people. They were:

1. Mike Kadish, defensive tackle; 6-5, 270; Notre Dame.
2. This round went to Cleveland in the 1971 trade for Bob Matheson.
3. Gary Kosins, running back; 6-1, 212; Dayton
4. (from San Diego, for Carl Mauck) Larry Ball, defensive end; 6-6, 225; Louisville
   Al Benton, offensive tackle; 6-5, 250; Ohio University
5. Charles Babb, defensive back; 6-0, 196; Memphis State
6. Ray Nettles, linebacker; 6-1, 212; Tennessee
7. (from Denver, for John Stofa) Bill Adams, offensive guard; 6-2, 240; Holy Cross
   Calvin Harrell, fullback; 6-2, 220; Arkansas State
8. Craig Curry, quarterback; 6-2, 195; Minnesota
9. Greg Johnson, defensive back; 6-0, 187; Wisconsin
10. This round went to Houston in the 1971 trade for Russell Price
11. Ed Jenkins, wide receiver; 6-2, 204; Holy Cross
12. Ashley Bell, tight end; 6-2, 212; Purdue
13. Archie Robinson, defensive back; 6-1, 215; Hillside
14. Willie Jones, linebacker; 6-1, 220; Tampa
15. Bill Davis, defensive tackle; 6-4, 255; William and Mary
16. Al Hannah, wide receiver; 6-2, 188; Wisconsin (Al played earlier at Miami's Mays High.)
17. Vern Brown, defensive back; 5-10, 187; Western Michigan

It figured that very few, if any, of these newcomers would break into the forty-man squad that carried the Miami Dolphins to Super Bowl VI.

But any Don Shula decided could help reach Super Bowl VII would be rewarded beyond anything possible with another squad— for the Dolphins are professional football's most exciting force, and they have reached the heights more quickly than any other young team in the game.

Appendix

DOLPHINS' ALL-TIME ROSTER
(*Including 1971 Season*)

COACHES

Coach, School, Assignment

Bill Arnsparger, Miami (Ohio)
  Assistant (head defensive coach, linebackers)   1970–71
Les Bingaman, Illinois
  Assistant (defensive line, special assignments)   1966–70
Ralph Hawkins, Maryland
  Assistant (receivers)   1966
Ernie Hefferle, Duquesne
  Assistant (offensive line)   1966–69
John Idzik, Maryland
  Assistant (offensive backfield)   1966–69
Tom Keane, West Virginia
  Assistant (defensive backfield)   1966–71
Bob Pellegrini, Maryland
  Assistant (linebackers)   1966–67
Mike Scarry, Waynesburg College
  Assistant (defensive line)   1970–71
Howard Schnellenberger, Kentucky
  Assistant (head offensive coach, receivers)   1970–71
Don Shula, John Carroll University
  Head Coach   1970–71
Carl Taseff, John Carroll University
  Assistant (offensive backfield)   1970–71
Bobby Walston, Georgia
  Assistant (receivers and place kickers)   1966–67
George Wilson, Northwestern
  Head Coach   1966–69

PLAYERS

PLAYER	POS.	COLLEGE	YEARS
Anderson, Dick	S	Colorado	1968–71
Auer, Joe	HB	Georgia Tech	1966–67
Barber, Rudy	LB	Bethune-Cookman	1968
Boutwell, Tom	WR-QB	Southern Mississippi	1969

PLAYER	POS.	COLLEGE	YEARS
Boynton, John	T	Tennessee	1969
Bramlett, John	LB	Memphis State	1967–68
Branch, Mel	DE	Louisiana State	1966–68
Brown, Dean	S	Fort Valley State	1970
Brownlee, Claude	DE	Benedict	1967
Bruggers, Bob	LB	Minnesota	1966–68
Buoniconti, Nick	LB	Notre Dame	1969–71
Canale, Whit	DE	Tennessee	1966
Carpenter, Preston	TE	Arkansas	1967
Casares, Rick	FB	Florida	1966
Chesser, George	FB	Delta State	1966–67
Clancy, Jack	WR	Michigan	1967, 1969
Cole, Terry	RB	Indiana	1971
Cooke, Ed	DE	Maryland	1966–67
Cornish, Frank	DT	Grambling	1971
Cox, Jim	TE	Miami (Fla.)	1968
Cronin, Bill	TE	Boston College	1966
Crusan, Doug	T	Indiana	1968–71
Csonka, Larry	FB	Syracuse	1968–71
Current, Mike	T	Ohio State	1967
Darnall, Bill	WR	North Carolina	1968–69
Davis, Ted	LB	Georgia Tech	1970
DeMarco, Bob	C	Dayton	1971
Den Herder, Vern	DE	Central (Iowa)	1971
Dotson, Al	DT	Grambling	1966
Edmunds, Randall	LB	Georgia Tech	1968–69
Emanuel, Frank	LB	Tennessee	1966–69
Erlandson, Tom	LB	Washington State	1966–67
Evans, Norm	T	Texas Christian	1966–71
Faison, Earl	DE	Indiana	1966
Fernandez, Manny	DE	Utah	1968–71
Fleming, Marv	TE	Utah	1970–71
Foley, Tim	DB	Purdue	1970–71
Fowler, Charlie	G	Houston	1967–68
Gilchrist, Cookie	FB	None	1966
Ginn, Hubert	RB	Florida A&M	1970–71
Goode, Tom	C	Mississippi State	1966–69

PLAYER	POS.	COLLEGE	YEARS
Grady, Garry	DB	Eastern Michigan	1969
Griese, Bob	QB	Purdue	1967–71
Hammond, Kim	QB	Florida State	1968
Harper, Jack	HB	Florida	1967–68
Haynes, Abner	HB	North Texas State	1967
Heinz, Bob	DT	Pacific	1969–71
Higgins, Jim	G	Xavier	1966
Hines, Jimmy	WR	Texas Southern	1969
Holmes, Johnny	DE	Florida A&M	1966
Hopkins, Jerry	LB	Texas A&M	1967–68
Hudock, Mike	C	Miami (Fla.)	1966
Hunter, Billy	HB	Syracuse	1966
Jackson, Frank	FL	Southern Methodist	1966–67
Jacobs, Ray	DT	Howard Payne	1967–68
Jaquess, Pete	DB	Eastern New Mexico	1966–67
Joe, Billy	FB	Villanova	1966
Johnson, Curtis	DB	Toledo	1970–71
Joswick, Bob	DE	Tulsa	1968–69
Keating, Bill	DT	Michigan	1967
Keyes, Jimmy	LB-K	Mississippi	1968–69
Kiick, Jim	RB	Wyoming	1968–71
Kocourek, Dave	TE	Wisconsin	1966
Kolen, Mike	LB	Auburn	1970–71
Kremser, Karl	K	Tennessee	1969–70
Kuechenberg, Bob	G	Notre Dame	1970–71
Lamb, Mack	DB	Tennessee A&I	1967–68
Langer, Jim	G	South Dakota State	1970–71
Leigh, Charles	RB	None	1971
Lusteg, Booth	K	Connecticut	1967
Little, Larry	G-T	Bethune-Cookman	1969–71
Mass, Wayne	OT	Clemson	1971
Mandich, Jim	TE	Michigan	1970–71
Matheson, Bob	LB	Duke	1971
Matthews, Wes	FL	Northeast Oklahoma	1966
Mauck, Carl	C	Southern Illinois	1970
McBride, Norm	DE	Utah	1969–70
McCullers, Dale	LB	Florida State	1969
McDaniel, Wahoo	LB	Oklahoma	1966–68

COLLEGE		YEARS	PLAYER	POS.
McGeever, John	DB	Auburn	1966
Mertens, Jim	TE	Fairmont State	1969
Milton, Gene	WR	Florida A&M	1968–69
Mingo, Gene	K	None	1966–67
Mira, George	QB	Miami (Fla.)	1971
Mitchell, Stan	RB	Tennessee	1966–71
Moore, Wayne	T	Lamar Tech	1970–71
Moreau, Doug	TE	Louisiana State	1966–69
Morris, Mercury	RB	West Texas State	1969–71
Mumphord, Lloyd	CB	Texas Southern	1969–71
Neff, Bob	DB	Stephen F. Austin	1966–68
Neighbors, Billy	G	Alabama	1966–71
Nomina, Tom	DT	Miami (Ohio)	1966–68
Noonan, Karl	WR	Iowa	1966–71
Norton, Rick	QB	Kentucky	1966–69
Park, Ernie	G	McMurray (Tex.)	1966
Pearson, Willie	CB	North Carolina A&T	1969
Petrella, Bob	DB	Tennessee	1966–71
Powell, Jesse	LB	West Texas State	1969–71
Price, Sam	FB	Illinois	1966–68
Pryor, Barry	RB	Boston University	1969–70
Pyburn, Jack	T	Texas A&M	1967–68
Rice, Ken	G	Auburn	1966–67
Richardson, Jeff	T	Michigan State	1969
Richardson, John	DT	UCLA	1967–71
Richardson, Willie	WR	Jackson State	1970–71
Riley, Jim	DE	Oklahoma	1967–71
Roberson, Bo	FL	Cornell	1966
Roberts, Archie	QB	Columbia	1967
Roderick, John	FL	Southern Methodist	1966–67
Rudolph, Jack	LB	Georgia Tech	1966
Scott, Jake	S	Georgia	1970–71
Seiple, Larry	TE-P	Kentucky	1967–71
Stanfill, Bill	DE	Georgia	1969–71
Stofa, John	QB	Buffalo	1966–67, 1969–71
Stowe, Otto	WR	Iowa State	1971
Thornton, Jack	LB	Auburn	1966

PLAYER	POS.	COLLEGE	YEARS
Torczon, Laverne	DE	Nebraska	1966
Tucker, Gary	RB	Chattanooga	1968
Twilley, Howard	WR	Tulsa	1966–71
Urbanek, Jim	DT	Mississippi	1968
Warfield, Paul	WR	Ohio State	1970–71
Warren, Jimmy	DB	Illinois	1966–69
Washington, Dick	DB	Bethune-Cookman	1968
Weisacosky, Ed	LB	Miami (Fla.)	1968–71
West, Willie	DB	Oregon	1966–68
Westmoreland, Dick	DB	North Carolina A&T	1966–69
Williams, Maxie	G-T	Southeastern Louisiana	1966–70
Wilson, George, Jr.	QB	Xavier	1966
Wood, Dick	QB	Auburn	1966
Woodson, Freddie	G	Florida A&M	1967–69
Yepremian, Garo	K	None	1971
Zecher, Rich	DT	Utah State	1966–67

DOLPHINS IN ALL-STAR GAMES

AMERICAN FOOTBALL LEAGUE

1966 Willie West, Jimmy Warren, Ed Cooke, Tom Erlandson
1967 John Bramlett, Bob Griese, Jack Clancy, Dick Westmoreland
1968 Jim Kiick, Bob Griese, Karl Noonan
1969 George Wilson (coach), Jim Kiick, Tom Goode, Larry Little, Bill Stanfill, Nick Buoniconti

NFL PRO-BOWL

1971 Bob Griese, Paul Warfield, Larry Csonka
1972 Paul Warfield, Larry Little, Bob Griese, Larry Csonka, Bill Stanfill, Jake Scott, Mercury Morris

COLLEGE ALL-STAR

1966 Frank Emanuel
1967 Bob Griese, Jack Clancy, Jim Riley
1968 Larry Csonka (voted game's outstanding player), Jim Kiick, Bob Heinz
1971 Ron Dickerson

COACHES' ALL-AMERICA

1966 Frank Emanuel, Bob Petrella, Hal Wantland
1967 Jon Brittenum (voted game's outstanding player), Bob Griese, Jim Riley, Tom Beier
1968 Larry Csonka (voted game's outstanding player), Dick Anderson (voted Ernie Davis Memorial Award for general excellence), Doug Crusan, Jimmy Keyes
1969 Bill Stanfill
1971 Otto Stowe

DOLPHINS' DRAFT CHOICES

1966: 1. Jim Grabowski, fb, Illinois; 1. (bonus) Rick Norton, qb, Kentucky; 2. Frank Emanuel, lb, Tennessee; 3. Larry Gagner, g, Florida; 4. Dick Leftridge, fb, West Virginia; 5. Grady Bolton, dt, Mississippi State; 6. Ed Weisacosky, lb, Miami (Fla.); 7. Don Hansen, lb, Illinois; 8. Bob Petrella, db, Tennessee; 9. Bill Matan, de, Kansas State;

10. Pat Killorin, c, Syracuse; 11. Sam Price, fb, Illinois; 12. Howard Twilley, se, Tulsa; 13. Kent Kramer, e, Minnesota; 14. Phil Scoggin, p, Texas A&M; 15. Jerry Oliver, t, Southwest Texas; 16. Don Lorenz, de, Stephen Austin; 17. Mike Bender, g, Arkansas; 18. Rick Kestner, e, Kentucky; 19. Doug Moreau, te, LSU; 20. John Tooker, db, Adams State.

1966 Redshirt: 1. John Roderick, fl, SMU; 2. Harold Fulford, e, Auburn; 3. Jack Clancy, e, Michigan; 4. Jim Mankins, fb, Florida State; 5. Fritz Greenlee, e, Arizona; 6. Bill Darnall, db, North Carolina; 7. Don Williams, de, Wofford; 8. Jon Brittenum, db, Arkansas; 9. Craig Baynham, fl, Georgia Tech; 10. Randy Winkler, t, Tarleton State; 11. Kai Anderson, c, Illinois.

1967: 1. Bob Griese, qb, Purdue; 2. Jim Riley, t, Oklahoma; 3. (to Denver); 4. Bob Greenlee, de, Yale; 5a. (to Denver); 5b. (from Buffalo) Gary Tucker, hb, Chattanooga; 6. Bud Norris, te, Washington State; 7. Larry Seiple, hb, Kentucky; 8. (to Oakland); 9. John Richardson, dt, UCLA; 10. Tom Beier, ss, Miami (Fla.); 11. Jack Pyburn, t, Texas A&M; 12a. Stan Juk, lb, South Carolina; 12b. (from Denver) Jim Whitaker, db, Missouri; 13. (to Buffalo); 14. Charles Stikes, db, Kent State; 15. Jake Ferro, lb, Youngstown; 16. Maurice Calhoun, fb, Central (Ohio) State; 17. Larry Kissam, t, Florida State.

1968: 1a. Larry Csonka, fb, Syracuse; 1b. (from Cincinnati) Doug Crusan, t, Indiana; 2a. Jim Keyes, lb, Mississippi; 2b. (from Cincinnati) Jim Cox, te, Miami (Fla.); 3a. Jim Urbanek, dt, Mississippi; 3b. (from San Diego) Dick Anderson, db, Colorado; 4. (to Denver); 5. Jim Kiick, hb, Wyoming; 6a. (from Denver) Kim Hammond, qb, Florida State; 6b. Jimmy Hines, fl, Texas Southern; 7. John Boynton, t, Tennessee; 8a. (to New York Jets); 8b. (from Oakland) Randall Edmunds, lb, Georgia Tech; 9a. Sam McDowell, t, Southwest Missouri; 9b. (from Houston) Tom Paciorek, db, Houston; 10. Joe Mirto, t, Miami (Fla.); 11. Cornelius Cooper, de, Prairie View; 12. Paul Paxton, t, Akron; 13. Bob Joswick, dt, Tulsa; 14. Ray Blunk, te, Xavier; 15. Ken Corbin lb, Miami (Fla.); 16. Henry Still, dt, Bethune-Cookman; 17. Bill Nemeth, c, Arizona.

1969: 1. Bill Stanfill, de, Georgia; 2. Bob Heinz, dt, Pacific (Calif.); 3. Mercury Morris, hb, West Texas State; 4. Norman McBride, lb,

Utah; 5a. Willie Pearson, db, North Carolina A&T; 5b. (from Oakland) Karl Kremser, k, Tennessee; 6. Ed Tuck, g, Notre Dame; 7a. John Egan, c, Boston College; 7b. (from San Diego) John Kulka, g, Penn State; 8. Bruce Weinstein, te, Yale; 9. Jesse Powell, lb, West Texas State; 10. Jim Mertens, te, Fairmont State; 11. Mike Berdis, dt, North Dakota State: 12. Dale McCullers, lb, Florida State; 13. Amos Ayers, db, Arkansas AM&N; 14. Glynn Thompson, dt, Troy State; 15. Chick McGeehan, fl, Tennessee; 16. Lloyd Mumphord, db, Texas Southern; 17. Tom Krallman, de, Xavier.

1970: 1. (to Cleveland); 2. Jim Mandich, te, Michigan; 3. Tim Foley, db, Purdue; 4. Curtis Johnson, db, Toledo; 5. (to Boston); 6. Dave Campbell, de, Auburn; 7. Jake Scott, db, Georgia; 8. Narvel Chavers, rb, Jackson State; 9. Hubert Ginn, rb, Florida A&M; 10. Dick Nittinger, g, Tampa; 11. Brownie Wheless, dt, Rice; 12. Mike Kolen, lb, Auburn; 13. Dave Buddington, rb, Springfield (Mass.); 14. Gary Brackett, g, Holy Cross; 15. Pat Hauser, wr, East Tennessee; 16. Charles Williams, g, Tennessee State; 17. George Myles, dt, Morris Brown.

1971: 1. (to Baltimore); 2. Otto Stowe, wr, Iowa State; 3. Dale Farley, de, West Virginia; 4. Joe Theismann, qb, Notre Dame; 5. (to Pittsburgh); 6. Dennis Coleman, mlb, Mississippi; 7. Ron Dickerson, db, Kansas State; 8. (to Pittsburgh); 9. Vern Den Herder, de, Central Iowa; 10. Ron Maree, dt, Purdue; 11. Vic Surma, ot, Penn State; 12. Leroy Byars, rb, Alcorn A&M; 13. Lonnie Hepburn, db, Texas Southern; 14. David Vaughn, te, Memphis State; 15. Bob Richards, og, California; 16. Chris Myers, wr, Kenyon; 17. Curt Mark, lb, Mayville State.

The Dolphins' 1972 draft choices were given in Chapter 15.

OWNERSHIP OF DOLPHINS
(*Chronological Digest*)

The Miami franchise in the American Football League was awarded to Joseph Robbie and Danny Thomas on August 16, 1965. It was announced at a press conference and a dinner for city officials and civic leaders at the Palm Bay Club in the evening.

Title to the franchise was transferred by Robbie and Thomas to Miami Dolphins, Ltd., on December 16, 1965. Miami Dolphins, Ltd., was formed on that date as a limited partnership under the laws of Florida.

Under the terms of the Articles of Limited Partnership, Robbie became the sole individual general partner and Danny Thomas Sports, Inc., became a corporate general partner. During the first year of operation, the limited partners were Martin M. Decker, Philadelphia, Pa.; George A. Hamid, Sr. and George A. Hamid, Jr., Atlantic City, N.J.; John H. O'Neil, Jr., Miami; E. R. Haggar and J. M. Haggar, Jr., Dallas, Tex. It was later disclosed that Max M. Kampelman, Washington, D.C., was assigned part of Decker's interest as a limited partner.

On January 31, 1967, W. H. Keland, Racine, Wis., became a limited partner. He assigned one-half of his ownership interest to George N. Gillett, Jr. for a brief period, but this interest was transferred back to Keland in June 1967. Keland later acquired the ownership interests of Decker, Kampelman, Hamid, Sr., and Hamid, Jr.

In June 1967, Robbie and Keland purchased all of the common stock in Danny Thomas Sports, Inc., in equal shares and entered into an equalization agreement that would prevent either from acquiring a majority position.

On May 20, 1970, after a six-month struggle for ultimate control of the Dolphins, Keland sold his entire holdings, casting a shadow on the position of John H. O'Neil, the Miami sportsman early in the partnership but soon at friction with Robbie. O'Neil was to keep his stock for another year but eventually withdrew. Robbie purchased all of the common stock owned by Keland in South Florida Sports Corporation (successor to Danny Thomas Sports, Inc.) and sufficient of Keland's limited partnership equity to become the first majority owner of Miami Dolphins, Ltd.

The remainder of Keland's limited partnership interests were bought by Harper Sibley, Jr., of Rochester, N.Y., and Miami, where he is the dominant figure in The Jockey Club and conducts extensive affairs in numerous enterprises across the country; H. Earl Smalley, longtime Miami business personality, who actually gathered the new partners and presented them to Robbie; Wilbur L. Morrison, former vice president of Pan American World Airways and executive officer of its Latin American Division, now a business consultant in Miami; James W. McLamore, a founder and chairman of the board of Burger King Corporation, the national quick-food chain, and Frank W. Callahan, industrialist of national stature residing in Miami.

Subsequently, William S. Frates, Peter T. Fay, Robert L. Floyd, and Ray S. Pearson, partners in a law firm that bore their names; Morris S. Burk, a Miami contractor associated with Sibley in several enterprises, and James L. Davis, a dairy company executive, were added as limited partners through purchases from individual members of the club.

The late Fred Gates, of Minneapolis, owned shares in Robbie's corporate partner holdings from its inception.

Don Shula's limited-partnership stock was made available to him when he became vice president, coach, and director of football operations in February 1970.

DOLPHINS' ATTENDANCE

YEAR	HOME	AWAY	PRESEASON	GAMES	TOTAL
1966	182,431	243,269	91,692	18	517,392
1967	202,849	255,143	126,107	19	584,099
1968	215,980	252,291	171,460	19	639,731
1969	242,815	280,967	220,855	20	744,637
1970	440,139	348,918	296,734	20	1,085,791
1971	484,379	413,166	340,997	20	1,238,539
Totals	1,766,593	1,793,754	1,247,842	116	4,810,189

AVERAGES AT HOME

YEAR	LEAGUE	PRESEASON	GAMES	OVER-ALL
1966	26,062	36,366	8	27,349
1967	28,978	43,346	9	32,171
1968	30,854	48,419	10	36,124
1969	34,688	46,838	10	38,333
1970	62,877	61,544	11	64,210
1971	69,197	61,452	11	66,380

SEASON TICKETS

1966	12,503
1967	13,050
1968	14,924
1969	17,478
1970	26,161
1971	46,000
1972 (as of May 15)	64,000

(A breakdown indicates that the Dolphins get 71 percent of their season ticket holders from Dade (Miami) County; 20 percent from Broward County (Fort Lauderdale) ; 6 percent from Palm Beach; 1 percent from Monroe County (Key West), 1 percent from the rest of Florida, and 2 percent from twenty-seven other states.)

DOLPHINS' GAME-BY-GAME SUMMARY, 1970

BOSTON 27, MIAMI 14

September 20 at Boston

DOLPHINS	7	7	0	0	14
PATRIOTS	3	17	0	7	27

Miami—Griese, 5, run (Kremser, kick)
Boston—Cappelletti, 41, fg
Miami—Kiick, 5, run (Kremser, kick)
Boston—Garrett, 10, run (Cappelletti, kick)
Boston—Nance, 1, run (Cappelletti, kick)
Boston—Cappelletti, 22, fg
Boston—Sellers, 24, pass from Taliaferro (Cappelletti, kick)

MIAMI 20, HOUSTON 10

September 27 at Houston

DOLPHINS	3	7	7	3	20
OILERS	3	0	0	7	10

Miami—Yepremian, 31, fg
Houston—Gerela, 10, fg
Miami—Mandich, 3, pass from Griese (Yepremian, kick)
Miami—Twilley, 5, pass from Griese (Yepremian, kick)
Miami—Yepremian, 42, fg
Houston—Granger, 9, run (Gerela, kick)

MIAMI 20, OAKLAND 13

October 3 at Miami

RAIDERS	0	3	3	7	13
DOLPHINS	0	10	0	10	20

Miami—Warfield, 49, pass from Griese (Yepremian, kick)
Oakland—Blanda, 12, fg
Miami—Yepremian, 47, fg
Oakland—Blanda, 17, fg
Miami—Warfield, 17, pass from Griese (Yepremian, kick)
Miami—Yepremian, 40, fg
Oakland—Wells, 36, pass from Blanda (Blanda, kick)

MIAMI 20, NEW YORK JETS 6

October 10 at New York

DOLPHINS	7	0	3	10	20
JETS	6	0	0	0	6

New York—Turner, 17, fg
Miami—Warfield, 9, pass from Griese (Yepremian, kick)
New York—Turner, 35, fg
Miami—Yepremian, 37, fg
Miami—Twilley, 3, pass from Griese (Yepremian, kick)
Miami—Yepremian, 11, fg

MIAMI 33, BUFFALO 14

October 18 at Buffalo

DOLPHINS	10	3	7	13	33
BILLS	0	7	7	0	14

Miami—Csonka, 4, run (Yepremian, kick)
Miami—Yepremian, 46, fg
Miami—Yepremian, 42, fg
Buffalo—Briscoe, 18, pass from Shaw (Guthrie, kick)
Miami—Csonka, 5, run (Yepremian, kick)
Buffalo—Briscoe, 16, run (Guthrie, kick)
Miami—Warfield, 43, pass from Griese (Yepremian, kick)
Miami—Yepremian, 47, fg
Miami—Yepremian, 30, fg

CLEVELAND 28, MIAMI 0

October 25 at Miami

BROWNS	0	14	7	7	28
DOLPHINS	0	0	0	0	0

Cleveland—Scott, 13, pass from Nelsen (Cockroft, kick)
Cleveland—Lindsey, 56, pass interception (Cockroft, kick)
Cleveland—Collins, 21, pass from Nelsen (Cockroft, kick)
Cleveland—Minniear, 1, run (Cockroft, kick)

BALTIMORE 35, MIAMI 0

November 1 at Baltimore

DOLPHINS	0	0	0	0	0
COLTS	7	7	14	7	35

Baltimore—Gardin, 80, punt return (O'Brien, kick)
Baltimore—Bulach, 1, run (O'Brien, kick)
Baltimore—Duncan, 99, kickoff return (O'Brien, kick)
Baltimore—Hinton, 32, pass from Unitas (O'Brien, kick)
Baltimore—Mitchell, 15, pass from Morrall (O'Brien, kick)

PHILADELPHIA 24, MIAMI 17

November 8 at Philadelphia

DOLPHINS	0	0	0	17	17
EAGLES	0	17	7	0	24

Philadelphia—Jackson, 31, pass from Snead (Moseley, kick)
Philadelphia—Moseley, 23, fg
Philadelphia—Jackson, 15, pass from Snead (Moseley, kick)
Philadelphia—Zabel, 2, pass from Snead (Moseley, kick)
Miami—Yepremian, 24, fg
Miami—Warfield, 52, pass from Stofa (Yepremian, kick)
Miami—W. Richardson, 27, pass from Stofa (Yepremian, kick)

MIAMI 21, NEW ORLEANS 10

November 15 at New Orleans

SAINTS	10	0	0	0	10
DOLPHINS	7	0	7	7	21

Miami—Mumphord, 32, pass interception (Yepremian, kick)
New Orleans—Barrington, 11, run (Dempsey, kick)
New Orleans—Dempsey, 10, fg
Miami—Kiick, 1, run (Yepremian, kick)
Miami—Csonka, 6, run (Yepremian, kick)

MIAMI 34, BALTIMORE 17

November 22 at Miami

COLTS	3	7	0	7	17
DOLPHINS	7	17	7	3	34

Baltimore—O'Brien, 38, fg
Miami—Scott, 77, punt return (Yepremian, kick)
Miami—Griese, 15, run (Yepremian, kick)
Miami—Warfield, 27, pass from Griese (Yepremian, kick)
Baltimore—Jefferson, 4, pass from Unitas (O'Brien, kick)
Miami—Yepremian, 43, fg
Miami—Noonan, 51, pass from Griese (Yepremian, kick)
Baltimore—Mitchell, 2, pass from Unitas (O'Brien, kick)
Miami—Yepremian, 46, fg

MIAMI 20, ATLANTA 7

November 30 at Atlanta

DOLPHINS	3	10	0	7	20
FALCONS	0	0	0	7	7

Miami—Yepremian, 9, fg
Miami—Kiick, 1, run (Yepremian, kick)
Miami—Yepremian, 43, fg
Atlanta—Gipson, 5, pass from Berry (Vinyard, kick)
Miami—Csonka, 1, run (Yepremian, kick)

MIAMI 37, BOSTON 20
December 6 at Miami

PATRIOTS	0	6	7	7	20
DOLPHINS	17	10	7	3	37

Miami—Morris, 96, kickoff return (Yepremian, kick)
Miami—Mumphord, 51, blocked fg (Yepremian, kick)
Miami—Yepremian, 15, fg
Boston—Nance, 10, run (Cappelletti, kick)
Miami—Yepremian, 39, fg
Miami—Twilley, 19, pass from Griese (Yepremian, kick)
Boston—Garrett, 6, run (Cappelletti, kick)
Miami—Csonka, 1, run (Yepremian, kick)
Miami—Yepremian, 30, fg
Boston—Knief, 22, pass from Taliaferro (Cappalletti, kick)

MIAMI 16, NEW YORK JETS 10
December 13 at Miami

JETS	3	7	0	0	10
DOLPHINS	0	10	0	6	16

New York—Turner, 21, fg
Miami—Twilley, 23, pass from Griese (Yepremian, kick)
Miami—Yepremian, 40, fg
New York—Bell, 8, pass from Woodall (Turner, kick)
Miami—Yepremian, 13, fg
Miami—Yepremian, 21, fg

MIAMI 45, BUFFALO 7
December 20 at Miami

BILLS	0	0	0	7	7
DOLPHINS	21	10	7	7	45

Miami—Kiick, 4, run (Yepremian, kick)
Miami—Twilley, 21, pass from Griese (Yepremian, kick)
Miami—Csonka, 2, run (Yepremian, kick)
Miami—Kiick, 2, run (Yepremian, kick)
Miami—Yepremian, 43, fg
Miami—Kiick, 2, run (Yepremian, kick)
Miami—Mitchell, 36, pass from Stofa (Yepremian, kick)
Buffalo—Grate, 30, pass from Harris (Guthrie, kick)

AFC FIRST-ROUND PLAYOFFS, 1970

OAKLAND 21, MIAMI 14

December 27 at Oakland

DOLPHINS	0	7	0	7	14
RAIDERS	0	7	7	7	21

Miami—Warfield, 16, pass from Griese (Yepremian, kick)
Oakland—Biletnikoff, 22, pass from Lamonica (Blanda, kick)
Oakland—Brown, 750, pass interception (Blanda, kick)
Oakland—Sherman, 82, pass from Lamonica (Blanda, kick)
Miami—W. Richardson, 7, pass from Griese (Yepremian, kick)

DOLPHINS' STATISTICS, 1970 (10–4–0)
(not including playoff)

	MIAMI	OPP.
First Downs	228	226
Rushing	106	82
Passing	100	128
Penalties	22	16
Net Total, Offense	4039	4004
Total plays	827	808
Average gain per play	4.9	5.0
Average gain per game	288.5	286.0
Net Rushing, Offense	2082	1453
Rushing plays	492	387
Average gain per play	4.2	3.8
Average gain per game	148.7	103.8
Net Passing, Offense	1957	2551
Tackled/Yards lost	36/327	18/157
Attempts/Completions	299/159	403/234
Percent completed	53.2	58.0
Had intercepted	19	23
Average gain per play	6.5	6.3
Average gain per completion	14.4	11.6
Average gain per game	139.8	182.2
Touchdowns	15	17

	MIAMI	OPP.
Punts/Average	58/41.2	63/41.7
Yards	2392	2624
Had blocked	0	0
Punt Returns/Yards	30/295	20/241
Average per return	9.8	12.1
Kickoff Returns/Yards	48/1036	55/1142
Average per return	21.6	20.8
Interceptions/Yards	23/414	19/258
Average per return	18.0	13.6
Penalties/Yards	77/834	68/704
Fumbles/No. Lost	24/11	24/15
Total Points	297	228
Touchdowns	33	28
Rushing	14	8
Passing	15	17
Returns	4	3
Safeties	0	0
PAT Made/Attempted	33/33	27/28
Field Goals Made/Attempted	22/30	11/22

INDIVIDUAL RUSHING

PLAYER	NO.	YDS.	AVG.	TD	LONG
Csonka	193	874	4.5	6	53
Kiick	191	658	3.4	6	56
Morris	60	409	6.8	0	40
Griese	26	89	3.4	2	16
Mitchell	8	23	2.9	0	9
Seiple	2	21	10.5	0	24
Warfield	2	13	6.5	0	16
Stofa	2	5	2.5	0	4
Pryor	2	0	0.0	0	5
Ginn	5	—1	—0.2	0	8
Noonan	1	—9	—9.0	0	—9
DOLPHINS	492	2082	4.2	14	56
OPPONENTS	387	1453	3.8	8	26

INDIVIDUAL PASSING

PLAYER	ATT.	COMP.	PCT.	YDS.	TD	LONG	INT.	PCT.
Griese	245	142	58.0	2019	12	54	17	6.9
Stofa	53	16	30.2	240	3	52+	2	3.8
Kiick	1	1	100.0	25	0	25	0	0.0
DOLPHINS	299	159	53.2	2284	15	54	19	6.7
OPPONENTS	403	234	58.0	2708	17	46	22	5.4

TIMES TACKLED ATTEMPTING PASS (SACKS)

PLAYER	NO.	YDS.	AVG. LOSS
Griese	31	282	9.1
Stofa	5	45	9.0
DOLPHINS	36	327	9.1
OPPONENTS	18	157	8.7

INDIVIDUAL RECEIVING

PLAYER	NO.	YDS.	AVG.	TD	LONG
Kiick	42	497	11.8	0	47
Warfield	28	703	25.1	6	54
Twilley	22	281	12.8	5	23
Fleming	18	205	11.4	0	36
Morris	12	149	12.4	0	50
Csonka	11	94	8.5	0	54
Noonan	10	186	18.6	1	51
Richardson, W	7	67	9.6	1	27
Mitchell	6	85	14.2	1	36
Seiple	2	14	7.0	0	7
Mandich	1	3	3.0	1	3
DOLPHINS	159	2284	14.4	15	54
OPPONENTS	234	2708	11.6	17	46

INTERCEPTIONS BY

PLAYER	NO.	YDS.	AVG.	TD	LONG
Anderson	8	191	23.9	0	86
Scott	5	112	22.4	0	47
Mumphord	5	35	7.0	1	32
Johnson	3	29	9.7	0	21
Brown	1	32	32.0	0	15
Davis	1	15	15.0	0	15
DOLPHINS	23	414	18.0	1	86
OPPONENTS	19	258	13.6	1	56

PUNTING

PLAYER	NO.	YDS.	AVG.	LONG	BLKD.
Seiple	58	2392	41.2	67	0
DOLPHINS	58	2392	41.2	67	0
OPPONENTS	63	2624	41.7	62	0

MISSED AND BLOCKED FIELD-GOAL RETURNS

PLAYER	NO.	YDS.	AVG.	TD	LONG
Scott	3	102	34.0	0	50
Mumphord	1	51	51.0	1	51
Johnson	1	3	3.0	0	3
DOLPHINS	5	156	31.2	1	51
OPPONENTS	1	44	44.0	0	44

KICK RETURNS

PLAYER	FC	NO.	YDS.	AVG.	TD	LONG
Scott	15	27	290	10.7	1	77
Morris	0	2	—1	—0.5	0	0
Anderson	0	1	6	6.0	0	6
DOLPHINS	15	30	295	9.8	1	77
OPPONENTS	25	21	241	12.1	1	80

SCORING

PLAYER	R/P/RET	PAT	FG/ATT. (LONG)	PTS.
Yepremian	0/0/0	31/31	22/29 (47)	97
Warfield	0/6/0	0/0	0/0	36
Csonka	6/0/0	0/0	0/0	36
Kiick	6/0/0	0/0	0/0	36
Twilley	0/5/0	0/0	0/0	30
Griese	2/0/0	0/0	0/0	12
Mumphord	0/0/2	0/0	0/0	12
Mandich	0/1/0	0/0	0/0	6
Noonan	0/1/0	0/0	0/0	6
Richardosn, W.	0/1/0	0/0	0/0	6
Scott	0/0/1	0/0	0/0	6
Morris	0/0/1	0/0	0/0	6
Mitchell	0/1/0	0/0	0/0	6
Kremser	0/0/0	2/2	0/1	2
DOLPHINS	14/15/4	33/33	22/30 (47)	297
OPPONENTS	8/17/3	27/28	11/22 (41)	228

FIELD-GOAL ACCURACY

		YARDS					
PLAYER	1–19	20–29	30–39	40–49	50–OVER	TOTAL	PCT.
Yepremian	4/4	2/3	5/6	11/15	0/1	22/29	75.7
Kremser	0/0	0/1	0/0	0/0	0/0	0/1	0.0
DOLPHINS	4/4	2/4	5/6	11/15	0/1	22/30	75.7
OPPONENTS	5/5	3/4	2/3	1/8	0/3	11/23	47.8

DEFENSIVE STATISTICS
(TACKLES-ASSISTS-TOTAL)

Buoniconti	96-49-145	Cornish	9-4-13
Anderson	72-34-106	Langer	10-1-11
Kolen	70-26-96	Palmer	6-2-8
Johnson	50-22-72	Mandich	5-0-5
Fernandez	54-17-71	Brown	4-1-5
Stanfill	51-16-67	Kuechenberg	4-0-4
Swift	48-19-67	Seiple	3-0-3
Richardson, J.	43-21-64	Evans	3-0-3
Scott	45-17-62	Mitchell	2-1-3
Mumphord	40-16-56	Warfield	2-0-2
Davis	39-15-54	Little	2-0-2
Riley	31-15-46	Weisacosky	2-0-2
Powell	16-4-20	Williams	1-1-2
Heinz	11-4-15	Yepremian	1-1-2
Foley	12-2-14	Kiick	1-0-1
Ginn	13-1-14	Crusan	1-0-1
Petrella	12-1-13	McBride	1-0-1

PASSES DEFENDED

Johnson 12, Anderson 11, Mumphord 9, Kolen 7, Buoniconti 7, Stanfill 6, Scott 5, Davis 2, Richardson J. 2, Cornish 2, Powell 2, Swift 1, Fernandez 1, Heinz 1, Foley 1, Petrella 1.

BLOCKED KICKS

Mumphord 2 FG; Cornish 2 FG, 1 PAT; Heinz 2 FG; Johnson 1 FG; Fernandez 1 FG.

TACKLED PASSER (SACKS)

Stanfill 6, Fernandez 4½, J. Richardson 2½, Riley 2, Anderson 1.

DOLPHINS' GAME-BY-GAME SUMMARY, 1971

DENVER 10, MIAMI 10

September 19 at Denver

DOLPHINS	3	0	0	7	10
BRONCOS	3	0	7	0	10

Miami—Yepremian, 22, fg
Denver—Turner, 10, fg
Denver—Harrison, 31, pass from Horn (J. Turner, kick)
Miami—Warfield, 31, pass from Griese (Yepremian, kick)

MIAMI 29, BUFFALO 14

September 26 at Buffalo

DOLPHINS	3	9	7	10	29
BILLS	7	0	7	0	14

Miami—Yepremian, 15, fg
Buffalo—Patrick, 1, run (Guthrie, kick)
Miami—Yepremian, 46, fg
Miami—Yepremian, 13, fg
Miami—Yepremian, 9, fg
Miami—Csonka, 1, run (Yepremian, kick)
Buffalo—Simpson, 46, run (Guthrie, kick)
Miami—Warfield, 23, pass from Griese (Yepremian, kick)
Miami—Yepremian, 48, fg

NEW YORK, 14, MIAMI 10

October 3 at Miami

JETS	0	0	0	14	14
DOLPHINS	10	0	0	0	10

Miami—Csonka, 16, run (Yepremian, kick)
Miami—Yepremian, 43, fg
New York—Nock, 1, run (Howfield, kick)
New York—Nock, 2, run (Howfield, kick)

MIAMI 23, CINCINNATI 13

October 10 at Cincinnati

DOLPHINS	7	3	7	4	23
BENGALS	0	3	3	7	13

Miami—Warfield, 43, pass from Griese (Yepremian, kick)
Miami—Yepremian, 19, fg
Cincinnati—Muhlmann, 16, fg
Miami—Twilley, 4, pass from Griese (Yepremian, kick)
Cincinnati—Muhlmann, 9, fg
Miami—Yepremian, 36, fg
Cincinnati—Trumpy, 11, pass from Anderson (Muhlmann, kick)
Miami—Yepremian, 16, fg

MIAMI 41, NEW ENGLAND 3

October 17 at Miami

PATRIOTS	0	3	0	0	3
DOLPHINS	21	10	7	3	41

Miami—Twilley, 22, pass from Griese (Yepremian, kick)
Miami—Warfield, 32, pass from Griese (Yepremian, kick)
Miami—Twilley, 14, pass from Griese (Yepremian, kick)
New England—Gogolak, 51, fg
Miami—Yepremian, 34, fg
Miami—Warfield, 14, pass from Griese (Yepremian, kick)
Miami—Kiick, 1, run (Yepremian, kick)
Miami—Yepremian, 42, fg

MIAMI 30, NEW YORK 14

October 24 at New York

DOLPHINS	0	10	7	13	30
JETS	7	0	0	7	14

New York—Boozer, 14, pass from Davis (Howfield, kick)
Miami—Yepremian, 25, fg
Miami—Warfield, 37, pass from Griese (Yepremian, kick)
Miami—Csonka, 2, run (Yepremian, kick)
Miami—Yepremian, 31, fg
Miami—Csonka, 2, run (Yepremian, kick)
New York—Lammons, 16, pass from Davis (Howfield, kick)
Miami—Yepremian, 14, fg

MIAMI 20, LOS ANGELES 14

October 31 at Los Angeles

DOLPHINS	7	7	3	3	20
RAMS	0	0	0	14	14

Miami—Warfield, 74, pass from Griese (Yepremian, kick)
Miami—Twilley, 11, pass from Griese (Yepremian, kick)
Miami—Yepremian, 20, fg
Los Angeles—L. Smith, 1, run (Ray, kick)
Los Angeles—Snow, 45, pass from Gabriel (Ray, kick)
Miami—Yepremian, 40, fg

MIAMI 34, BUFFALO 0

November 7 at Miami

BILLS	0	0	0	0	0
DOLPHINS	7	7	7	13	34

Miami—Csonka, 12, run (Yepremian, kick)
Miami—Warfield, 3, pass from Griese (Yepremian, kick)
Miami—Mandich, 10, pass from Griese (Yepremian, kick)
Miami—Morris, 45, run (Yepremian, kick)
Miami—Yepremian, 38, fg
Miami—Yepremian, 24, fg

MIAMI 24, PITTSBURGH 21

November 14 at Miami

STEELERS	14	7	0	0	21
DOLPHINS	3	14	0	7	24

Miami—Yepremian, 43, fg
Pittsburgh—Smith, 30, pass from Bradshaw (Gerela, kick)
Pittsburgh—Shanklin, 28, pass from Bradshaw (Gerela, kick)
Pittsburgh—Smith, 16, pass from Bradshaw (Gerela, kick)
Miami—Warfield, 12, pass from Griese (Yepremian, kick)
Miami—Warfield, 86, pass from Griese (Yepremian, kick)
Miami—Warfield, 60, pass from Griese (Yepremian, kick)

MIAMI 17, BALTIMORE 14

November 21 at Miami

COLTS	7	0	7	0	14
DOLPHINS	0	0	14	3	17

Baltimore—Nottingham, 4, run (O'Brien, kick)
Miami—Kiick, 1, run (Yepremian, kick)
Miami—Fleming, 10, pass from Griese (Yepremian, kick)
Baltimore—Bulaich, 4, run (O'Brien, kick)
Miami—Yepremian, 20, fg

MIAMI 34, CHICAGO 3

November 29 at Miami

BEARS	0	0	3	0	3
DOLPHINS	10	10	7	7	34

Miami—Yepremian, 43, fg
Miami—Csonka, 2, run (Yepremian, kick)
Miami—Fleming, 6, pass from Griese (Yepremian, kick)
Miami—Yepremian, 35, fg
Miami—Csonka, 10, pass from Griese (Yepremian, kick)
Chicago—Percival, 15, fg
Miami—Stowe, 13, pass from Mira (Yepremian, kick)

NEW ENGLAND 34, MIAMI 13

December 5 at Boston

DOLPHINS	7	3	3	0	13
PATRIOTS	17	3	14	0	34

Miami—Morris, 94, kickoff return (Yepremian, kick)
New England—Nance, 6, run (Gogolak, kick)
New England—Vataha, 26, pass from Plunkett (Gogolak, kick)
New England—Gogolak, 37, fg
Miami—Yepremian, 26, fg
New England—Gogolak, 35, fg
Miami—Yepremian, 30, fg
New England—Vataha, 25, pass from Plunkett (Gogolak, kick)
New England—Carwell, 53, interception return (Gogolak, kick)

BALTIMORE 14, MIAMI 3

December 11 at Baltimore

DOLPHINS	0	0	3	0	3
COLTS	7	7	0	0	14

Baltimore—Matte, 7, run (O'Brien, kick)
Baltimore—Matte, 1, run (O'Brien, kick)
Miami—Yepremian, 17, fg

MIAMI 27, GREEN BAY 6

December 19 at Miami

PACKERS	3	0	3	0	6
DOLPHINS	3	3	14	7	27

Green Bay—Webster, 14, fg
Miami—Yepremian, 26, fg
Miami—Yepremian, 27, fg
Green Bay—Webster, 24, fg
Miami—Kiick, 1, run (Yepremian, kick)
Miami—Csonka, 1, run (Yepremian, kick)
Miami—Johnson, 47, blocked field goal (Yepremian, kick)

PLAYOFFS, 1971–72

Preliminary Round
MIAMI 27, KANSAS CITY 24
December 25 at Kansas City

DOLPHINS	0	10	7	7	0	3	27
CHIEFS	10	0	7	7	0	0	24

Kansas City—Stenerud, 24, fg
Kansas City—Podolak, 7, pass from Dawson (Stenerud, kick)
Miami—Csonka, 1, run (Yepremian, kick)
Miami—Yepremian, 14, fg
Kansas City—Otis, 1, run (Stenerud, kick)
Miami—Kiick, 1, run (Yepremian, kick)
Kansas City—Podolak, 3, run (Stenerud, kick)
Miami—Fleming, 5, pass from Griese (Yepremian, kick)
Miami (Second Overtime Period)—Yepremian, 37, fg

AFC CHAMPIONSHIP GAME
MIAMI 21, BALTIMORE 0
January 2 at Miami

COLTS	0	0	0	0	0
DOLPHINS	7	0	7	7	21

Miami—Warfield, 75, pass from Griese (Yepremian, kick)
Miami—Anderson, 62, interception (Yepremian, kick)
Miami—Csonka, 5, run (Yepremian, kick)

SUPER BOWL
NFL CHAMPIONSHIP GAME
DALLAS 24, MIAMI 3
January 16 at New Orleans

COWBOYS	3	7	7	7	24
DOLPHINS	0	3	0	0	3

Dallas—Clark, 9, fg
Dallas—Alworth, 7, pass from Staubach (Clark, kick)
Miami—Yepremian, 31, fg
Dallas—D. Thomas, 3 (Clark, kick)
Dallas—Ditka, 7, pass from Staubach (Clark, kick)

DOLPHINS' STATISTICS, 1971
(not including playoff)

SCORES

MIAMI		OPP.	ATT.
10	At Denver	10	51,200
29	At Buffalo	14	45,139
10	New York Jets	14	70,670
23	At Cincinnati	13	60,099
41	New England	3	58,822
30	At New York Jets	14	62,130
20	At L. A. Rams	14	72,903
34	Buffalo	0	61,016
24	Pittsburgh	21	66,435
17	Baltimore	14	75,312
34	Chicago	3	75,312
13	At New England	34	61,457
3	At Baltimore	14	60,238
27	Green Bay	6	76,812

Average at home: 69,197; Average away: 59,023

Scores by Quarter

DOLPHINS	81	76	79	79	315
OPPONENTS	65	23	44	42	174

TEAM STATISTICS

	MIAMI	OPP.
First Downs	232	214
Rushing	121	93
Passing	94	111
Penalties	17	10
Net Total, Offense	4412	3661
Total Plays	803	791
Average gain per play	5.4	4.7
Average gain per game	315.1	261.5

	MIAMI	OPP.
Net Rushing, Offense	2429	1661
Rushing plays	486	403
Average gain per play	5.0	4.1
Average gain per game	173.5	118.7
Net Passing, Offense	1983	2000
Tackled/Yards lost	25/256	34/293
Attempts/Completions	293/156	363/206
Percent completed	53.2	56.8
Had intercepted	10	17
Touchdowns	20	10
Average gain per play	6.8	5.5
Average gain per comp	12.7	9.7
Average gain per game	141.6	142.9
Punts/Average	52/40.1	72/40.7
Yardage	2087	2935
Had blocked	1	0
Punt Returns/Yards	41/423	26/106
Average per return	10.5	4.1
Kickoff Returns/Yards	32/806	59/1180
Average per return	25.2	20.0
Interceptions/Yards	17/143	10/166
Penalties/Yards	65/632	64/561
Fumbles/No. Lost	22/13	38/14
Total Points	315	174
Touchdowns	33	21
Rushing	11	10
Passing	20	10
Returns	2	1
PAT Made/Attempted	33/33	22/22
Field Goals Made/Attempted	28/40	9/21
Safeties	0	0

INDIVIDUAL RUSHING

PLAYER	NO.	YDS.	AVG.	TD	LONG
Csonka	195	1051	5.4	7	28
Kiick	161	738	4.5	3	34
Morris	57	315	5.5	1	51
Warfield	9	115	12.8	0	39
Ginn	22	97	4.5	0	46
Griese	26	82	3.2	0	21
Leigh	5	15	3.0	0	7
Seiple	1	14	14.0	0	14
Cole	3	11	3.7	0	4
Mira	6	—9	—1.5	0	0
DOLPHINS	486	2429	4.9	11	51
OPPONENTS	403	1661	4.1	10	46

INDIVIDUAL PASSING

PLAYER	ATT.	COMP.	INT.	YDS.	AVG.	TD	LONG
Griese	263	145	9	2089	55.1	19	86
Mira	30	11	1	159	36.6	1	43
DOLPHINS	293	156	10	2248	53.2	20	86
OPPONENTS	363	206	17	2153	56.8	10	51

TIMES TACKLED ATTEMPTING PASS (SACKS)

PLAYER	NO.	YDS.	AVG. LOSS
Griese	23	248	10.8
Mira	2	17	8.5
DOLPHINS	25	265	10.6
OPPONENTS	34	293	8.6

INDIVIDUAL RECEIVING

PLAYER	NO.	YDS.	AVG.	TD	LONG
Warfield	43	996	23.2	11	86
Kiick	40	338	8.5	0	27
Twilley	23	349	15.2	4	41
Fleming	13	137	10.5	2	23
Csonka	13	113	8.7	1	25
Noonan	10	180	19.4	0	43
Stowe	5	68	13.6	1	21
Morris	5	16	3.6	0	11
Mandich	3	19	6.3	1	10
Seiple	1	32	32.0	0	32
DOLPHINS	156	2248	14.4	20	86
OPPONENTS	206	2153	10.4	10	51

INTERCEPTIONS BY

PLAYER	NO.	YDS.	AVG.	TD	LONG
Scott	7	34	4.9	0	21
Foley	4	14	3.5	0	18
Johnson	2	34	17.0	0	34
Anderson	2	33	16.5	0	33
Buoniconti	1	16	16.0	0	16
Swift	1	12	12.0	0	12
DOLPHINS	17	143	9.0	0	34
OPPONENTS	10	166	16.6	1	53

PUNTING

PLAYER	NO.	YDS.	AVG.	LONG	BLKD.
Seiple	52	2087	40.1	73	1
DOLPHINS	52	2087	40.1	73	1
OPPONENTS	72	2935	40.4	58	0

PUNT RETURNS

PLAYER	FC	NO.	YDS.	AVG.	TD	LONG
Scott	18	33	318	9.6	0	31
Anderson	4	7	105	15.0	0	47
DOLPHINS	22	40	423	10.5	0	31
OPPONENTS	14	26	106	4.1	0	29

KICKOFF RETURNS

PLAYER	NO.	YDS.	AVG.	TD	LONG
Morris	15	423	28.2	1	94
Ginn	10	252	25.2	0	35
Leigh	4	99	24.9	0	31
Matheson	3	32	10.2	0	16
DOLPHINS	32	806	25.2	1	94
OPPONENTS	59	1180	20.0	0	35

SCORING

PLAYER	R/P/RET.	PAT	FG/ATT.	(LONG)	PTS.
Yepremian	0/0/0	33/33	28/40	(48)	117
Warfield	0/11/0	0/0	0/0		66
Csonka	7/1/0	0/0	0/0		48
Twilley	0/4/0	0/0	0/0		24
Kiick	3/0/0	0/0	0/0		18
Fleming	0/2/0	0/0	0/0		12
Morris	1/0/1	0/0	0/0		12
Mandich	0/1/0	0/0	0/0		6
Stowe	0/1/0	0/0	0/0		6
Johnson	0/0/1	0/0	0/0		6
DOLPHINS	11/20/2	33/33	28/40	(48)	315
OPPONENTS	10/10/1	22/22	9/20	(51)	174

FIELD-GOAL ACCURACY

PLAYER	YARDS					TOTAL
	1–19	20–29	30–39	40–49		
Yepremian	7/7	8/8	6/11	7/12	0/2	28/40

DOLPHINS	7/7	8/8	6/11	7/12	0/2	28/40
OPPONENTS	5/5	1/4	2/2	0/6	1/4	9/21

Yepremian sequence (italicized indicates good): 22, 41, 36, 35, *15*, *46*, 9, *48*, *13*, 35, *43*, 49, 40, *19*, *36*, *16*, *34*, 46, *42*, *25*, *31*, *14*, 51, *20*, *40*, *38*, *24*, *43*, 54, *20*, *43*, *35*, 39, *26*, *30*, 31, *17*, *26*, 40, *27*.

DEFENSIVE STATISTICS
(TACKLES-ASSISTS-TOTAL)

Buoniconti	86-40-126	Ginn	13-3-16
Anderson	52-22-74	Den Herder	13-3-16
Kolen	54-17-71	Richardson	12-4-16
Scott	49-21-70	Leigh	7-2-9
Fernandez	47-20-67	Petrella	2-7-9
Johnson	50-16-66	Mandich	5-1-6
Stanfill	42-22-64	Langer	4-0-4
Swift	41-20-61	Evans	3-0-3
Matheson	42-17-59	Twilley	2-0-2
Foley	36-22-58	Kuechenberg	2-0-2
Riley	33-19-52	Csonka	2-0-2
Heinz	24-27-51	Farley	2-0-2
Powell	43-5-48	Noonal	1-0-1
Mumphord	17-5-22	Little	1-0-1
Cornish	13-7-20	Cole	0-1-1

PASSES DEFENDED

Foley 11, Swift 8, Scott 6, Anderson 5, Kolen 5, Buoniconti 4, Mumphord 3, Powell 2, Johnson 2, Stanfill 2, Petrella 2, Matheson 1, Richardson 1, Den Herder 1, Cornish 1.

BLOCKED FG

Johnson 2, Mumphord 2, Riley 1.

TACKLED PASSER (SACKS)

Fernandez 8, Riley 7½, Stanfill 6½, Heinz 5½, Cornish 2, Swift 2, Powell 1, Anderson 1, Den Herder 1, Buoniconti 1.

FUMBLES LOST

Griese 3, Warfield 2, Ginn 2, Scott 1, Buoniconti 1, Anderson 1, Morris 1, Kiick 1.

OPP. FUMBLES RECOVERED

Anderson 4, Stanfill 3, Riley 2, Scott 1, Fernandez 1, Johnson 1, Leigh 1, Langer 1, Matheson 1.

DOLPHINS' ROSTER, 1971

(As of December 12, 1971)

(Age as of September 1971)

NO.	NAME	POS.	HT.	WT.	AGE	YR.	COLLEGE
1	Yepremian, Garo	K	5-8	172	27	4	None
10	Mira, George	QB	5-11	192	29	7	Miami (Fla.)
12	Griese, Bob	QB	6-1	190	26	5	Purdue
13	Scott, Jake	S	6-0	188	26	2	Georgia
15	Leigh, Charlie	RB	5-11	205	25	3	None
20	Seiple, Larry	TE-P	6-0	215	26	5	Kentucky
21	Kiick, Jim	RB	5-11	215	25	4	Wyoming
22	Morris, Mercury	RB	5-10	190	24	3	West Texas State
25	Foley, Tim	CB	6-0	194	22	2	Purdue
26	Mumphord, Lloyd	CB	5-10	180	24	3	Texas Southern
31	Cole, Terry	RB	6-1	220	26	4	Indiana
32	Ginn, Hubert	RB	5-10	188	24	2	Florida A&M
39	Csonka, Larry	RB	6-2	237	24	4	Syracuse
40	Anderson, Dick	S	6-2	196	25	4	Colorado
42	Warfield, Paul	WR	6-0	185	28	8	Ohio State
45	Johnson, Curtis	CB	6-1	196	23	2	Toledo
48	Petrella, Bob	S	5-11	190	26	6	Tennessee
53	Matheson, Bob	LB	6-4	240	26	5	Duke
56	Powell, Jesse	LB	6-2	215	24	3	West Texas State
57	Kolen, Mike	LB	6-2	220	23	2	Auburn
59	Swift, Doug	LB	6-3	228	23	2	Amherst
61	DeMarco, Bob	C	6-2	250	31	11	Dayton
62	Langer, Jim	G	6-2	250	23	2	South Dakota
66	Little, Larry	G	6-1	265	25	5	Bethune-Cookman
67	Kuechenberg, Bob	G	6-2	247	23	2	Notre Dame
70	Riley, Jim	DE	6-4	250	26	5	Oklahoma
71	Cornish, Frank	DT	6-3	285	27	6	Grambling
72	Heinz, Bob	DT	6-6	280	24	3	Pacific
73	Evans, Norm	T	6-3	252	28	7	TCU
75	Fernandez, Manny	DT	6-2	248	25	4	Utah
77	Crusan, Doug	T	6-4	250	25	4	Indiana
78	Mass, Wayne	T	6-4	255	25	4	Clemson
80	Fleming, Marv	TE	6-4	235	29	9	Utah

NO.	NAME	POS.	HT.	WT.	AGE	YR.	COLLEGE
81	Twilley, Howard	WR	5-10	185	28	6	Tulsa
82	Stowe, Otto	WR	6-2	188	22	R	Iowa State
84	Stanfill, Bill	DE	6-5	250	24	3	Georgia
85	Buoniconti, Nick	LB	5-11	220	30	10	Notre Dame
86	Den Herder, Vern	DE	6-6	250	22	R	Central College (Iowa)
88	Mandich, Jim	TE	6-2	224	23	2	Michigan
89	Noonan, Karl	WR	6-2	198	27	6	Iowa

TAXI SQUAD

NO.	NAME	POS.	HT.	WT.	AGE	YR.	COLLEGE
11	Del Gaizo, Jim	QB	6-1	198	24	R	Tampa
24	Clancy, Jack	WR	6-1	195	27	5	Michigan
58	Farley, Dale	LB	6-3	235	22	R	West Virginia
64	Griffin, Bill	T	6-5	255	23	R	Catawba (N.C.)
65	Moore, Maulty	DT	6-5	265	25	R	Bethune-Cookman
75	Richardson, John	DT	6-2	248	26	5	UCLA
79	Moore, Wayne	T	6-6	265	25	2	Lamar Tech

DEPTH CHART

(As of December 11, 1971)

OFFENSE

POS.	NO.		NO.		NO.	
WR	42	Paul Warfield	89	Karl Noonan		
LT	77	Doug Crusan	78	Wayne Mass		
LG	67	Bob Kuechenberg	62	Jim Langer		
C	61	Bob DeMarco	62	Jim Langer		
RG	66	Larry Little	62	Jim Langer		
RT	73	Norm Evans	78	Wayne Mass		
TE	80	Marv Fleming	88	Jim Mandich	20	Larry Seiple
WR	81	Howard Twilley	82	Otto Stowe		
QB	12	Bob Griese	22	Mercury Morris		
RB	21	Jim Kiick	10	George Mira	32	Hubert Ginn
RB	39	Larry Csonka	15	Charlie Leigh	31	Terry Cole

DEFENSE

POS.	NO.		NO.	
LE	70	Jim Riley	86	Vern Den Herder
LT	75	Manny Fernandez	71	Frank Cornish
RT	72	Bob Heinz	71	Frank Cornish
RE	84	Bill Stanfill	86	Vern Den Herder
LLB	59	Doug Swift	53	Bob Matheson
MLB	85	Nick Buoniconti	53	Bob Matheson
RLB	57	Mike Kolen	56	Jesse Powell
LCB	25	Tim Foley	45	Curtis Johnson
RCB	45	Curtis Johnson	26	Lloyd Mumphord
LS	40	Dick Anderson	48	Bob Petrella
FS	13	Jake Scott	48	Bob Petrella

SPECIALISTS

POS.	NO.		NO.	
Punter	20	Larry Seiple	40	Dick Anderson
Placements	1	Garo Yepremian		
Kickoffs	1	Garo Yepremian		
Holder	89	Karl Noonan	10	George Mira
Punt Returns	13	Jake Scott	40	Dick Anderson
			15	Charlie Leigh
Kickoff Returns	22	Mercury Morris	32	Hubert Ginn
			15	Charlie Leigh

NFL TEAM STATISTICS, SUMMARY, 1971

AMERICAN FOOTBALL CONFERENCE

(The final team statistics for the thirteen clubs of the American Football Conference in the six major offensive and defensive categories for the 1971 regular season, *not* including playoffs.)

TOTAL OFFENSE

TEAM	YDS. R.	YDS. P.	TOT. YDS.	AV. PER GAME
San Diego	1604	3134*	4738*	338.4*
Miami	2429*	1983	4412	315.1
Cincinnati	2142	2124	4266	304.7
Oakland	2130	2128	4258	304.1
Kansas City	1843	2347	4190	299.3
Denver	2093	2065	4158	297.0
Baltimore	2149	1922	4071	290.8
Pittsburgh	1758	2124	3882	277.3
Cleveland	1558	2299	3857	275.5
New England	1669	1887	3556	254.0
Houston	1106	2409	3515	251.1
Buffalo	1337	1989	3326	237.6
New York Jets	1888	1379	3267	233.4

RUSHING OFFENSE

TEAM	ATT.	YDS.	AVG.	AVG. PER GAME
Miami	486	2429*	5.0*	173.5*
Baltimore	512*	2149	4.2	153.5
Cincinnati	462	2142	4.6	153.0
Oakland	473	2130	4.5	152.1
Denver	512	2093	4.1	149.5
New York Jets	485	1888	3.9	134.9
Kansas City	487	1843	3.8	131.6
Pittsburgh	416	1758	4.2	125.6
New England	420	1669	4.0	119.2
San Diego	390	1604	4.1	114.6
Cleveland	461	1558	3.4	111.3
Buffalo	320	1337	4.2	95.5
Houston	364	1106	3.0	79.0

*Conference leader.

PASSING OFFENSE

TEAM	ATT.	COMP.	PCT.	LAP/YDS.	NET YDS.	TD	INT.	INT. PCT.	AV. PER GAME
San Diego	450*	244*	54.2*	19/171*	3134*	23*	28	.062	223.9*
Houston	423	194	45.9	31/234	2409	12	37	.087	172.1
Kansas City	337	183	54.3	35/347	2347	15	13	.039	167.6
Cleveland	376	188	50.0	22/222	2299	14	27	.072	164.2
Oakland	348	174	50.0	24/235	2128	21	26	.075	152.0
Cincinnati	365	214	58.6*	40/303	2124	15	11	.030*	151.7
Pittsburgh	414	214	51.7	37/322	2124	15	26	.063	151.7
Denver	358	175	48.9	22/178	2065	8	27	.075	147.5
Buffalo	401	202	50.4	49/421	1989	12	32	.080	142.1
Miami	293	156	53.2	25/265	1983	20	10*	.034	141.6
Baltimore	344	176	51.2	27/230	1922	10	21	.061	137.3
New England	330	159	48.2	36/319	1887	19	16	.048	134.8
New York Jets	278	119	42.8	23/177	1379	15	16	.058	98.5

* Conference leader.

TOTAL DEFENSE

TEAM	YDS. R.	YDS. P.	TOT. YDS.	AVG. PER GAME
Baltimore	1113*	1739*	2852*	203.7*
Miami	1661	2000	3661	261.5
Kansas City	1300	2468	3768	269.1
Houston	1723	2072	3795	271.1
Denver	1834	1985	3819	272.8
Cincinnati	1778	2128	3906	279.0
New England	1918	2154	4072	290.9
Oakland	1751	2386	4137	295.5
Cleveland	2227	1967	4194	299.6
Pittsburgh	1482	2766	4248	303.4
New York Jets	2302	2055	4357	311.2
San Diego	2296	2262	4558	325.6
Buffalo	2496	2108	4604	328.9

RUSHING DEFENSE

TEAM	ATT.	YDS.	AVG.	AVG. PER GAME
Baltimore	353*	1113*	3.2*	79.5*
Kansas City	367	1300	3.5	92.9
Pittsburgh	443	1482	3.3	105.9
Miami	403	1661	4.1	118.6
Houston	489	1723	3.5	123.1
Oakland	480	1751	3.6	125.1
Cincinnati	446	1778	4.0	127.0
Denver	426	1834	4.3	131.0
New England	481	1918	4.0	137.0
Cleveland	484	2227	4.6	159.1
San Diego	493	2296	4.7	164.0
New York Jets	472	2302	4.9	164.4
Buffalo	2496	2108	4.4	178.3

*Conference leader.

PASSING DEFENSE

TEAM	ATT.	COMP.	PCT.	LAP/YDS.	NET YDS.	TD	INT.	INT. PCT.	AVG. PER GAME
Baltimore	361	185	51.2	33/288	1739*	9*	28*	.078	124.2*
Cleveland	339	156	46.0	25/203	1967	12	24	.071	140.5
Denver	356	150*	42.1*	44*/435*	1985	18	20	.056	141.8
Miami	363	206	56.7	34/293	2000	10	17	.047	142.9
New York Jets	342	163	47.7	27/230	2055	17	13	.038	146.8
Houston	354	180	50.8	37/344	2072	11	23	.065	148.0
Buffalo	303*	157	51.8	30/225	2108	20	11	.036	150.6
Cincinnati	335	157	46.9	30/254	2128	19	27	.081*	152.0
New England	350	170	48.6	25/249	2154	16	15	.043	153.9
San Diego	347	193	55.6	19/177	2262	15	22	.063	161.6
Oakland	359	184	51.3	32/223	2386	15	23	.064	170.4
Kansas City	418	209	50.0	28/235	2468	11	27	.065	176.3
Pittsburgh	408	235	57.6	33/294	2766	16	17	.042	197.6

* Conference leader.

NATIONAL FOOTBALL CONFERENCE

(The final team statistics for the thirteen clubs of the National Football Conference in the six major offensive and defensive categories for the 1971 regular season, *not* including playoffs.)

TOTAL OFFENSE

TEAM	YDS. R.	YDS. P.	TOT. YDS.	AVG. PER GAME
Dallas	2249	2786*	5035*	359.6*
San Francisco	2129	2577	4706	336.1
Detroit	2376*	2201	4577	326.9
Los Angeles	2139	2094	4233	302.4
New York Giants	1461	2714	4175	298.2
Washington	1757	2273	4030	287.9
St. Louis	1530	2471	4001	285.8
Atlanta	1703	2256	3959	282.8
Green Bay	2229	1685	3914	279.6
New Orleans	1711	1955	3666	261.9
Philadelphia	1248	2323	3571	255.1
Minnesota	1695	1655	3350	239.3
Chicago	1434	1902	3336	238.3

RUSHING OFFENSE

TEAM	ATT.	YDS.	AVG.	AVG. PER GAME
Detroit	532*	2376*	4.5	169.7*
Dallas	512	2249	4.4	160.6
Green Bay	500	2229	4.5	159.2
Los Angeles	460	2139	4.7*	152.8
San Francisco	498	2129	4.3	152.1
Washington	477	1757	3.7	125.5
New Orleans	452	1711	3.8	122.2
Atlanta	494	1703	3.4	121.6
Minnesota	484	1695	3.5	121.1
St. Louis	417	1530	3.7	109.3
New York Giants	394	1461	3.7	104.4
Chicago	305	1434	3.9	102.4
Philadelphia	407	1248	3.1	89.1

*Conference leader.

PASSING OFFENSE

TEAM	ATT.	COMP.	PCT.	LAP/YDS.	NET YDS.	TD	INT.	INT. PCT.	AVG. PER GAME
Dallas	361	206	57.1	32/251	2786*	22*	14	.039	199.0*
New York Giants	462*	268*	58.0	40/348	2714	14	25	.054	193.9
San Francisco	391	209	53.5	11*/111*	2577	18	24	.065	184.1
St. Louis	385	170	44.2	19/185	2471	14	25	.065	176.5
Philadelphia	390	200	51.3	26/229	2323	13	20	.051	165.9
Washington	334	182	54.5	17/118	2273	13	15	.045	162.4
Atlanta	285	167	58.6	31/239	2256	16	21	.074	161.1
Detroit	299	157	52.5	31/252	2201	17	14	.047	157.2
Los Angeles	370	185	50.0	26/210	2094	18	11*	.030*	149.6
New Orleans	387	182	47.0	50/400	1955	12	14	.036	139.6
Chicago	443	186	42.0	49/392	1902	12	28	.063	135.9
Green Bay	254	121	47.6	18/157	1685	12	24	.094	120.4
Minnesota	334	157	47.0	28/255	1655	9	18	.054	118.2

* Conference leader.

TOTAL DEFENSE

TEAM	YDS. R.	YDS. P.	TOT. YDS.	AVG. PER GAME
Minnesota	1600	1806	3406*	243.3*
Dallas	1144*	2324	3468	247.7
Washington	1396	2127	3523	251.6
San Francisco	1668	2011	3679	262.8
Atlanta	2149	1638*	3787	270.5
Detroit	1842	2017	3859	275.6
Green Bay	1707	2301	4008	286.3
Los Angeles	1658	2379	4037	288.4
St. Louis	1985	2380	4365	311.8
New York Giants	2059	2307	4366	311.9
New Orleans	2200	2238	4438	317.0
Chicago	2116	2404	4520	322.9
Philadelphia	1962	2660	4622	330.1

RUSHING DEFENSE

TEAM	ATT.	YDS.	AVG.	AVG. PER GAME
Dallas	353*	1144*	3.2*	81.7*
Washington	408	1396	3.4	99.7
Minnesota	447	1600	3.6	114.3
Los Angeles	455	1658	3.6	118.4
San Francisco	408	1668	4.1	119.1
Green Bay	489	1707	3.5	121.9
Detroit	432	1842	4.3	131.6
Philadelphia	450	1962	4.4	140.1
St. Louis	486	1985	4.1	141.8
New York Giants	449	2059	4.6	147.1
Chicago	509	2116	4.2	151.1
Atlanta	500	2149	4.3	153.5
New Orleans	495	2200	4.4	157.1

*Conference leader.

PASSING DEFENSE

TEAM	ATT.	COMP.	PCT.	LAP/YDS.	NET YDS.	TD	INT.	INT. PCT.	AVG. PER GAME
Atlanta	343	164	47.8	31/257	1638*	9*	20	.058	117.0
Minnesota	405	206	50.9	27/216	1806	10	27	.067	129.0
San Francisco	341	152*	44.6*	38/298	2011	17	14	.041	143.6
Detroit	306*	163	53.3	18/146	2017	17	22	.072*	144.1
Washington	411	191	46.5	36/321	2127	11	29*	.071	151.9
New Orleans	333	175	52.6	24/234	2238	20	20	.060	159.9
Green Bay	353	186	52.7	19/168	2301	21	16	.045	164.4
New York Giants	333	173	52.0	18/151	2307	25	15	.045	164.8
Dallas	421	209	49.6	43*/336*	2324	15	25	.059	166.0
Los Angeles	387	200	51.7	37/314	2379	15	27	.070	169.9
St. Louis	375	212	56.5	20/166	2380	12	17	.045	170.0
Chicago	362	192	53.0	28/203	2404	12	22	.061	171.7
Philadelphia	407	220	54.1	32/311	2660	16	22	.054	190.0

* Conference leader.

FINAL STANDINGS, 1971
AMERICAN FOOTBALL CONFERENCE

EASTERN DIVISION

	W.	L.	T.	PCT.	PTS.	OP.
Miami	10	3	1	.769	315	174
*Baltimore	10	4	0	.714	313	140
New England	6	8	0	.429	238	325
New York Jets	6	8	0	.429	212	299
Buffalo	1	13	0	.071	184	394

WESTERN DIVISION

	W.	L.	T.	PCT.	PTS.	OP.
Kansas City	10	3	1	.769	302	208
Oakland	8	4	2	.667	344	278
San Diego	6	8	0	.429	311	341
Denver	4	9	1	.308	203	275

CENTRAL DIVISION

	W.	L.	T.	PCT.	PTS.	OP.
Cleveland	9	5	0	.643	285	273
Pittsburgh	6	8	0	.429	246	292
Houston	4	9	1	.308	251	330
Cincinnati	4	10	0	.286	284	265

* Fourth qualifier for playoffs.

GAME RESULTS BY TEAM, AFC, 1971

BALTIMORE (10–4)

22	*New York Jets	0
13	*Cleveland	14
23	New England	3
43	Buffalo	0
31	New York Giants	7
3	Minnesota	10
34	*Pittsburgh	21
24	*Los Angeles	17
14	New York Jets	13
14	Miami	17
37	Oakland	14
24	*Buffalo	0
14	*Miami	3
17	*New England	21
313		140

BUFFALO (1–13)

37	*Dallas	49
14	*Miami	29
0	Minnesota	19
0	*Baltimore	43
17	New York Jets	28
3	San Diego	20
23	*St. Louis	28
0	Miami	34
33	New England	38
7	*New York Jets	20
27	*New England	20
0	Baltimore	24
14	*Houston	20
9	Kansas City	22
184		394

CINCINNATI (4–10)

37	*Philadelphia	14
10	Pittsburgh	21
17	Green Bay	20
13	*Miami	23
24	*Cleveland	27
27	Oakland	31
6	Houston	10
6	*Atlanta	9
24	Denver	10
28	*Houston	13
31	*San Diego	0
27	Cleveland	31
13	*Pittsburgh	21
21	New York Jets	35
284		265

CLEVELAND (9–5)

31	*Houston	0
14	Baltimore	13
20	*Oakland	34
27	*Pittsburgh	17
27	Cincinnati	24
0	*Denver	27
14	*Atlanta	31
9	Pittsburgh	26
7	Kansas City	13
27	*New England	7
37	Houston	24
31	*Cincinnati	27
21	New Orleans	17
20	Washington	13
285		273

*Home game.

DENVER (4–9–1)

10	*Miami	10
13	Green Bay	
	(at Milw.)	34
3	*Kansas City	16
16	*Oakland	27
20	*San Diego	16
27	Cleveland	0
16	Philadelphia	17
20	*Detroit	24
10	*Cincinnati	24
10	Kansas City	28
22	Pittsburgh	10
6	*Chicago	3
17	San Diego	45
13	Oakland	21
203		275

HOUSTON (4–9–1)

0	Cleveland	31
16	*Kansas City	20
13	*New Orleans	13
13	Washington	22
7	*Detroit	31
16	Pittsburgh	23
10	*Cincinnati	6
20	New England	28
21	Oakland	41
13	Cincinnati	28
24	*Cleveland	37
29	*Pittsburgh	3
20	Buffalo	14
49	*San Diego	33
251		330

KANSAS CITY (10–3–1)

14	San Diego	21
20	Houston	16
16	Denver	3
31	*San Diego	10
38	*Pittsburgh	16
27	*Washington	20
20	Oakland	20
10	New York Jets	13
13	*Cleveland	7
28	*Denver	10
21	Detroit	32
26	San Francisco	17
16	*Oakland	14
22	*Buffalo	9
302		208

MIAMI (10–3–1)

10	Denver	10
29	Buffalo	14
10	*New York Jets	14
23	Cincinnati	13
41	*New England	3
30	New York Jets	14
20	Los Angeles	14
34	*Buffalo	0
24	*Pittsburgh	21
17	*Baltimore	14
34	*Chicago	3
13	New England	34
3	Baltimore	14
27	*Green Bay	6
315		174

*Home game.

NEW ENGLAND (6-8)

20	*Oakland	6
7	*Detroit	34
3	*Baltimore	23
20	*New York Jets	0
3	Miami	41
21	Dallas	44
10	San Francisco	27
28	*Houston	20
38	*Buffalo	33
7	Cleveland	27
20	Buffalo	27
34	*Miami	13
6	New York Jets	13
21	Baltimore	17
238		325

NEW YORK JETS (6-8)

0	Baltimore	22
10	St. Louis	17
14	Miami	10
0	New England	20
28	*Buffalo	17
14	*Miami	30
21	San Diego	49
13	*Kansas City	10
13	*Baltimore	14
20	Buffalo	7
21	*San Francisco	24
10	Dallas	52
13	*New England	6
35	*Cincinnati	21
212		299

OAKLAND (8-4-2)

6	New England	20
34	San Diego	0
34	Cleveland	20
27	Denver	16
34	*Philadelphia	10
31	*Cincinnati	27
20	*Kansas City	20
21	New Orleans	21
41	*Houston	21
34	*San Diego	33
14	*Baltimore	37
13	Atlanta	24
14	Kansas City	16
21	*Denver	13
344		278

PITTSBURGH (6-8)

15	Chicago	17
21	*Cincinnati	10
21	*San Diego	17
17	Cleveland	27
16	Kansas City	38
23	*Houston	16
21	Baltimore	34
26	*Cleveland	9
21	Miami	24
17	*New York Giants	13
10	*Denver	22
3	Houston	29
21	Cincinnati	13
14	*Los Angeles	23
246		292

*Home game.

SAN DIEGO (6–8)

21	*Kansas City	14
0	*Oakland	34
17	Pittsburgh	21
10	Kansas City	31
16	Denver	20
20	*Buffalo	3
49	*New York Jets	21
17	New York Giants	35
20	*St. Louis	17
33	Oakland	34
0	Cincinnati	31
30	*Minnesota	14
45	*Denver	17
33	Houston	49
311		341

* Home game.

TEAM RANKINGS, OFFENSE/DEFENSE, 1971
AMERICAN FOOTBALL CONFERENCE

| | *Offense* | | | *Defense* | | |
	TOTAL	RUSH.	PASS.	TOTAL	RUSH.	PASS.
Baltimore	7	2	11	1	1	1
Buffalo	12	12	9	13	13	7
Cincinnati	3	3	6	6	7	8
Cleveland	9	11	4	9	10	2
Denver	6	5	8	5	8	3
Houston	11	13	2	4	5	6
Kansas City	5	7	3	3	2	12
Miami	2	1	10	2	4	4
New England	10	9	12	7	9	9
New York Jets	13	6	13	11	12	5
Oakland	4	4	5	8	6	11
Pittsburgh	8	8	6	10	3	13
San Diego	1	10	1	12	11	10

FINAL STANDINGS, 1971
NATIONAL FOOTBALL CONFERENCE

EASTERN DIVISION

	W.	L.	T.	PCT.	PTS.	OP.
Dallas	11	3	0	.786	406	222
*Washington	9	4	1	.692	276	190
Philadelphia	6	7	1	.462	221	302
St. Louis	4	9	1	.308	231	279
New York Giants	4	10	0	.286	228	362

WESTERN DIVISION

	W.	L.	T.	PCT.	PTS.	OP.
San Francisco	9	5	0	.643	300	216
Los Angeles	8	5	1	.615	313	260
Atlanta	7	6	1	.538	274	277
New Orleans	4	8	2	.333	266	347

CENTRAL DIVISION

	W.	L.	T.	PCT.	PTS.	OP.
Minnesota	11	3	0	.786	245	139
Detroit	7	6	1	.538	341	286
Chicago	6	8	0	.429	185	276
Green Bay	4	8	2	.333	274	298

* Fourth qualifier for playoffs.

GAME RESULTS BY TEAM, NFC, 1971

ATLANTA (7–6–1)

20	*San Francisco	17
20	Los Angeles	20
38	Detroit	41
9	*St. Louis	26
16	*Los Angeles	24
28	*New Orleans	6
31	Cleveland	14
9	Cincinnati	6
17	*New York Giants	21
28	*Green Bay	21
7	Minnesota	24
24	*Oakland	13
3	San Francisco	24
24	New Orleans	20
274		277

CHICAGO (6–8)

17	*Pittsburgh	15
20	Minnesota	17
3	Los Angeles	17
35	*New Orleans	14
0	San Francisco	13
28	Detroit	23
23	*Dallas	19
14	*Green Bay	17
16	*Washington	15
3	*Detroit	28
3	Miami	34
3	Denver	6
10	Green Bay	31
10	*Minnesota	27
185		276

DALLAS (11–3)

49	Buffalo	37
42	Philadelphia	7
16	*Washington	20
20	*New York Giants	13
14	New Orleans	24
44	*New England	21
19	Chicago	23
16	St. Louis	13
20	*Philadelphia	7
13	Washington	0
28	*Los Angeles	21
52	*New York Jets	10
42	New York Giants	14
31	*St. Louis	12
406		222

DETROIT (7–6–1)

13	*Minnesota	16
34	New England	7
41	*Atlanta	28
31	*Green Bay	28
31	Houston	7
23	*Chicago	28
14	Green Bay (at Milw.)	14
24	Denver	20
13	*Los Angeles	21
28	Chicago	3
32	*Kansas City	21
20	*Philadelphia	23
10	Minnesota	29
27	San Francisco	31
341		286

*Home game.

GREEN BAY (4–8–2)

40	*New York Giants	42
34	*Denver (at Milw.)	13
20	*Cincinnati	17
28	Detroit	31
13	*Minnesota	24
13	Los Angeles	30
14	*Detroit (at Milw.)	14
17	Chicago	14
0	Minnesota	3
21	Atlanta	28
21	*New Orleans (at Milw.)	29
16	St. Louis	16
31	*Chicago	10
6	Miami	27
$\overline{274}$		$\overline{298}$

MINNESOTA (11–3)

16	Detroit	13
17	*Chicago	20
19	*Buffalo	0
13	Philadelphia	0
24	Green Bay	13
10	*Baltimore	3
17	New York Giants	10
9	*San Francisco	13
3	*Green Bay	0
23	New Orleans	10
24	*Atlanta	7
14	San Diego	30
29	*Detroit	10
27	Chicago	10
$\overline{245}$		$\overline{139}$

*Home game.

LOS ANGELES (8–5–1)

20	New Orleans	24
20	*Atlanta	20
17	*Chicago	3
20	San Francisco	13
24	Atlanta	16
30	*Green Bay	13
14	*Miami	20
17	Baltimore	24
21	Detroit	13
17	*San Francisco	6
21	Dallas	28
45	*New Orleans	28
24	*Washington	38
23	Pittsburgh	14
$\overline{313}$		$\overline{260}$

NEW ORLEANS (4–8–2)

24	*Los Angeles	20
20	*San Francisco	38
13	Houston	13
14	Chicago	35
24	*Dallas	14
6	Atlanta	28
14	Washington	24
21	*Oakland	21
26	San Francisco	20
10	*Minnesota	23
29	Green Bay (at Milw.)	21
28	Los Angeles	45
17	*Cleveland	21
20	*Atlanta	24
$\overline{266}$		$\overline{347}$

NEW YORK GIANTS
(4–10)

42	Green Bay	40
3	*Washington	30
21	St. Louis	20
13	Dallas	20
7	*Baltimore	31
7	Philadelphia	23
10	*Minnesota	17
35	*San Diego	17
21	Atlanta	17
13	Pittsburgh	17
7	*St. Louis	24
7	Washington	23
14	*Dallas	42
28	*Philadelphia	41
228		362

PHILADELPHIA
(6–7–1)

14	Cincinnati	37
7	*Dallas	42
3	*San Francisco	31
0	*Minnesota	13
10	Oakland	34
23	*New York Giants	7
17	*Denver	16
7	Washington	7
7	Dallas	20
37	St. Louis	20
13	*Washington	20
23	Detroit	20
19	*St. Louis	7
41	New York Giants	28
221		302

ST. LOUIS (4–9–1)

17	*Washington	24
17	*New York Jets	10
20	*New York Giants	21
26	Atlanta	9
0	Washington	20
14	*San Francisco	26
28	Buffalo	23
13	*Dallas	16
17	San Diego	20
20	*Philadelphia	37
24	New York Giants	7
16	*Green Bay	16
7	Philadelphia	19
12	Dallas	31
231		279

SAN FRANCISCO
(9–5)

17	Atlanta	20
38	New Orleans	20
31	Philadelphia	3
13	*Los Angeles	20
13	*Chicago	0
26	St. Louis	14
27	*New England	10
13	Minnesota	9
20	*New Orleans	26
6	Los Angeles	17
24	New York Jets	21
17	*Kansas City	26
24	*Atlanta	3
31	*Detroit	27
300		216

*Home game.

WASHINGTON
(9–4–1)

24	St. Louis	17
30	New York Giants	3
30	Dallas	16
22	*Houston	13
20	*St. Louis	0
20	Kansas City	27
24	*New Orleans	14
7	*Philadelphia	7
15	Chicago	16
0	*Dallas	13
20	Philadelphia	13
23	*New York Giants	7
38	Los Angeles	24
13	*Cleveland	20
276		190

* Home game.

DOLPHINS' THREE-GAME PLAYOFF STATISTICS, 1971–72

SCORES

MIAMI		OPP.	ATT.
27	at Kansas City	24	50,374
21	Baltimore Colts	0	78,629
3	Dallas Cowboys (at New Orleans)	24	81,035

TEAM STATISTICS

	MIAMI	OPP.
First Downs	45	62
Rushing	17	34
Passing	25	28
Penalties	3	0
Net Total, Offense	878	1105
Total plays	167	208
Average gain per play	5.3	5.3
Net Rushing, Offense	368	558
Rushing plays	98	121
Average gain per play	3.8	4.6
Net Passing, Offense	510	547
Tackled/Yards lost	3/45	6/42
Attempts/Completions	66/36	81/50
Percent completed	54.5	61.7
Had intercepted	4	5
Touchdowns	2	3
Average gain per play	7.4	6.3
Average gain per completion	14.2	10.9
Punts/Average	17/40.9	10/42.4
Yards	696	424
Had blocked	0	0
Punt Returns/Yards	4/59	8/20
Average per return	14.7	2.5
Kickoff Returns/Yards	8/205	8/246
Average per return	25.6	30.7
Interceptions/Yards	5/86	4/58
Penalties/Yards	6/38	11/79
Fumbles/No. Lost	3/2	5/3
Total Points	51	48
Touchdowns	6	6
Rushing	3	3
Passing	2	3
Returns	1	1
PAT Made/Attempted	6/6	6/6
Field Goals Made/Attempted	3/5	2/8
Safeties	0	0

SCORES BY QUARTER

	1	2	3	4	1OT	2OT	TOTAL
MIAMI	7	13	14	0	0	3	51
OPPONENTS	13	7	14	14	0	0	48

INDIVIDUAL RUSHING

PLAYER	NO.	YDS.	AVG.	TD	LONG
Csonka	48	189	3.9	2	29
Kiick	40	162	4.1	1	15
Griese	4	21	5.2	0	12
Morris	1	3	3.0	0	3
Warfield	2	—7	—3.5	0	—3
DOLPHINS	95	368	3.8	3	29
OPPONENTS	121	558	4.6	3	32

INDIVIDUAL PASSING

PLAYER	ATT.	COMP.	INT.	YDS.	AVG.	TD	LONG
Griese	66	36	4	555	54.5	2	75
DOLPHINS	66	36	4	555	54.5	2	75
OPPONENTS	71	50	5	589	61.7	3	63

TIMES TACKLED ATTEMPTING PASS (SACKS)

PLAYER	NO.	YDS.	AVG. LOSS
Griese	3	45	15.0
DOLPHINS	3	45	15.0
OPPONENTS	6	42	7.0

INDIVIDUAL RECEIVING

PLAYER	NO.	YDS.	AVG.	TD	LONG
Warfield	13	306	23.5	1	75
Twilley	8	111	13.9	0	23
Fleming	5	64	12.8	1	27
Kiick	6	45	7.5	0	21
Csonka	2	18	9.0	0	16
Mandich	2	13	6.5	0	9
DOLPHINS	36	555	15.4	2	75
OPPONENTS	50	589	11.8	3	63

INTERCEPTIONS BY

PLAYER	NO.	YDS.	AVG.	TD	LONG
Scott	2	13	6.5	0	13
Anderson	1	62	62.0	1	62
Kolen	1	11	11.0	0	11
Johnson	1	0	0.0	0	0
DOLPHINS	5	86	17.2	1	62
OPPONENTS	4	58	14.5	0	41

PUNTING

PLAYER	NO.	YDS.	AVG.	LONG	BLKD.
Seiple	12	496	41.3	52	0
DOLPHINS	12	496	41.3	52	0
OPPONENTS	6	279	46.5	52	0

PUNT RETURNS

PLAYER	FC	NO.	YDS.	AVG.	TD	LONG
Scott	1	4	59	14.7	0	21
DOLPHINS	1	4	59	14.7	0	21
OPPONENTS	8	8	20	2.5	0	6

KICKOFF RETURNS

PLAYER	NO.	YDS.	AVG.	TD	LONG
Morris	7	173	24.7	0	37
Ginn	1	32	32.0	0	32
DOLPHINS	8	205	29.1	0	37
OPPONENTS	8	246	30.8	0	78

SCORING

PLAYER	R/P/RET.	PAT	FG/ATT.	(LONG)	PTS.
Yepremian	0/0/0	6/6	3/5	(37)	15
Csonka	2/0/0	0/0	0/0		12
Anderson	0/0/1	0/0	0/0		6
Kiick	1/0/0	0/0	0/0		6
Warfield	0/1/0	0/0	0/0		6
Fleming	0/1/0	0/0	0/0		6
DOLPHINS	3/2/1	6/6	3/5	(37)	51
OPPONENTS	3/3/0	6/6	2/8	(24)	48

FIELD-GOAL ACCURACY

PLAYER	YARDS					TOTAL
	1–19	20–29	30–39	40–49	50–OVER	
Yepremian	1/1	0/0	2/2	0/1	0/1	3/5
DOLPHINS	1/1	0/0	2/2	0/1	0/1	3/5
OPPONENTS	1/1	1/2	0/2	0/3	0/0	2/8

Yepremian sequence (italicized indicates good): *14,* 52, *37,* 49, *31.*

DEFENSIVE STATISTICS
(TACKLES-ASSISTS-TOTAL)

Buoniconti	23-20-43	Matheson	4-2-6
Kolen	18-11-29	Den Herder	2-3-5
Anderson	17-8-25	Mumphord	4-1-5
Fernandez	15-9-24	Langer	3-0-3
Swift	11-11-22	Kiick	1-0-1
Johnson	17-3-20	Ginn	1-0-1
Heinz	7-10-17	Little	1-0-1
Riley	9-7-16	Csonka	1-0-1
Foley	11-2-13	Mandich	1-0-1
Stanfill	9-4-13	Cole	1-0-1
Scott	5-5-10	Petrella	0-1-1
Cornish	5-4-9		

PASSES DEFENDED

Foley 4, Johnson 2, Heinz 2, Anderson 2, Buoniconti 2, Scott 1, Swift 1.

BLOCKED FG

Buoniconti 1, Mumphord 1.

TACKLED PASSER

Fernandez 2½, Riley 2, Heinz 1½.

OPP. FUMBLES RECOVERED

Anderson 1, Fernandez 1, Buoniconti 1.

ALL-NFL TEAM, 1971

(Selected by Professional Football Writers Association,
Associated Press, Newspaper Enterprise Association)

OFFENSE

Otis Taylor, Kansas City (PFWA, AP, NEA)	wide receiver
PAUL WARFIELD, Miami (PFWA, AP, NEA)	wide receiver
Charlie Sanders, Detroit (PFWA, AP, NEA)	tight end
Ron Yary, Minnesota (PFWA, AP, NEA)	tackle
Rayfield Wright, Dallas (PFWA, AP)	tackle
Bob Brown, Oakland (NEA)	tackle
LARRY LITTLE, Miami (PFWA, AP)	guard
John Niland, Dallas (PFWA, AP)	guard
Gale Gillingham, Green Bay (NEA)	guard
Tom Mack, Los Angeles (NEA)	guard
Forest Blue, San Francisco (PFWA, AP)	center
Jim Otto, Oakland (NEA)	center
BOB GRIESE, Miami (PFWA, AP, NEA)	quarterback
John Brockington, Green Bay (PFWA, AP, NEA)	running back
LARRY CSONKA, Miami (PFWA, AP)	running back
Leroy Kelly, Cleveland (NEA)	running back

DEFENSE

Carl Eller, Minnesota (PFWA, AP, NEA)	end
Bubba Smith, Baltimore (PFWA, AP)	end
Claude Humphrey, Atlanta (NEA)	end
Bob Lilly, Dallas (PFWA, AP, NEA)	tackle
Alan Page, Minnesota (PFWA, AP, NEA)	tackle
Ted Hendricks, Baltimore (PFWA, AP, NEA)	outside linebacker
Dave Wilcox, San Francisco (PFWA, AP, NEA)	outside linebacker
Willie Lanier, Kansas City (PFWA, AP, NEA)	middle linebacker
Jim Johnson, San Francisco (PFWA, AP, NEA)	cornerback
Willie Brown, Oakland (PFWA, AP)	cornerback
Mel Renfro, Dallas (NEA)	cornerback
Rick Volk, Baltimore (PFWA, AP, NEA)	safety
Bill Bradley, Philadelphia (PFWA, AP)	safety
Paul Krause, Minnesota (NEA)	safety

SPECIALISTS

Curt Knight, Washington (NEA)	placekicker
GARO YEPREMIAN, Miami (PFWA, AP)	placekicker
Jerrel Wilson, Kansas City (PFWA)	punter

AMERICAN FOOTBALL CONFERENCE
PRO BOWL TEAM, 1972
(Listed alphabetically; Vote by coaches)

OFFENSE

Fred Biletnikoff, Oakland; Gary Garrison, San Diego; Otis Taylor, Kansas City; PAUL WARFIELD, Miami—wide receivers

Raymond Chester, Oakland; Milt Morin, Cleveland—tight ends

Bob Brown, Oakland; Winston Hill, New York Jets; Jim Tyrer, Kansas City—tackles

Ed Budde, Kansas City; LARRY LITTLE, Miami; Walter Sweeney, San Diego—guards

Bill Curry, Baltimore; Jim Otto, Oakland—centers

Len Dawson, Kansas City; BOB GRIESE, Miami—quarterbacks

Norm Bulaich, Baltimore; LARRY CSONKA, Miami; Leroy Kelly, Cleveland; Floyd Little, Denver—running backs

DEFENSE

Elvin Bethea, Houston; Bubba Smith, Baltimore; BILL STANFILL, Miami—ends

Buck Buchanan, Kansas City; Curly Culp, Kansas City; Joe Greene, Pittsburgh—tackles

Bobby Bell, Kansas City; Ted Hendricks, Baltimore; Andy Russell, Pittsburgh—outside linebackers

Mike Curtis, Baltimore; Willie Lanier, Kansas City—middle linebackers

Willie Brown, Oakland; Lemar Parrish, Cincinnati; Emmitt Thomas, Kansas City—cornerbacks

Ken Houston, Houston; JAKE SCOTT, Miami; Rick Volk, Baltimore—safeties (Scott withdrew, injured, and was replaced by Jerry Logan, Baltimore.)

SPECIALISTS

Jerrel Wilson, Kansas City—punter

Jan Stenerud, Kansas City—placekicker

MERCURY MORRIS, Miami—kick returner